Lecture Notes in Computer Science 6910

Commenced Publication in 1973
Founding and Former Series Editors:
Gerhard Goos, Juris Hartmanis, and Jan van Leeuwen

W0192942

Ngoc Thanh Nguyen (Ed.)

Transactions on Computational Collective Intelligence V

 Springer

Volume Editor

Ngoc Thanh Nguyen
Wroclaw University of Technology
Wyb. Wyspianskiego 27
50-370 Wroclaw, Poland
E-mail: ngoc-thanh.nguyen@pwr.edu.pl

ISSN 0302-9743 (LNCS)   e-ISSN 1611-3349 (LNCS)
ISSN 2190-9288 (TCCI)
ISBN 978-3-642-24015-7   e-ISBN 978-3-642-24016-4
DOI 10.1007/978-3-642-24016-4

Springer Heidelberg Dordrecht London New York

Library of Congress Control Number: 2011935943

CR Subject Classification (1998): I.2, C.2.4, I.2.11, H.3-5, D.2, I.5

Typesetting: Camera-ready by author, data conversion by Scientific Publishing Services, Chennai, India

Printed on acid-free paper

Springer is part of Springer Science+Business Media (www.springer.com)

Preface

Welcome to the fifth volume of Springer's *Transactions on Computational Collective Intelligence* (TCCI). It is the third issue in 2011 of this journal which is devoted to research in computer-based methods of computational collective intelligence (CCI) and their applications in a wide range of fields such as group decision making, knowledge integration, consensus computing, the Semantic Web, social networks and multi-agent systems. TCCI strives to cover new computational, methodological, theoretical and practical aspects of collective intelligence understood as the form of intelligence that emerges from the collaboration and competition of many individuals (artificial and/or natural).

This volume of TCCI includes ten interesting and original papers. The first of them, entitled "Improved N-grams Approach for Web Page Language Identification" by Ali Selamat, presents an improved N-grams approach for Web page language identification, which is based on a combination of an original N-grams approach and a modified N-grams approach that has been used for language identification of Web documents. In the second paper with the title "Image-Edge Detection Using Variation-Adaptive Ant Colony Optimization" the authors, Jing Tian, Weiyu Yu, Li Chen, and Lihong Ma, present a novel image-edge detection approach using ant colony optimization techniques, in which a pheromone matrix representing edges at pixel positions of an image is built according to the movements of a number of ants which are dispatched to move on the image. The next paper, "An Iterative Process for Component-Based Software Development Centered on Agents" by Yves Wautelet, Sodany Kiv, and Manuel Kolp, includes a formalization of the process for component-based software development through the use of the agent paradigm. In the fourth paper entitled "Cellular Gene Expression Programming Classifier Learning" the authors, Joanna Jędrzejowicz and Piotr Jędrzejowicz, present a method for integrating two collective computational intelligence techniques: gene expression programming and cellular evolutionary algorithms with a view to inducing expression trees. This paper also includes a discussion of the validating experiment results confirming the high quality of the proposed ensemble classifiers. The next paper, "A Situation-Aware Computational Trust Model for Selecting Partners" by Joana Urbano, Ana Paula Rocha, and Eugenio Oliveira, contains the description of a model for selecting partners in a society, in which the authors focus on contextual fitness, a component of the model that adds a contextual dimensional to existing trust aggregation engines. The sixth paper entitled "Using the Perseus System for Modelling Epistemic Interactions" by Magdalena Kacprzak et al., includes a model for agent knowledge acquisition, using a logical puzzle in which agents increase their knowledge about the hats they wear and the software tool named Perseus. In the seventh paper, "Reduction of Faulty Detected Shot Cuts and Cross-Dissolve Effects in Video Segmentation Process of Different Categories of Digital Videos," the author, Kazimierz Choroś, presents a description of experiments confirming the effectiveness of four methods of faulty video detection referring to five different categories of movie: TV talk-show, documentary movie, animal video, action and adventure, and pop music video. In the next paper, "Using Knowledge-Integration Techniques for User Profile Adaptation Methods in Document Retrieval Systems" by Bernadetta Mianowska and Ngoc Thanh Nguyen, a model for integrating the archival knowledge included in a user profile with the new knowledge delivered to an information retrieval system, detecting and proving its properties, is presented. The ninth paper entitled "Modeling Agents and Agent Systems," by Theodor Lettmann et al., contains a universal and formal description for agent systems that can be used as a core model with other existing models as special cases. The authors show that owing to this core model a clear specification of agent systems and their properties can be achieved. The last paper, "Online News Event Extraction for Global Crisis Surveillance" by Jakub Piskorski et al., presents a real-time and multilingual news event extraction system developed at the Joint Research Centre of the European Commission. The authors show that with this system it is possible to accurately and efficiently extract violent and natural disaster events from online news.

TCCI is a peer-reviewed and authoritative reference dealing with the working potential of CCI methodologies and applications as well as emerging issues of interest to academics and practitioners. The research area of CCI has been growing significantly in recent years and we are very thankful to everyone within the CCI research community who has supported the TCCI and its affiliated events including the International Conferences on Computational Collective Intelligence (ICCCI). The first ICCCI event was held in Wroclaw, Poland, in October 2009. ICCCI 2010 was held in Kaohsiung, Taiwan, in November 2010 and ICCCI 2011 took place in Gdynia, Poland, in September 2011. For ICCCI 2011 around 300 papers from 25 countries were submitted and only 105 papers were selected for inclusion in the proceedings published by Springer in LNCS/LNAI series. We will invite authors of the ICCCI papers to extend them and submit them for publication in TCCI.

We are very pleased that TCCI and the ICCCI conferences are strongly cemented as high-quality platforms for presenting and exchanging the most important and significant advances in CCI research and development. It is also our pleasure to announce the creation of the new Technical Committee on Computational Collective Intelligence within the Systems, Man and Cybernetics Society (SMC) of IEEE.

We would like to thank all the authors for their contributions to TCCI. This issue would not have been possible without the great efforts of the editorial board and many anonymously acting reviewers. We would like to express our sincere thanks to all of them. Finally, we would also like to express our gratitude to the LNCS editorial staff of Springer, in particular Alfred Hofmann, Ursula Barth, Peter Strasser and their team, who supported the TCCI journal.

July 2011   Ngoc Thanh Nguyen

Transactions on Computational Collective Intelligence

This Springer journal focuses on research in applications of the computer-based methods of computational collective intelligence (CCI) and their applications in a wide range of fields such as the Semantic Web, social networks and multi-agent systems. It aims to provide a forum for the presentation of scientific research and technological achievements accomplished by the international community.

The topics addressed by this journal include all solutions of real-life problems for which it is necessary to use computational collective intelligence technologies to achieve effective results. The emphasis of the papers published is on novel and original research and technological advancements. Special features on specific topics are welcome.

Table of Contents

Improved N-grams Approach for Web Page Language Identification

Ali Selamat

Software Engineering Research Group,
Faculty of Computer Science & Information Systems,
Universiti Teknologi Malaysia, UTM Johor Baharu Campus,
81310, Johor, Malaysia
aselamat@utm.my

Abstract. Language identification has been widely used for machine translations and information retrieval. In this paper, an improved N-grams (ING) approach is proposed for web page language identification. The improved N-grams approach is based on a combination of original N-grams (ONG) approach and a modified N-grams (MNG) approach that has been used for language identification of web documents. The features selected from the improved N-grams approach are based on N-grams frequency and N-grams position. The features selected from the original N-grams approach are based on a distance measurement and the features selected from the modified N-grams approach are based on a Boolean matching rate for language identification of Roman and Arabic scripts web pages. A large real-world document collection from British Broadcasting Corporation (BBC) website, which is composed of 1000 documents on each of the languages (e.g., Azeri, English, Indonesian, Serbian, Somali, Spanish, Turkish, Vietnamese, Arabic, Persian, Urdu, Pashto) have been used for evaluations. The precision, recall and $F1$ measures have been used to determine the effectiveness of the proposed improved N-grams (ING) approach. From the experiments, we have found that the improved N-grams approach has been able to improve the language identification of the contents in Roman and Arabic scripts web page documents from the available datasets.

Keywords: Monolingual, multilingual, web page language identification, N-grams approach.

1 Introduction

Language identification (LID) is the process of identifying the predefined language that has been used to write various types of documents. In order to identify the content of web documents, humans are the most accurate language identifier. Within seconds of reading a passage of a text, humans can determine whether it is a language they can understand. If it is a language that they are unfamiliar with, they often can make subjective judgments as to its similarity to a language that they already know. In this research, a term "language" is used to refer to

N.T. Nguyen (Ed.): Transactions on CCI V, LNCS 6910, pp. 1–26, 2011.

a natural communication system used by humans either in spoken or written forms. There are 7000 languages that have been reported in *Ethnologue* [1] that indicate a widely cited reference works on the languages available in the world.

Globalization has led to unlimited information sharing across the Internet, where communication among people in a bilingual environment is a critical challenge to be faced. Abd Rozan et al. [2] have noted the importance of monitoring the behavior and activities of world languages in cyberspace. The information collected from such studies has implications for customized ubiquitous learning[1], in which Information and Communication Technology (ICT) has to cope with the "digital divides"[2] that exist both within countries and regions and between countries. In addition, MacLean [3] has reasserted the status of language as a topic of major concern for researchers in the light of the rise in transnational corporations. Also, Redondo-Bellon [4] has analyzed the effects of bilingualism on the consumers in Spain. From the study, the author has found that language segmentation in various sectors and regions in Spain is very important in order to reach each linguistic group more efficiently. All of these examples reflect the significance of multi-languages identification and understanding between various ethnic groups in the world that will bring people together.

Therefore, in this paper we analyze the important of language identification of web documents as one of the crucial tasks in identifying the language belongs to the document. The same words may appear in many languages which use similar scripts for written communication. This is usually happen when the countries that are using the Arabic scripts for their written language (i.e., Saudi Arabia, Pakistan, Iran, Iraq, Turkey, etc.) and also the countries that use Roman scripts for written communications such as United Kingdom, France, Germany, Australia, Indonesia, Malaysia, etc. Many researchers have proposed different solutions in language identification problems of web documents such as support vector machine (SVM), neural networks (NN), rough-set theory, N-grams [5], etc. However, the effectiveness of the proposed algorithms in identifying the languages exist in the documents remain as important research area to be investigated.

In this paper we proposed an improved N-grams approach (ING) for web page language identification. The improved N-grams approach is based on a combination of an original N-grams (ONG) approach and a modified N-grams (MNG) approach used for language identification of web documents. The original N-grams (ONG) approach is based on a distance measurement while the modified N-grams (MNG) approach uses a Boolean matching rate for language identification. The improved N-grams approach uses both N-grams frequency and N-grams position in order to identify the languages that have been written in Roman and Arabic scripts web pages. The precision, recall, and $F1$ measures

---

[1] According to AbdRozan et al. [2], customized ubiquitous learning means that the learning is best conducted in the natural language of the student and present everywhere at once.

[2] Digital divide refers to the disparity between those who have use of and access to ICT versus those who do not [2].

have been used to evaluate the effectiveness of the approaches. From the experiments, we have found that the improved N-grams approach has been able to improve the language identification of the contents in Roman and Arabic scripts web page documents with then accuracy is above 96%.

This paper is organized as follows: Related works on language identification and recent development of N-grams approach for language identifications are discussed in Section 2. Section 3 describes the proposed improved N-grams approach (ING) for web page language identification. Section 4 explains the experimental setup used to evaluate the proposed improved N-grams approach for web page language identifications. The experimental results and discussions are explained in Section 5. Finally, the conclusion is discussed in Section 6.

2   Related Works on N-grams Used For Language Identification

Language identification is frequently used as an initial step in a text processing system that may involve machine translation, semantic understanding, categorization, searching, routing or storage for information retrieval [6]. In order to produce correct dictionaries, sentence parsers, profiles, distribution lists, and stop-word list to be used, the main pre-requisite is to know the language belongs to the given text. Incorrect identification of the language may resulted in garbled translations, faulty or no information analysis, and poor precision or recall during searching for the related documents of interest [7]. Language identification has been typically performed by trained professionals [8]. Manual language identification process is time consuming and costly if is performed by many language experts. In order to overcome the inefficiency of the manual process, the learning-based language identification methods using computational approaches have emerged. Although existing computational methods can produce reasonable results, they often resulted in a huge computational cost [8]. Also, many computational methods require large lists of words or N-grams with associated frequency counts for each of characters in the documents that belong to certain language. Calculations on large lists and matrices make these methods expensive to use [9]. Therefore, there is a need to improve the usage of N-grams approach for language identifications of web documents.

Many related works have been done on language identifications of web documents using N-grams approach. For example, Ng et al. [10] have investigated total N-grams, N-grams frequency, N-grams frequency document frequency, and N-grams frequency inverse document frequency of web page language identification. However, the authors found that the N-grams approach is not suitable to be used for language identification of web documents due to the required algorithm having dimensional and feature selectivity problems. Therefore, a machine learning method namely a fuzzy ARTMAP approach has been used for supervised language identification of web documents. Barroso et al. [11] have used N-grams and compare it with the support vector machines (SVM) and multilayer perceptron (MLP) classifiers for language identification of web documents.

However, the authors state that the proposed approach only satisfactorily identify three different languages written in Roman scripts that are Basque, Spanish and French. Wang et al. [12] have proposed a hierarchical system design for a language identification system. The authors claim that the hierarchical system has outperformed the N-grams based approach. Amine et al. [13] have proposed a language identification of text documents using hybrid algorithm based on a combination of the K-means and the artificial ants. The authors claim that the results are very promising and offer many perspectives.

Xiao et al. [14] have proposed the LVQ approach for language identification of web documents and the authors claim that the performance is five times better than the N-grams approach. Rehurek et al. [15] have proposed an improve N-grams based on the constructs language models based on word relevance and addresses these limitations. You et al. [16] have proposed an inclusion of morphological information in a web document including letter or letter-chunk N-grams and web-based page counts that are used to enhance the performance of language identification of web documents. The accuracy increases from 75.0% to 86.3%, or a 45.2% relative error reduction. Ng and Lee [17] have proposed a language identification of web documents of four Chinese dialects such as Wu, Cantonese, Min and Mandarin using N-gram features. Deng and Liu [18] have proposed automatic language identification using support vector machines and phonetic N-gram approaches. Botha et al. [19] have investigated the performance of text-based language identification systems on the 11 official languages of South Africa, where the N-gram statistics have been used as features for classification.

Cordoba et al. [20] have presented a novel approach for language identification based on a text categorization technique, namely an N-gram frequency ranking based on 5-gram. Thomas and Verma [21] have proposed a language identification of web documents using substrings of a person name based on letter N-grams to identify the language of its origin. Suo et al. [22] have proposed backend classifiers for for classifying the phone recognition and language modeling. Moscola et al. [23] have proposed hardware language identifier based on N-gram based language identifier. Yang and Siu et al. [24] have used N-best tokenization in a GMM-SVM language identification system and the n-best tokenization gives good performance improvement. Rouas [25] has analyzed the problem of prosodic differences among languages or dialects can be automatically determined for language identification using N-grams approach. The proposed model has been able to identify the dialectal areas, leading to the hypothesis that those dialects have prosodic differences. Hanif et al. [26] have studied on unicode aided language identification across multiple scripts and heterogeneous data using N-grams approach. Li et al. [27] have proposed a vector space modeling (VSM) approach to spoken language identification. The authors claimed that the VSM approach leads to a discriminative classifier backend, which is demonstrated to give superior performance over likelihood-based N-gram language modeling (LM) backend for long utterances.

However, the research done by the above researchers are mainly focusing on language identification of English and Chinese text documents. The studies on language identification of Arabic web documents have mainly been done by [10]. Therefore, the scalability and effectiveness of the proposed method on Arabic scripts related languages have not been widely investigated. Therefore, in this research an improved N-grams approach has been proposed in order to identify the languages belonging to Arabic and Roman scripts web based documents. The detail of the proposed improved N-grams approach is discussed in the following section.

3   Proposed Improved N-grams Approach

The proposed improved N-grams (INA) approach is based on a combination of original N-grams (ONG) approach and a modified N-grams (MNG) approach that has been used for language identification of web documents. The improved N-grams approach is based on N-grams frequency and N-grams position. The original N-grams is based on distance measurement and the modified N-grams approach uses a Boolean matching rate for language identification of Roman and Arabic scripts web pages. Before the proposed improved N-grams approach is discussed in detail in Section 3.4, the original N-grams approach is described in Section 3.4 and the modified N-grams approach is described in Section 3.3 to highlight the processes involved in the existing works of N-grams. The detail explanations are as follows:

3.1   N-grams Approach

The N-grams approach can be viewed as a sub-sequence of N items from a longer sequence of words. The item mentioned can refer to a letter, word, syllable or any logical data type that is defined by the application. Because of its simplicity in implementation and high accuracy in predicting the next possible sequence from a known sequence, the N-grams probability model is one of the most popular methods in statistical natural language processing [28]. The principal idea of using N-grams for language identification is that every language contains its own unique N-grams and tends to use certain N-grams more frequently than others, hence providing a clue about the language [29].

An N-gram order 1 (i.e., $N = 1$) is referred to as a monogram, N-gram order 2 as a bigram and N-gram order 3 as a trigram. The rest is generally referred to as "N-grams". For instance, a string "Hello World" that is written in Arabic scripts can be composed as a number of unigram and bigram as shown in Fig. 1. The fine dotted line means to shift the token to the next targeted gram according to the size of N-grams. Therefore, the tokens of unigram after processing are م, رر, ح, ب, ا, ل, ع, ا, ل, م; whereas bigrams after processing are م رر, رر ح, ح ب, ب ا, ا ل ا, ل, ل ع, ع ا, ا ل, ل م (the meaning of العالم مرحبا is "hello world").

Figure 2 shows the N-grams calculation between the testing and training profiles. Each language has its own training profile. The testing profile generated from the testing data is compared with certain training profile either in terms of distance, matching or frequency rates. The winner is selected based on the

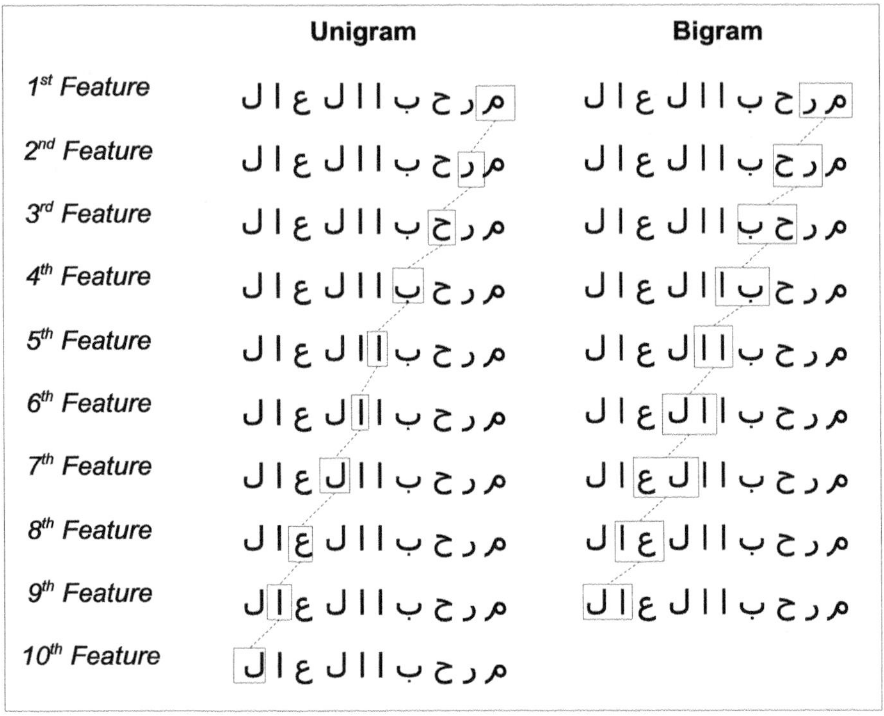

	Unigram	Bigram
1st Feature	ل ا ع ل ا ا ب ح ر مر	ل ا ع ل ا ا ب ح رر م
2nd Feature	ل ا ع ل ا ا ب ح ر مر	ل ا ع ل ا ا ب ح ر مر
3rd Feature	ل ا ع ل ا ا ب ح ر ر م	ل ا ع ل ا ا ب ح ر ر م
4th Feature	ل ا ع ل ا ا ب ح ر ر م	ل ا ع ل ا ا ب ح ر ر م
5th Feature	ل ا ع ل ا ا ب ح ر ر م	ل ا ع ل ا ا ب ح ر ر م
6th Feature	ل ا ع ل ا ا ب ح ر ر م	ل ا ع ل ا ا ب ح ر ر م
7th Feature	ل ا ع ل ا ا ب ح ر ر م	ل ا ع ل ا ا ب ح ر ر م
8th Feature	ل ا ع ل ا ا ب ح ر ر م	ل ا ع ل ا ا ب ح ر ر م
9th Feature	ل ا ع ل ا ا ب ح ر ر م	ل ا ع ل ا ا ب ح ر ر م
10th Feature	ل ا ع ل ا ا ب ح ر ر م	

Fig. 1. A simulation of the N-grams approach

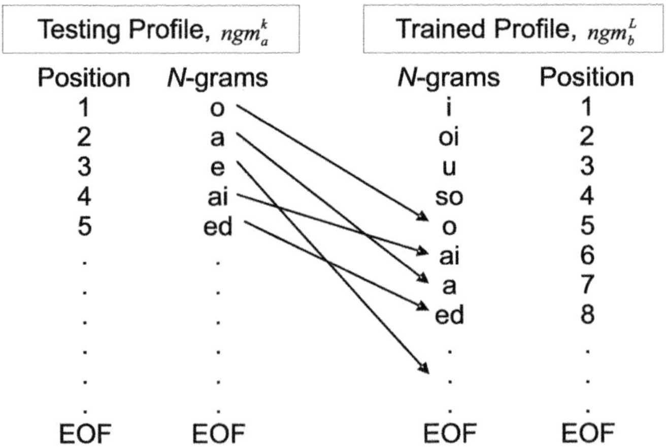

Testing Profile, ngm_a^k		Trained Profile, ngm_b^L	
Position	N-grams	N-grams	Position
1	o	i	1
2	a	oi	2
3	e	u	3
4	ai	so	4
5	ed	o	5
.	.	ai	6
.	.	a	7
.	.	ed	8
.	.	.	.
.	.	.	.
EOF	EOF	EOF	EOF

Fig. 2. Rank order statistics of N-grams (note: EOF is the end of file either in training or testing profile

algorithm used. For example, the winner is selected from a minimum distance rate and maximum matching or frequency rate. The detail of the calculations can be found in Cavnar [28].

3.2   Original N-grams Approach

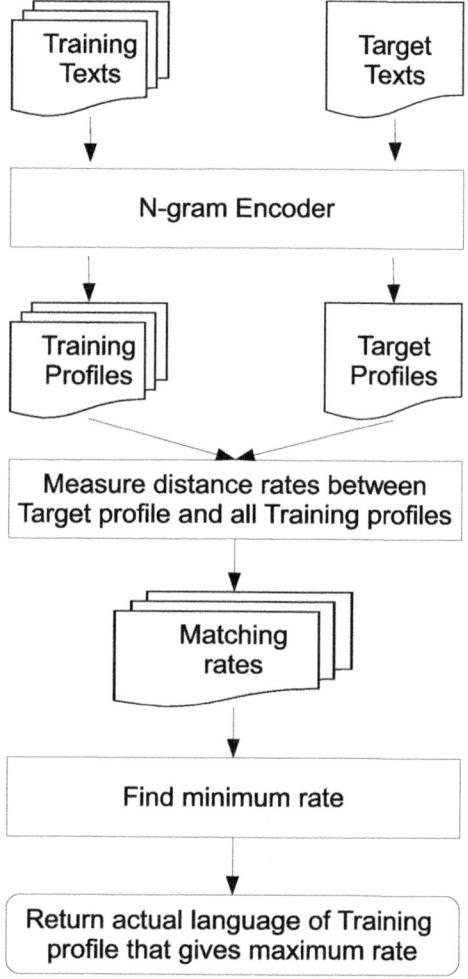

Fig. 3. System flow of the original N-grams [28]

The original N-grams (ONG) approach has been initially introduced by Cavnar [28] and the authors have use it for addressing the problem of text categorization and language identification. They have reported very high correct classification rate, 92.9% - 99.8% on eight Roman script languages of a Usenet newsgroup article. The algorithm is based on rank-order statistics on N-grams profile. In their experiments, the shortest text used for language identification was 300 bytes, whereas the training data sets were between 20 kilobytes (KB) to 120 KB. They have classified documents by calculating the distances of a testing document profile with all training documents profiles and then the shortest one has been selected as a winner. To perform the distance measurement, both training and testing profiles have to be sorted in descending order, which is from the highest score to the lowest score. It is illustrated in Fig. 3. The distance measurement is given in Eq. 1 where L is the particular language-trained profile, K is the total N-grams found in the testing profile, ngm_a is the particular N-grams in the testing profile, and ngm_b is the particular N-grams in the training profile. The actual output or testing of document language is selected among the $DM(L)$ with the minimum distance. The problem of original N-grams approach is the curse of dimensionality. At least 300 bytes of data are needed to produce a reasonable result and a particular threshold is also needed to be declared to avoid huge dimension of features in calculating the distance measurement. Otherwise, rank order statistics N-grams will fail to perform language identification.

$$DM(L) = \sum_{k=1}^{K} \sqrt{\left(ngm_a^k - ngm_b^L\right)^2} \tag{1}$$

Fig. 4 shows the algorithm that has been applied on the orignal N-grams (ONG) approach. The input is a dataset of experiments (D), the parameter of d_j represents the particular document j. The parameter L_i, represents the particular language of i and $\hat{S}$ represents the particular script of languages. The $\hat{S}_{begin}$ is representing the beginning of codepoint for a particular script, and the $\hat{S}_{end}$ is representing the end of codepoint for a particular script. The outputs are given as NF, which is the particular N-grams frequency of a particular training or a target profile. The ngm_b^L is the N-grams of the training profile and the ngm_a^k is the N-grams of the target profile. The $DM(L)$ is the distance measurement between the training and target profiles.

At the beginning of experiment, the experimental dataset is set to a particular script, $D \leftarrow \hat{S}$, and the boundary of that script is set to $\hat{S}_{begin}$ and $\hat{S}_{end}$ as shown on line 8 and 9 in Fig. 4. For each of a particular language, L_i which is a subset of a particular script, do the looping from line 11 to 22 until the end of the languages of that script. Then, for each particular document, d_j, do the looping from line 12 to 18 until the end of the document in the dataset. If the particular N-grams, ngm is between the boundary of $\hat{S}_{begin}$ and $\hat{S}_{end}$, then find the total of that particular N-grams, $\sum ngm_d$, in the particular document, d_j. Next, find the N-grams weighting as line 18 and proceed to next document. Otherwise, set the particular document, d_j as problematic document and proceed to next document. For line 19 until 21, it is used to find out the N-grams sequence of particular language and then set the features as the N-grams are ordered in descending. The process of N-grams feature selection is repeated until the end of the other languages in that script as shown in line 23. The training process is ended on line

1.	**INPUT:**
2.	D, is a data set of experiments
3.	**PARAMETERS:**
4.	d_j, is the particular document j. L_i, is the particular language i. $\hat{S}$, is the particular script. $\hat{S}_{begin}$, is the begin codepoint of a particular script. $\hat{S}_{end}$, is the end codepoint of particular script.
5.	**OUTPUT:**
6.	NF, Particular N-grams frequency in a document or data set. ngm_b^l, N-grams of the training profiles. ngm_a^k, N-grams of the target profiles. $DM(L)$, distance measurement between training profiles and target profiles, and minimum $DM(L)$ is selected as the winner or actual output.
7.	**BEGIN**
8.	$D \leftarrow \hat{S}$; //set the training data set to a particular script.
9.	set $\hat{S}_{begin}$ and $\hat{S}_{end}$; //based on the selected script
10.	**for each** $L_i \in \hat{S}$ **do**
11.	**for each** $d_j \in D$ **do**
12.	**if** $\hat{S}_{begin} \le ngm \le \hat{S}_{end}$ **then**
13.	**find** $\sum ngm_d$;
14.	$d_j + 1$;
15.	**else**
16.	set d_j as error document;
17.	$d_j + 1$; **continue;** //proceed to next document
18.	**find** $\sum ngm_d/T_d$;
19.	$NF_L(ngm) = \sum_{d=1}^{D} ngm_d/T_d$; //refer to N-grams approach
20.	**sort** $NF_L(ngm) \rightarrow ngm_b^l$;
21.	set $features = ngm_b^l$; //trained features of a language is set to ngm_b^l
22.	$L_i + 1$; //set to other languages of that particular script
23.	**repeat** the process from line 11 to 22 until the end of the languages of script;
24.	**end training**
25.	set d_z as testing document
26.	**if** $\hat{S}_{begin} \le ngm \le \hat{S}_{end}$ **then**
27.	**find** $\sum ngm_d$;
28.	**else**
29.	set d_z as error document;
30.	$NF(ngm) = \sum ngm_d/T_d$; //refer to N-grams approach
31.	**sort** $NF(ngm) \rightarrow ngm_a^k$;
32.	set $features = ngm_a^k$; //testing features of a document is set to ngm_a^k
33.	**find** $DM(L) = \sum_{k=1}^{K} \left(\sqrt{\left(ngm_a^k - ngm_b^l \right)^2} \right)$, where $L \in [1, i]$
34.	set minimum $DM(L)$ as the winner
35.	**END**

Fig. 4. Algorithm of original N-grams (ONG) approach [28]

24. We have to set the testing document as d_z, then the weight of one particular N-grams, $\sum ngm_d$ if figured out. If the ngm is between the boundary of $\hat{S}_{begin}$ and $\hat{S}_{end}$ the it is a candidate language, otherwise the set of d_z is treated as problematic document. After that, the testing features of a document is set to ngm_a^k. Finally, the process of finding the distance measurement between the training and testing profiles is represented as $DM(L)$ where the smallest one is selected as a winner.

3.3   Modified N-grams Approach

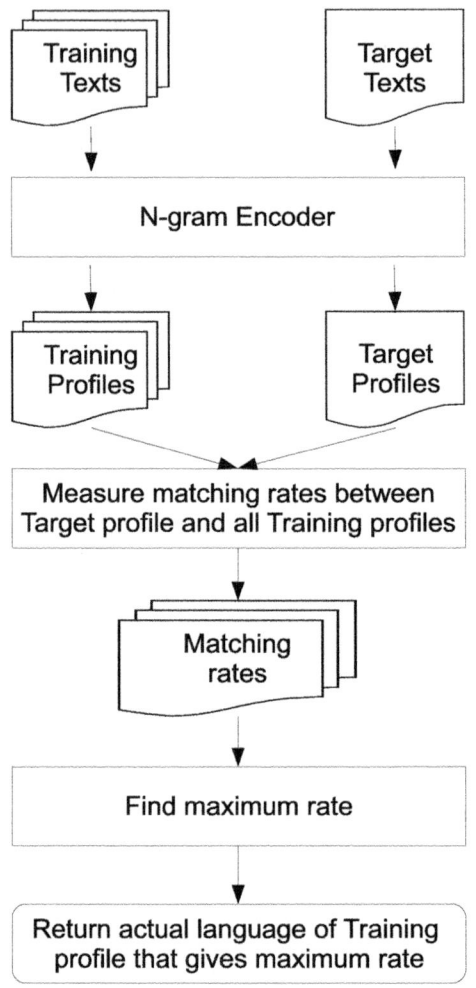

Fig. 5. System flow of the language identification process [29]

The modified N-grams (MNG) approach has been proposed by Choong et al. [29], which is an enhancement of original N-grams (ONG) approach. In the process design, a set of training profiles has been constructed by converting the training texts in various languages, scripts, and character encoding schemes into the N-grams. The generated training profile contained a set of distinct N-grams without frequency of occurrence of the N-grams. In the same way, the system has converted the target text into a target profile. The system then measured the matching rates of N-grams between the target profile and the training profiles. The system classified the target profile belonging to the training profile that yield the highest matching rate [29]. Fig. 5 shows the process flow of modified N-grams.

Unlike many other N-grams based approach, the modified N-grams approach does not depending on the N-grams frequency. Instead, the modified N-grams approach uses a Boolean method to decide the output of the matching. The Boolean method returns a value of 1 if the N-grams from the target profiles are found among the training profiles. The Boolean method returns a value of 0 if there is no match from the target profiles. After all of the N-grams in the target profiles have been compared with the training profiles, the system derives the matching rate by dividing the total match values and the total number of distinct N-grams in the target profiles as follows:

$$R(L) = \sum_{x=1}^{n} \frac{B(x)}{n} \tag{2}$$

where $B(x) = 0$ if s_x did not match with t_y and $B(x) = 1$ if s_x match with t_y where $y \in [1, m]$. Equation 2 shows the matching mechanism has been used by Choong et al. [29], where the target profile is s; the number of distinct N-grams in s is n; the list of N-grams in $s = \{s_1, s_2, s_3, \cdots, s_n\}$; the training profile is t; the number of distinct N-grams in training profile is m; the list of N-grams in $t = \{t_1, t_2, t_3, \cdots, t_m\}$. $R(L)$ is the rate of a particular language, L, at which the xth distinct N-grams in the target profile matches with the yth distinct N-grams in the training profile. $B(x)$ is the Boolean value that corresponds to the matching rates between s_x and t_y. The highest value of a particular language, $R(L)$, is selected as the winner. As the modified N-grams approach is having problems with the accuracy of language identification, this method cannot perform a correct identification if two or more languages found with the same matching rate.

Fig. 6 shows the algorithm that has been applied on the modified N-grams approach. The input is a dataset of experiments, D. The parameter d_j is used to represent the particular document. The j and L_i are the particular language i and the $\hat{S}$ represents the particular script of languages. The parameter $\hat{S}_{begin}$ represents the beginning of codepoint of a particular script, and the $\hat{S}_{end}$ represents the end of codepoint of a particular script. The output of NF is referring to the particular N-grams frequency of a particular training or target profile. The t_y represents the N-grams of the training profile and the s_x represents the N-grams of the target profile. The $R(L)$ represents the matching rates between the training and target profiles.

The process involved in modified N-grams approach is similar to the original N-grams approach except the steps shown on line 20, 21, 31, 32, 33, and 34 in Fig. 6. The t_y and s_x are two paraments that represent the modified N-grams in the training and testing profiles. The steps that are shown on line 33 are used to find the $R(L)$ based on the matching rate of a particular language. If a Boolean rate $B(x)$, is equivalent to true then the $B(x)$ is set to true.

1.	**INPUT**:
2.	D, is a data set of experiments
3.	**PARAMETERS**:
4.	d_j, is the particular document j. L_i, is the particular language i. $\hat{S}$, is the particular script. $\hat{S}_{begin}$, is the begin codepoint of a particular script. $\hat{S}_{end}$, is the end codepoint of particular script.
5.	**OUTPUT:**
6.	NF, Particular N-grams frequency in a document or data set. t_y, N-grams of the training profiles. s_x, N-grams of the target profiles. $R(L)$, distance measurement between training profiles and target profiles, and maximum $R(L)$ is selected as the winner or actual output.
7.	**BEGIN**
8.	$D \leftarrow \hat{S}$; //set the training data set to a particular script.
9.	**set** $\hat{S}_{begin}$ and $\hat{S}_{end}$; //based on the selected script
10.	**for each** $L_i \in \hat{S}$ **do**
11.	**for each** $d_j \in D$ **do**
12.	**if** $\hat{S}_{begin} \leq ngm \leq \hat{S}_{end}$ **then**
13.	**find** $\sum ngm_d$;
14.	$d_j + 1$;
15.	**else**
16.	set d_j as error document;
17.	$d_j + 1$; **continue**; //proceed to next document
18.	**find** $\sum ngm_d/T_d$;
19.	$NF_L(ngm) = \sum_{d=1}^{D} ngm_d/T_d$; //refer to N-grams approach
20.	**sort** $NF_L(ngm) \rightarrow t_y$;
21.	**set** $features = t_y$; //trained features of a language is set to t_y
22.	$L_i + 1$; //set to other languages of that particular script
23.	**repeat** the process from line 11 to 22 until the end of the languages of script;
24.	**end training**
25.	set d_z as testing document
26.	**if** $\hat{S}_{begin} \leq ngm \leq \hat{S}_{end}$ **then**
27.	**find** $\sum ngm_d$;
28.	**else**
29.	set d_z as error document;
30.	$NF(ngm) = \sum ngm_d/T_d$; //refer to N-grams approach
31.	**sort** $NF(ngm) \rightarrow s_x$;
32.	**set** $features = s_x$; //testing features of a document is set to s_x
33.	**find** $R(L) = \sum_{x=1}^{n} \frac{B(x)}{n}$, where $B(x) = \begin{cases} 0 \text{ if } s_x \text{ did not matched with } t_y \\ 1 \text{ if } s_x \text{ matched with } t_y \end{cases}$
34.	set maximum $R(L)$ as the winner
35.	**END**

Fig. 6. Algorithm of modified N-grams (MNG) approach [29]

3.4   Improved N-grams Approach

The improved N-grams (ING) approach is an enhancement of the original N-grams approach. The ING approach makes use of the N-grams frequency (NF), and the minimum feature position (FP). Fig. 7 shows the flow of the proposed improved N-grams approach by using the NF and FP. Similar to the original

N-grams (ONG) approach, the ING approach uses rank order statistics in order to produce the training and testing profiles. However, the proposed improved N-grams (ING) approach uses the N-grams frequency (NF_q) that has been obtained in the testing document and feature position (FP_p) of the training profile. The N-grams frequency of the training profile (NF_p) is given by Eq. 6 and the feature position of the training profile (FP_p) is given by the index of feature after rank order statistics. The ING approach will show that different languages will produce different feature position (FP) although the particular feature is using the same N-grams. Initially, the maximum N-grams frequency, NF_q will be identified using the Eq. 4 if the true condition is becoming the predicted output. Otherwise, the feature position, FP_p will be identified when the type of language is identified. If these two parameters fail to identify the type of language in the document, then the values of NF and FP will be produced again by reducing 10% of the end of the particular testing datasets. Finally, the actual output, $\omega(L)$ will be predicted through the maximum N-grams frequency, NF. The minimum feature position, FP, is given by Eq. 3.

$$\omega(L) = \{\max(NF(L)) \,|\min(FP(L))\}\qquad(3)$$

$$NF(L) = \sum NF_q \quad where \; ngm_q \; found \; in \; ngm_p\qquad(4)$$

$$FP(L) = \sum FP_p \quad where \; ngm_q \; found \; in \; ngm_p\qquad(5)$$

Fig. 8 shows the algorithm that has been applied on the proposed improved N-grams (ING) approach. The input is a dataset of experiments (D) and the parameter of d_j represents the particular document j . The parameter L_i represents the particular language of i. The parameter $\hat{S}$ represents the particular script of languages and the $\hat{S}_{begin}$ represents the beginning of codepoint for a particular script. The parameter $\hat{S}_{end}$ represents the end of codepoint for a particular script. The output (NF) is used to represent the particular N-grams frequency of a particular training or target profile. The FP is used to represent the feature position of the training and testing profiles and the $\omega(L)$ represents the output of the decision.

Similarly, the process of the proposed improved N-grams (ING) approach is similar to the original N-grams (ONG) approach as shown in Fig. 6 except the conditions state on lines 20, 21, 31, 32, 33, and 34, respectively. The NP_p and FP_p represent the N-grams frequency and feature position of training profile, respectively. The NP_q and FP_q are N-grams frequency and feature position of target profile, respectively. On line 33, the algorithm it is used to find out the $\omega(L)$ by selecting the value from the maximum value of $NF_q(L)$ followed by the minimum value of $FP_p(L)$. If both $NF_q(L)$ and $FP_p(L)$ are failed to produce

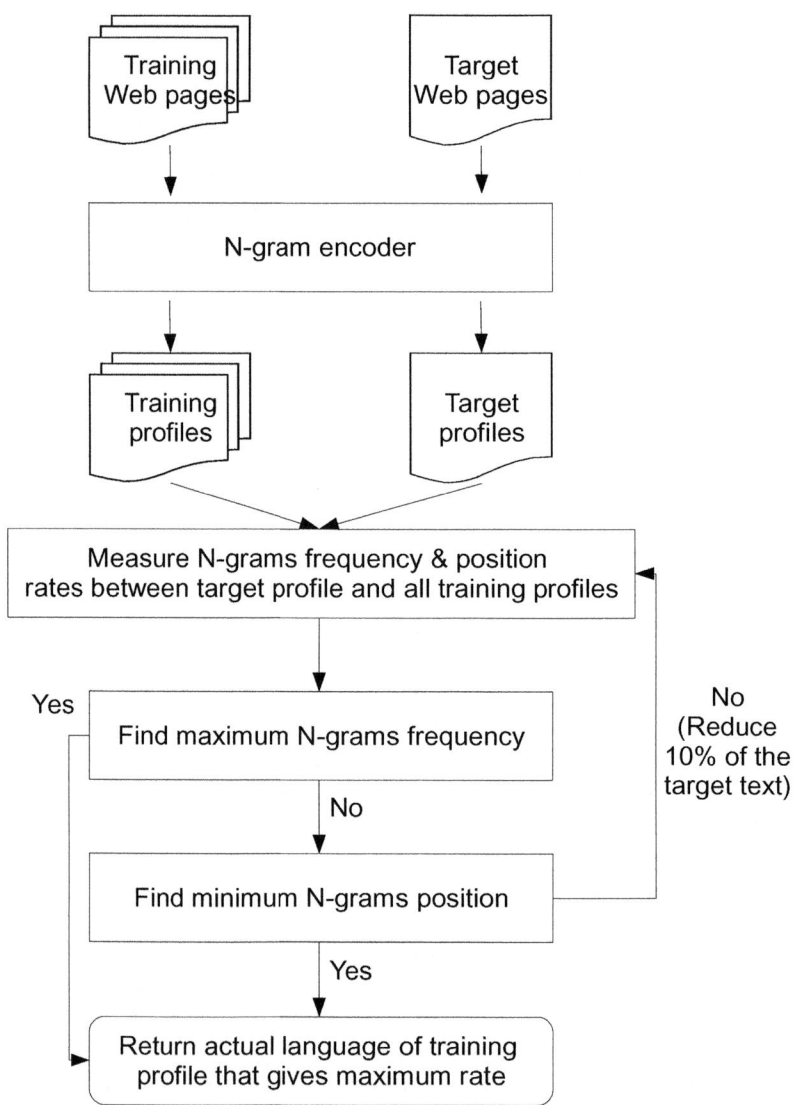

Fig. 7. The flow of the proposed improved N-grams (ING) approach

1.	**INPUT**:
2.	D, is a data set of experiments
3.	**PARAMETERS**:
4.	d_j, is the particular document j. L_i, is the particular language i. $\hat{S}$, is the particular script. $\hat{S}_{begin}$, is the begin codepoint of a particular script. $\hat{S}_{end}$, is the end codepoint of particular script.
5.	**OUTPUT**:
6.	NF, Particular N-grams frequency of training of target profile. FP, is the feature position of training or target profile. Winner is selected from maximum $NF(L)$ or minimum $FP(L)$ as $\omega(L)$.
7.	**BEGIN**
8.	$D \leftarrow \hat{S}$; //set the training data set to a particular script.
9.	set $\hat{S}_{begin}$ and $\hat{S}_{end}$; //based on the selected script
10.	**for each** $L_i \in \hat{S}$ **do**
11.	**for each** $d_j \in D$ **do**
12.	**if** $\hat{S}_{begin} \leq ngm \leq \hat{S}_{end}$ **then**
13.	**find** $\sum ngm_d$;
14.	$d_j + 1$;
15.	**else**
16.	set d_j as error document;
17.	$d_j + 1$; **continue**; //proceed to next document
18.	**find** $\sum ngm_d / T_d$;
19.	$NF_L(ngm) = \sum_{d=1}^{D} ngm_d / T_d$; //refer to N-grams approach
20.	**sort** $NF_L(ngm) \rightarrow \{NF_p, FP_p\}$;
21.	set $features = \{NF_p, FP_p\}$; //training profile features are set to NF_p, FP_p
22.	$L_i + 1$; //set to other languages of that particular script
23.	**repeat** the process from line 11 to 22 until the end of the languages of script;
24.	**end training**
25.	set d_z as testing document
26.	**if** $\hat{S}_{begin} \leq ngm \leq \hat{S}_{end}$ **then**
27.	**find** $\sum ngm_d$;
28.	**else**
29.	set d_z as error document;
30.	$NF(ngm) = \sum ngm_d / T_d$; //refer to N-grams approach
31.	**sort** $NF(ngm) \rightarrow \{NF_q, FP_q\}$;
32.	set $features = \{NF_q, FP_q\}$; //target profile features are set to NF_q, FP_q
33.	**find** $\omega(L) = \{max(NF(L)) | min(FP(L))\}$
34.	set $\omega(L)$ as the winner, **otherwise repeat** line 25 by reducing 10% of the data, d_z
35.	**END**

Fig. 8. Algorithm of the proposed improved N-grams (ING) approach

the output then process will be repeated based on the statement on line 25 by reducing 10% datasets at the end of d_z.

4 Experimental Setup

Figure 9 shows the methodology that has been designed for web page language identification. It is divided into several stages: pre-processing process, script determination process, sentence segmentation process, feature selection process, feature extraction process, and language identification process. The details on each of the process are explained as follows:

4.1 Dataset Preparations Process

In this stage, the datasets with the predefined languages have been collected from the BBC (British Broadcasting) news website. The datasets have been divided into two categories, training and testing sets. The training dataset is used to determine the features of a particular language through certain statistical analysis that will be explained in the section on feature selection. The testing dataset is used to validate the features found in the training process. The total dataset of each language is 1000 pages and the validation process is done based on two particular language scripts belonging to the Arabic and Roman web documents.

The languages used for Arabic scripts document identification are Arabic, Persian, Urdu, and Pashto. The languages used for Roman scripts documents language identifications are Azeri, English, Indonesian, Serbian, Somali, Spanish, Turkish, and Vietnamese. The dataset that has been collected contain a monolingual web page will be used for testing the monolingual language identification of web document. The multilingual validation of web document is done based on sentences that have been derived from the monolingual web page because a sentence is the smallest unit of a text that gives a certain meaning.

4.2 Training Documents Process

After the preparation of the dataset has been completed, the training and testing documents will be used in the pre-processing process in order to filter out the noise exist in the text documents. Example of noises are programming code, broken string, and unrecognized string, etc. Initially, the programming codes along with the downloaded web page will be removed by using the HTMLEditorKit.ParserCallback open source toolkit [5] . It is followed by the unicode conversion from the original encoding [29]. After the conversion process has been completed, the broken or unrecognized strings are removed for preventing the bias during a statistical analysis process. Then, the pre-processed dataset will be used for further processing that will be explained in Section 4.3.

4.3   Preprocessing of Documents Process

The pre-processed document will be passed to script determination process in order to verify whether that document comprises the same script characters or different scripts. It is assumed that a text with the same script characters is written using one particular language only and a text with different scripts characters is written in a multilingual web page. However, it may happen that a text with same script characters is written in multiple languages. However, this situation has not been taken into consideration in this study. There are certain scripts that belong to one particular language only such as a unicode script of Hangul compatibility Jamo belongs to the Hangul language only [29]. As it is a monolingual script, it can easily be associated with the corresponding language.

4.4   Sentence Segmentations Process

The sentence segmentation process is done in order to derive the sentences of the texts. It is done based on the punctuation such as full stop, question mark, exclamation mark, etc. Sentences are basically used on the multilingual web page identification. In any particular web page, if the content of the texts contain about 70% of English and 30% of Mandarin languages, then these sentences can be considered as the smallest units for language identification process. In other words, a sentence in the text must belong to a particular script and language. It is assumed that the words and phrases are not practical to be considered as the smallest unit to be used for a language identification process because of the similar attributes may exist in more than one languages [29]. The complexity of segmenting the Chinese and Japanese sentences is that the Chinese and Japanese sentences are composed of characters without any spaces and even none of any punctuation in Chinese classiscal texts. Therefore Chinese character segmentation which is to find the final word boundaries is the crucial task for Chinese language identification. Research has been done to solve this problems address by Ng and Lee [17].

4.5   Feature Selections Process

The feature selection process is particularly used for training process. It is a process to reduce the dimension of features that can be used for language prediction. The N-grams approach has been proposed by Cavnar et al. [28] that used the algorithm to derive the sub-sequence string of a text. In this study, the mixed of unigram, bigrams, and trigrams are used as the feature selection algorithm. The mixed unigram, bigrams, and trigrams are referred as mixed N-grams, ngm. The mixed N-grams frequency of a particular language, $NF_L(ngm)$, is the frequency of a particular N-grams in the texts against the total frequency of equivalent sized of N-grams as shown in Eq. 6. The features will be selected from among the high mixed N-grams frequency of average training dataset. The feature selection process on each of the documents belonging to different languages has been done separately to ensure the process is done accurately.

4.6   Feature Extractions Process

The feature extraction process is used on the testing dataset for language prediction of the web documents. It is based on the mixture of N-grams frequency as shown in Eq. 6. However, the mixed N-grams frequency used for testing dataset does not take into account the average value of the whole data set based on Eq. 6 as follows:

$$NF_L\,(ngm) = \sum_{d=1}^{D}(ngm_d/T_d) \tag{6}$$

where the N-grams frequency of the learning profile (NF_L), from a set of documents $(d = 1, \ldots, D)$ and T_d represents the target documents. In other words, the feature extraction process will use of all the N-grams that have been produced from testing dataset. The feature selection process will only choose the features of the training dataset that matched with the threshold values. The features that have been produced in the feature extraction process will be compared to the features of each language found in the feature selection.

4.7   Language Identification Algorithms

The language identification algorithms are used to determine the predefined language of a particular data. Three language models are selected for performance evaluation: the original N-grams (ONG) approach [28], the modified N-grams (MNG) approach [29], and the proposed improved N-grams (ING) approach are used to identify the language belongs to a web document as described in Section 3.2, 3.3, and 3.4, respectively . Basically, these algorithms are based on the feature position, appearance, and frequencies. The proposed algorithm will compare the score that has been produced by each of the languages and the output will be the winner or the so-called actual output. Then, the actual output will be compared to the desired output in order to justify the performance of identifier as stated in the Section 4.8.

Table 1. The definitions of the parameters a, b, and c which are used in Table 2

Value	Meaning
a	The system and the expert agree with the assigned category
b	The system disagrees with the assigned category but the expert did
c	The expert disagrees with the assigned category but the system did
d	The system and the expert disagree with the assigned category

4.8   Evaluation Measurements

The proposed approaches are evaluated using the standard of information retrieval measurements that are precision (p), recall (r), and $F1$. They are defined as follows:

$$\text{precision} = \frac{a}{a + b} \tag{7}$$

Table 2. The decision matrix for calculating the classification accuracies

Expert System		
	Yes	No
Yes	a	b
No	c	d

$$\text{recall} = \frac{a}{a+c} \tag{8}$$

$$F1 = \frac{2}{\frac{1}{\text{precision}} + \frac{1}{\text{recall}}} \tag{9}$$

where the values of a, b, and c are defined in Table 1. The relationship between the classifier and the expert adjustment is expressed using four values as shown in Table 2. The $F1$ measure is a kind of average of precision and recall.

The precision describes the probability that a web document (randomly selected) retrieved document is relevant to the certain language. The recall describes the probability that a relevant web document is retrieved. The overall evaluation measure of the language identification on Arabic and Roman scripts is $F1$ that describes the average between precision and recall.

5   Experimental Results and Discussions

In this study, two experiments have been conducted to examine the proposed approaches in identifying the languages exist in the given web pages. The first experiment is to measure the effectiveness of web page language identification using Arabic and Romans scripts based web documents based on the precision, recall, and $F1$ measurements. Second, the experiment is done based on sentence-based identification of multilingual web page. The experimental results are stated as follows:

5.1   Effectiveness of Web Page Language Identification

The effectiveness of web page language identification as shown in Table 3 has been evaluated using precision, recall, and $F1$ measures of Arabic scripts used for language identification. Four Arabic languages such as Arabic, Persian, Urdu, and Pashto have been used in the experiment. Each language dataset is divided into training and testing datasets. From the experiments, the average precision, recall, and $F1$ measures of the original N-grams (ONG) approach is 66.60%, 61.41%, and 61.63%, respectively. However, the results of the experiments using the modified and the proposed improved N-grams approaches are 100% on both approaches. Table 2 shows the precision, recall, and $F1$ measures of Roman script web page language identification. Eight languages of Roman script such as Azeri,

Table 3. The precision, recall, and $F1$ measures of Arabic script web page language identification

Language Class	Arabic	Persian	Urdu	Pashto	Average (%)
Original N-grams (ONG) Approach					
Precision (%)	93.80	99.60	0.00	73.00	66.60
Recall (%)	48.00	97.65	0.00	100.00	61.41
$F1$ (%)	63.50	98.62	0.00	84.39	61.63
Modified N-grams (MNG) Approach					
Precision (%)	100.00	100.00	100.00	100.00	100.00
Recall (%)	100.00	100.00	100.00	100.00	100.00
$F1$ (%)	100.00	100.00	100.00	100.00	100.00
Improved N-grams (ING) Approach					
Precision (%)	100.00	100.00	100.00	100.00	100.00
Recall (%)	100.00	100.00	100.00	100.00	100.00
$F1$ (%)	100.00	100.00	100.00	100.00	100.00

English, Indonesian, Serbian, Somali, Spanish, Turkish, and Vietnamese have been used in the experiment. The average precision, recall, and $F1$ measures of the original N-grams approach are 74.75%, 89.37%, and 72.33%, respectively. However, the other methods have shown 100% in average precision, recall, and $F1$ measures. Therefore, it is concluded that original N-grams approach give the worst results compared to other methods in terms of precision, recall, and $F1$ measures.

5.2   Accuracy of Web Page Language Identification

Figures 10 and 11 show the results of web page language identification accuracy against the threshold value used. For the Arabic scripts web page language identification, the accuracy of original N-grams (ONG) approach on the threshold values of 10, 20, 30, 40, 50, 100, 200, 300, 400, and 500 are 85.40%, 97.85%, 85.05%, 85.65%, 91.40%, 88.55%, 26.20%, 5.85%, 1.55%, and 0.60%, respectively. However, for the modified N-grams (MNG) approach, the accuracy are 38.90%, 99.90%, 99.90%, 99.90%, 99.90%, 99.90%, 100.00%, 99.90%, 99.90%, and 99.90%, respectively. Furthermore, for the proposed improved N-grams (ING) approach, the accuracies are 99.55%, 99.90%, 99.90%, 100.00%, 100.00%, 100.00%, 100.00%, 99.90%, 99.90%, and 99.90%, respectively.

For the Roman script web page language identification, the accuracy of original N-grams (ONG) approach on threshold values of 10, 20, 30, 40, 50, 100, 200, 300, 400, and 500 are 95.95%, 96.65%, 97.48%, 98.18%, 98.38%, 90.45%, 52.55%, 24.38%, 15.22%, and 6.98% respectively. However, when the modified N-grams (MNG) approach has been used for the experiments, the accuracies are 25%, 39.2%, 74.38%, 89%, 91.9%, 92.42%, 99.58%, 99.58%, 99.58%, and 99.85%, respectively. For the proposed improved N-grams (ING) approach, the accuracies

Table 4. The precision, recall, and $F1$ measures of Roman script web page language identification

Language Class	Azeri	English	Indonesian	Serbian	Somali	Spanish	Turkish	Vietnamese	Average (%)
Original N-grams (ONG) Approach									
Precision (%)	15.60	100.00	100.00	100.00	100.00	34.40	88.20	59.80	74.75
Recall (%)	100.00	99.01	81.17	98.62	36.18	100.00	100.00	100.00	89.37
$F1$ (%)	26.99	99.50	89.61	89.61	53.14	51.19	93.73	74.84	72.33
Modified N-grams (MNG) Approach									
Precision (%)	100.00	100.00	100.00	100.00	100.00	100.00	100.00	100.00	100.00
Recall (%)	100.00	100.00	100.00	100.00	100.00	100.00	100.00	100.00	100.00
$F1$ (%)	100.00	100.00	100.00	100.00	100.00	100.00	100.00	100.00	100.00
Improved N-grams (ING) Approach									
Precision (%)	100.00	100.00	100.00	100.00	100.00	100.00	100.00	100.00	100.00
Recall (%)	100.00	100.00	100.00	100.00	100.00	100.00	100.00	100.00	100.00
$F1$ (%)	100.00	100.00	100.00	100.00	100.00	100.00	100.00	100.00	100.00

for Roman script web page language identification are 91.57%, 90.58%, 99.7%, 99.65%, 99.75%, 99.8%, 99.82%, 99.8%, 99.78%, and 99.75%, respectively. From these two experiments, it is observed that the proposed improved N-grams approach performs better than original N-grams approach and the modified N-grams approach.

5.3   Sentence-Based Identification of Multilingual Web Page

Fig. 12 shows the result of sentence-based identification of multilingual web page. The experiment is based on the sentences extracted from a particular text that has randomly been selected for training and testing of the datasets. The size of the dataset is 1000 units. Threshold used in this experiment is 50. The average accuracies of the original, modified, and proposed improved N-grams approaches are 39.57%, 97.09%, and 97.95%, respectively. It is noticed that the proposed improved N-grams (ING) approach performs better than the modified N-grams (MNG) approach.

5.4   Noise Tolerance of Language Identifier

An algorithm in computer science is consider as a robust algorithm if it continues to operate despite noises in the input dataset. In this study, the measurements used in the experiments such as precision, recall, and $F1$ have been used to justify the robustness of the stated approaches. The modified and proposed improved N-grams approaches are more robust than original N-grams (ONG) approach for web page language identification. In other words, these methods perform more reliably against the noises in the web pages. As observed from the experiment, the significant difference is that the proposed N-grams approach takes into consideration both the N-grams frequency and the N-grams position in producing

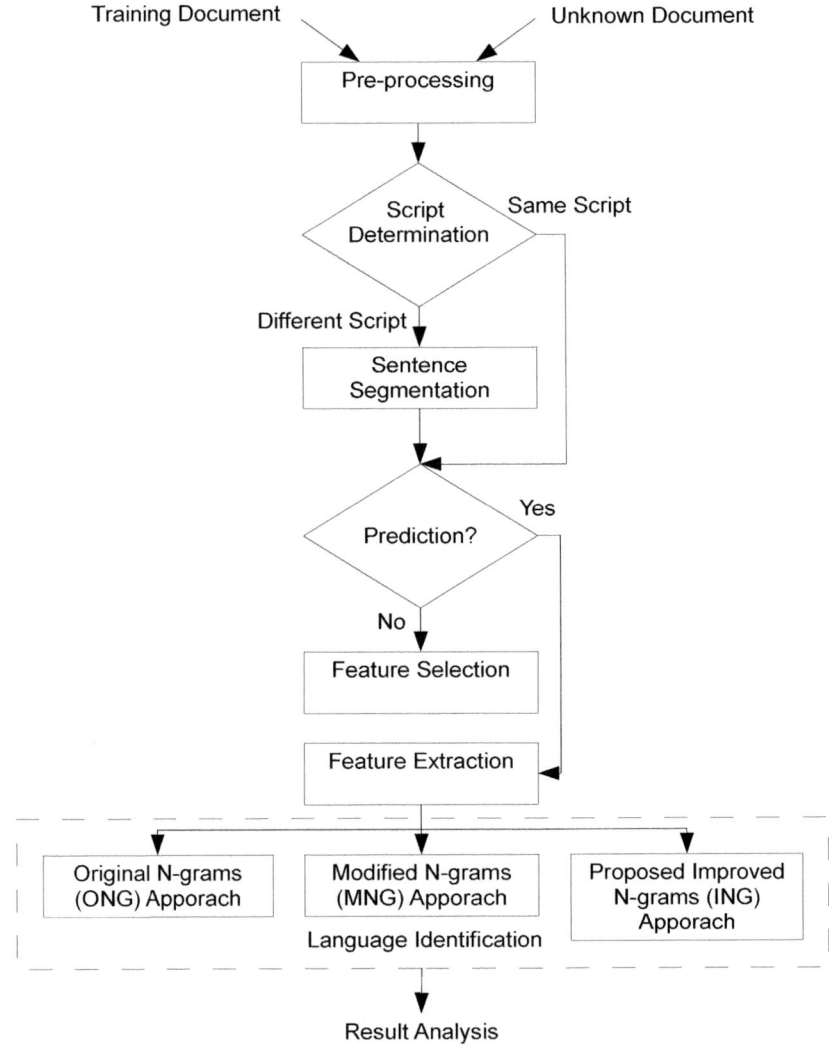

Fig. 9. The process flow of language identification

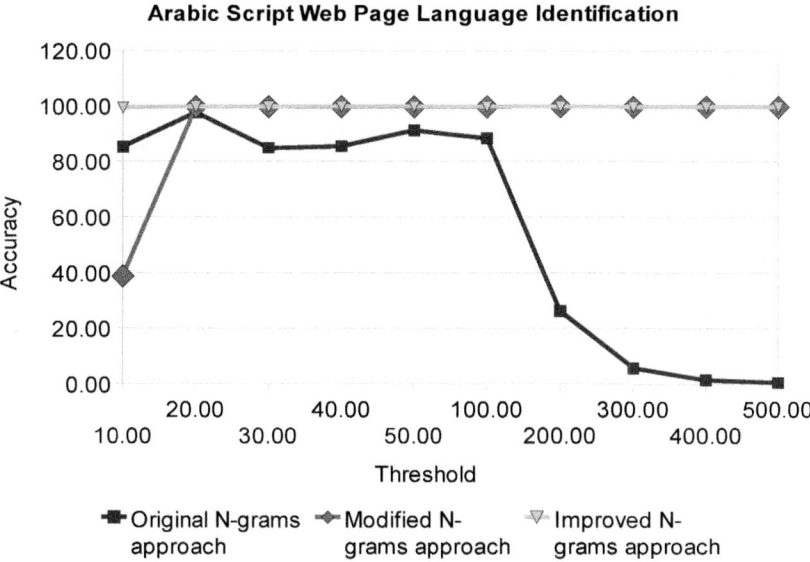

Fig. 10. Accuracy of Arabic script web page language identification

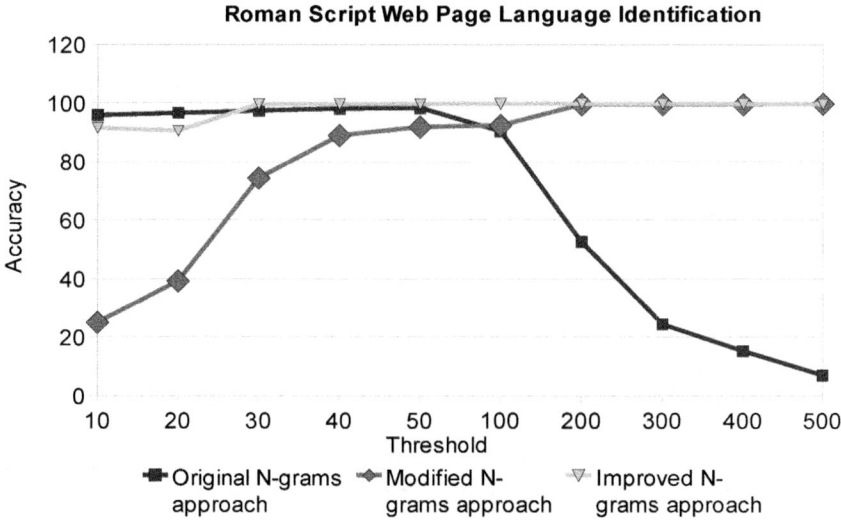

Fig. 11. Accuracy of Roman script web page language identification

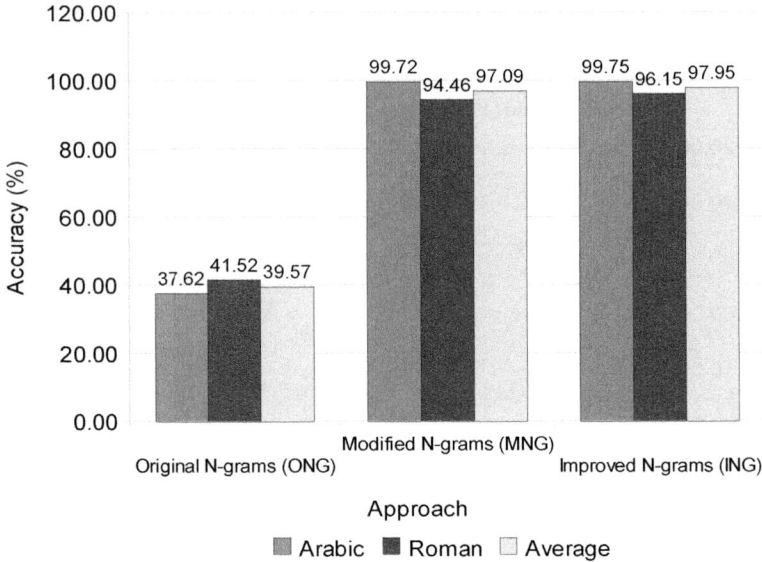

Fig. 12. Accuracy of sentence based language identification

the accurate results. However, this situation may be different if other domain dataset is used for the experiments.

6   Conclusion

Language identification is a core technology in various multilingual applications, especially in web services. This is a challenging task because of the ever increasing numbers of internet users and web documents existed in the internet. There are tremendous number of web pages emerging everyday. The problem is further aggravated by the complexity and diversity of the emerging of web applications and services. In this study, a web page language identification system has been proposed using an improved modified N-grams approach. The proposed improved N-grams approach has been compared using the conventional methods namely the original N-grams approach and the modified N-grams approach. The proposed improved N-grams approach has been able to determine the accuracy of the experimental datasets. The issues of computational cost and the scalability limitations have not been addressed in this study due to constraint of the existing computational facilities. In future studies, it is necessary to analyze such parameters to increase the reliability of the proposed approach used for web page language identification.

Acknowledgments. The author wishes to thank Mr. Ng Choon Ching for developing the experiments for this research. This work is supported by the Ministry of Higher Education Malaysia (MOHE) under Fundamental Research

Grant Scheme (FRGS) and Universiti Teknologi Malaysia under the Research University Funding Scheme (Q.J130000.7110.02H47). The author is also grateful to the anonymous reviewers for their valuable and insightful comments.

References

1. Gordon, R.G.: Ethnologue: Languages of the world. In: SIL International Dallas, TX (2005)
2. Abd Rozan, M.Z., Mikami, Y., Abu Bakar, A.Z., Vikas, O.: Multilingual ict education: Language observatory as a monitoring instrument. In: Proceedings of the South East Asia Regional Computer Confederation 2005: ICT Building Bridges Conference, Sydney, Australia, vol. 46, pp. 53–61 (2005)
3. Maclean, D.: Beyond english: Transnational corporations and the strategic management of language in a complex multilingual business environment. Management Decision 44(10), 1377–1390 (2006)
4. Redondo-Bellon, I.: The effects of bilingualism on the consumer: The case of spain. European Journal of Marketing 33(11/12), 1136–1160 (1999)
5. Selamat, A., Ng, C.C.: Arabic script web page language identifications using decision tree neural networks. Pattern Recognition, Elsevier Science (2010), doi:10.1016/j.patcog.2010.07.009
6. Chowdhury, G.G.: Natural language processing. Annual Review of Information Science and Technology 37(1), 51–89 (2003)
7. Lewandowski, D.: Problems with the use of web search engines to find results in foreign languages. Online Information Review 32(5), 668–672 (2008)
8. Jin, H., Wong, K.F.: A chinese dictionary construction algorithm for information retrieval. ACM Transactions on Asian Language Information Processing 1(4), 281–296 (2002)
9. Botha, G., Zimu, V., Barnard, E.: Text-based language identification for the south african languages. In: Proceedings of the 17th Annual Symposium of the Pattern Recognition Association of South Africa 2006, Parys, South Africa, pp. 7–13 (2006)
10. Ng, C.-C., Selamat, A.: Improve feature selection method of web page language identification using fuzzy artmap. International Journal of Intelligent Information and Database Systems 4(6), 629–642 (2010)
11. Barroso, N., de Ipiña, K.L., Ezeiza, A., Barroso, O., Susperregi, U.: Hybrid approach for language identification oriented to multilingual speech recognition in the basque context. In: Graña Romay, M., Corchado, E., Garcia Sebastian, M.T. (eds.) HAIS 2010. LNCS (LNAI), vol. 6076, pp. 196–204. Springer, Heidelberg (2010)
12. Wang, H., Xiao, X., Zhang, X., Zhang, J., Yan, Y.: A hierarchical system design for language identification. In: 2nd International Symposium on Information Science and Engineering, ISISE 2009, pp. 443–446 (2010)
13. Amine, A.B., Elberrichi, Z., Simonet, M.: Automatic language identification: an alternative unsupervised approach using a new hybrid algorithm. International Journal of Computer Science and Applications 7(1), 94–107 (2010)
14. Xiao, H., Yu, L., Chen, K.: An efficient method of language identification using lvq network. In: International Conference on Signal Processing Proceedings, ICSP, pp. 1690–1694 (2008)
15. Řehůřek, R., Kolkus, M.: Language identification on the web: Extending the dictionary method. In: Gelbukh, A. (ed.) CICLing 2009. LNCS (LNAI), vol. 5449, pp. 357–368. Springer, Heidelberg (2009)

16. You, J.-L., Chen, Y.-N., Chu, M., Soong, F.K., Wang, J.-L.: Identifying language origin of named entity with multiple information sources. IEEE Transactions on Audio, Speech and Language Processing 16(6), 1077–1086 (2008)
17. Ng, R., Lee, T.: Entropy-based analysis of the prosodic features of chinese dialects. In: Proceedings - 2008 6th International Symposium on Chinese Spoken Language Processing, ISCSLP 2008, pp. 65–68 (2008)
18. Deng, Y., Liu, J.: Automatic language identification using support vector machines and phonetic n-gram. In: ICALIP 2008, Proceedings of 2008 International Conference on Audio, Language and Image Processing, pp. 71–74 (2008)
19. Botha, G., Zimu, V., Barnard, E.: Text-based language identification for south african languages. Transactions of the South African Institute of Electrical Engineers 98(4), 141–148 (2007)
20. Cordoba, R., D'Haro, L., Fernandez-Martinez, F., Macias-Guarasa, J., Ferreiros, J.: Language identification based on n-gram frequency ranking. In: 8th Annual Conference of the International Speech Communication Association, Interspeech 2007., vol. 3, pp. 1921–1924 (2007)
21. Thomas, S., Verma, A.: Language identification of person names using cf-iof based weighing function. In: 8th Annual Conferenceof the International Speech Communication Association, Interspeech 2007, vol. 1, pp. 361–364 (2007)
22. Suo, H., Li, M., Liu, T., Lu, P., Yan, Y.: The design of backend classifiers in pprlm system for language identification. In: Proceedings of Third International Conference on Natural Computation, ICNC 2007, vol. 1, pp. 678–682 (2007)
23. Moscola, J., Cho, Y., Lockwood, J.: Hardware-accelerated parser for extraction of metadata in semantic network content. In: IEEE Aerospace Conference Proceedings (2007)
24. Yang, X., Siu, M.: N-best tokenization in a gmm-svm language identification system. In: ICASSP, Proceedings of IEEE International Conference on Acoustics, Speech and Signal Processing, vol. 4, pp. IV1005–IV1008 (2007)
25. Rouas, J.L.: Automatic prosodic variations modeling for language and dialect discrimination. IEEE Transactions on Audio, Speech and Language Processing 15(6), 1904–1911 (2007)
26. Hanif, F., Latif, F., Sikandar Hayat Khiyal, M.: Unicode aided language identification across multiple scripts and heterogeneous data. Information Technology Journal 6(4), 534–540 (2007)
27. Li, H., Ma, B., Lee, C.H.: A vector space modeling approach to spoken language identification. IEEE Transactions on Audio, Speech and Language Processing 15(1), 271–284 (2007)
28. Cavnar, W.B., Trenkle, J.M.: N-gram-based text categorization. In: Proceedings of the 3rd Annual Symposium on Document Analysis and Information Retrieval 1994, Las Vegas, Nevada, USA, pp. 161–175 (1994)
29. Choong, C., Mikami, Y., Marasinghe, C., Nandasara, S.: Optimizing n-gram order of an n-gram based language identification algorithm for 68 written languages. International Journal on Advances in ICT for Emerging Regions 2(2), 21–28 (2009)

Image Edge Detection Using Variation-Adaptive Ant Colony Optimization

Jing Tian[1], Weiyu Yu[2], Li Chen[3], and Lihong Ma[4]

[1] School of Computer Science and Technology, Wuhan University of Science and Technology, P.R. China, 430081
eejtian@gmail.com
[2] School of Electronic and Information Engineering, South China University of Technology, Guangzhou, P.R. China, 510641
yuweiyu@scut.edu.cn
[3] School of Computer Science and Technology, Wuhan University of Science and Technology, P.R. China, 430081
chenli@ieee.org
[4] Guangdong Key Lab of Wireless Network and Terminal, School of Electronic and Information Engineering, South China University of Technology, Guangzhou, P.R. China, 510641
eelhma@scut.edu.cn

Abstract. *Ant colony optimization* (ACO) is an optimization algorithm inspired by the natural collective behavior of ant species. The ACO technique is exploited in this paper to develop a novel image edge detection approach. The proposed approach is able to establish a pheromone matrix that represents the edge presented at each pixel position of the image, according to the movements of a number of ants which are dispatched to move on the image. Furthermore, the movements of ants are driven by the local variation of the image's intensity values. Extensive experimental results are provided to demonstrate the superior performance of the proposed approach.

1 Introduction

Ant colony optimization (ACO) is a nature-inspired optimization algorithm [8] motivated by the natural collective behavior of real-world ant colonies. The major collective behavior is the foraging behavior that guides ants on short paths to their food sources, since ants can deposit pheromone on the ground in order to mark some favorable path that should be followed by other members of the colony. Inspired by this, the first ACO algorithm, called the *ant system*, was proposed by Dorigo *et al.* [7]. Since then, a number of ACO algorithms have been developed [3], such as the *Max-Min ant system* [16] and the *ant colony system* [5]. The ACO technique has been widely applied to tackle various real-world applications [2, 4, 6, 19].

Image edge extraction aims to extract the edge presented in the image, which is crucial to understand the image's content [9]. Conventional image edge detection algorithms usually perform a linear filtering operation (or with a smoothing

N.T. Nguyen (Ed.): Transactions on CCI V, LNCS 6910, pp. 27–40, 2011.

pre-processing operation to remove noise from the image) on the image [9], such as *Sobel* and *Canny* operators. These operators yield low computational load and are suitable for real-time applications. However, these operators usually result in artifacts (e.g., broken edges) in the resulted edge image [9]. To overcome the above drawback, inspired by natural behavior of ants, various ant-based image edge detection methods have been developed [11, 13, 20]. Zhuang [20] proposed to utilize the perceptual graph to represent the relationship among neighboring image pixels, then use the ant colony system to build up the perceptual graph. Nezamabadi-Pour *et al.* [13] proposed to use the ant system to detect edges from images by formulating the image as a directed graph. Lu and Chen [11] proposed to use the ACO technique as a post-processing to compensate broken edges, which are usually incurred in the conventional image edge detection algorithms.

The ACO technique is exploited in this paper to develop a new image edge detection approach. The contribution of this paper is highlighted as follows. The proposed approach aims to establish a pheromone matrix, whose entries represent the edge at each pixel location of the image, by exploiting the ant colony system. The ant colony evolves on the image via moving to adjacent pixels according to the local features of the image. In the context of image edge extraction, the local feature used in the propose approach is the local variation of the image's intensity values (the more contrasted the most favorable a region is).

It is important to note that there are fundamental differences between our proposed approach and the conventional ones [1, 11, 13, 20]. First, our proposed approach exploits the pheromone that is established by ant colony to extract the edge from images; while Zhuang's algorithm [20] exploits a perceptual graph to represent the edge and further applies the ACO technique to construct this graph. Second, our proposed approach exploits the *ant colony system* [5]; on the contrary, Nezamabadi-Pour *et al.*'s method [13] applies the *ant system* [7]. It has been shown that the above fundamental difference (ant colony system *v.s.* ant system) is crucial to the respective designed ACO-based algorithms [3]. Third, ACO is exploited to 'directly' extract the edge in our proposed method, in contrast to that the ACO technique serves as a 'post-processing' in [11] to enhance the edge that has already been extracted by conventional edge detection algorithms.

The paper is organized as follows. An ACO-based image edge detection approach is proposed in Section 2. Extensive experimental results and discussions are presented in Section 3. Finally, Section 4 concludes this paper.

2   Proposed ACO-Based Image Edge Detection Approach

The proposed approach aims to utilize a number of ants to evolve on a 2-D image for constructing a pheromone matrix, each entry of which represents the edge at each pixel location of the image. Furthermore, the movements of the ants are steered by the local variation of the image's intensity values. That is, the ants prefer to move towards positions with larger variations (i.e., edge region).

The proposed approach starts from the *initialization process* and runs for N iterations to construct the pheromone matrix by iteratively performing both the *construction process*, which constructs the pheromone matrix, and the *update process*, which updates the pheromone matrix. Finally, the *decision process* is performed to determine the edge by applying a binary thresholding on the constructed pheromone matrix. Each of the above four process is presented in detail as follows.

2.1   Initialization Process

Totally K ants are randomly assigned on an image $\mathbf{I}$ with a size of $M_1 \times M_2$, each pixel of which can be viewed as a node. The initial value of each component of the pheromone matrix $\boldsymbol{\tau}^{(0)}$ is set to be a constant τ_{init}.

2.2   Construction Process

At the n-th construction-step, one ant is randomly selected from the above-mentioned total K ants, and this ant will consecutively move on the image for L movement-steps. This ant moves from the node (l, m) to its neighboring node (i, j) according to a transition probability, which is defined as

$$p_{(l,m),(i,j)}^{(n)} = \frac{\left(\tau_{i,j}^{(n-1)}\right)^{\alpha} (\eta_{i,j})^{\beta}}{\sum_{(s,q)\in\Omega_{(l,m)}} \left(\tau_{s,q}^{(n-1)}\right)^{\alpha} (\eta_{s,q})^{\beta}}, \tag{1}$$

where $\tau_{i,j}^{(n-1)}$ is the pheromone value of the node (i, j), $\Omega_{(l,m)}$ is the neighborhood nodes of the node (l, m), $\eta_{i,j}$ represents the heuristic information at the node (i, j). The constants α and β represent the influence of the pheromone matrix and the heuristic information matrix, respectively.

There are two crucial issues in the construction process. The first issue is the determination of the heuristic information $\eta_{i,j}$ in (1). In this paper, it is proposed to be determined by the local statistics at the pixel position (i, j) as

$$\eta_{i,j} = \frac{1}{Z} V_c(I_{i,j}), \tag{2}$$

where Z is a normalization factor as

$$Z = \sum_{i=1:M_1} \sum_{j=1:M_2} V_c(I_{i,j}), \tag{3}$$

$I_{i,j}$ is the intensity value of the pixel at the position (i, j) of the image $\mathbf{I}$, the function $V_c(I_{i,j})$ is a function of a local group of pixels c, and its value depends on the variation of image's intensity values on the clique c (as shown in Figure 1). More specifically, for the pixel $I_{i,j}$ under consideration, the function $V_c(I_{i,j})$ is

$$\begin{aligned} V_c(I_{i,j}) = f\,(& |I_{i-2,j-1} - I_{i+2,j+1}| + |I_{i-2,j+1} - I_{i+2,j-1}| + |I_{i-1,j-2} - I_{i+1,j+2}| \\ & + |I_{i-1,j-1} - I_{i+1,j+1}| + |I_{i-1,j} - I_{i+1,j}| + |I_{i-1,j+1} - I_{i-1,j-1}| \\ & + |I_{i-1,j+2} - I_{i-1,j-2}| + |I_{i,j-1} - I_{i,j+1}|\,). \end{aligned} \tag{4}$$

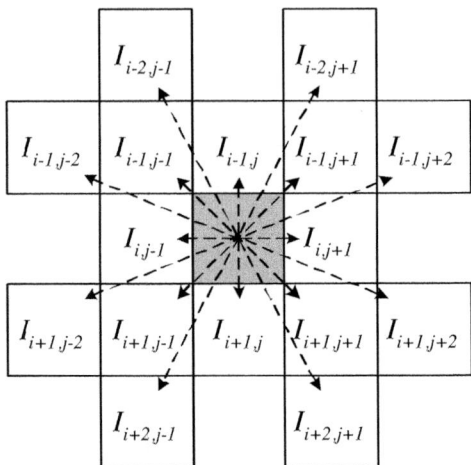

Fig. 1. A local configuration at the pixel position $I_{i,j}$ for computing the variation $V_c(I_{i,j})$ defined in (4). The pixel $I_{i,j}$ is marked as gray square.

The key issue is to establish the function $f(\cdot)$ used in (4), which is defined as

$$f(x) = \begin{cases} \sin\left(\frac{\pi x}{2\lambda}\right) & 0 \leq x \leq \lambda; \\ 0 & \text{else}, \end{cases} \qquad (5)$$

where the parameter λ adjusts the function's shape. The discussion of various functions is provided in Section 4.2.1.

2.3   Update Process

The proposed approach performs two updates operations for updating the pheromone matrix.

- The first update is performed after the movement of each ant within each construction-step. Each component of the pheromone matrix is updated according to

$$\tau_{i,j}^{(n-1)} \leftarrow \begin{cases} (1-\rho) \cdot \tau_{i,j}^{(n-1)} + \rho \cdot \Delta_{i,j}^{(k)}, & \text{if } (i,j) \text{ is visited by} \\ & \qquad\quad \text{the current } k\text{-th ant;} \\ \tau_{i,j}^{(n-1)}, & \text{otherwise.} \end{cases} \qquad (6)$$

  where ρ is evaporation rate, $\Delta_{i,j}^{(k)}$ is determined by the heuristic matrix; that is, $\Delta_{i,j}^{(k)} = \eta_{i,j}$.
- The second update is carried out after the movement of all ants within each construction-step according to

$$\boldsymbol{\tau}^{(n)} = (1-\psi) \cdot \boldsymbol{\tau}^{(n-1)} + \psi \cdot \boldsymbol{\tau}^{(0)}, \qquad (7)$$

where ψ is pheromone decay coefficient.

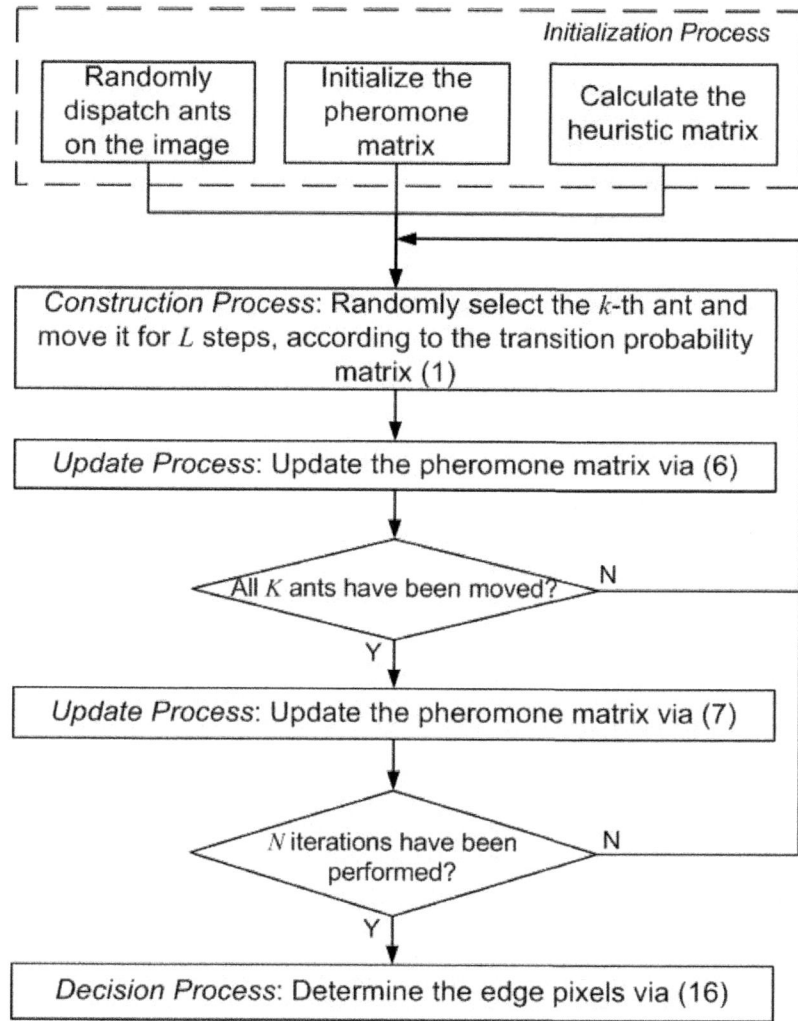

Fig. 2. A summary of the implementation of the proposed approach

2.4   Decision Process

In this step, a binary decision is made at each pixel location to determine whether it is edge or not, by applying a threshold T on the final pheromone matrix $\tau^{(N)}$. This threshold can be either manually determined by users or automatically determined by any binary thresholding algorithm (e.g., Otsu's algorithm in [14]). In this paper, the above-mentioned T is proposed to be adaptively computed based on the method developed in [14] as follows.

The initial threshold $T^{(0)}$ is selected as the mean value of the pheromone matrix. Next, the entries of the pheromone matrix is classified into two categories

(a)   (b)

Fig. 3. Test images used in this paper: (a) *Camera* (128×128) and (b) *House* (128×128)

according to the criterion that its value is lower than $T^{(0)}$ or larger than $T^{(0)}$. Then the new threshold is computed as the average of two mean values of each of above two categories. The above process is repeated until the threshold value does not change any more (in terms of a user-defined tolerance ϵ).

2.5   The Summary of the Proposed Approach

A summary of the implementation of the proposed image edge extraction approach is presented in Figure 2.

3   Experimental Results

3.1   Experimental Setup and Implementation

Experiments are conducted to evaluate the performance of the proposed approach using two test images, *Camera* and *House*, which are shown in Figure 3. Furthermore, various parameters of the proposed approach are set as follows. The total number of ants K is set to be $\lfloor \sqrt{M_1 \times M_2} \rfloor$, where the function $\lfloor x \rfloor$ represents the highest integer value that is smaller than or equals to x. The initial value of each component of the pheromone matrix τ_{init} is set to be 0.0001. The weighting factors of the pheromone and the heuristic information in (1) are set to be $\alpha = 10$ and $\beta = 0.01$, respectively. The permissable ant's movement range in (1) is selected to be 8-connectivity neighborhood. The adjusting factor of the function in (5) is $\lambda = 1$. The evaporation rate in (6) ρ is 0.1. Total number of ant's movement-steps within each construction-step L is 40. The pheromone decay coefficient in (7) $\psi = 0.05$. The user-defined tolerance value used in the decision process of the proposed method $\epsilon = 0.1$. Total number of construction-steps N is experimentally selected to be 4.

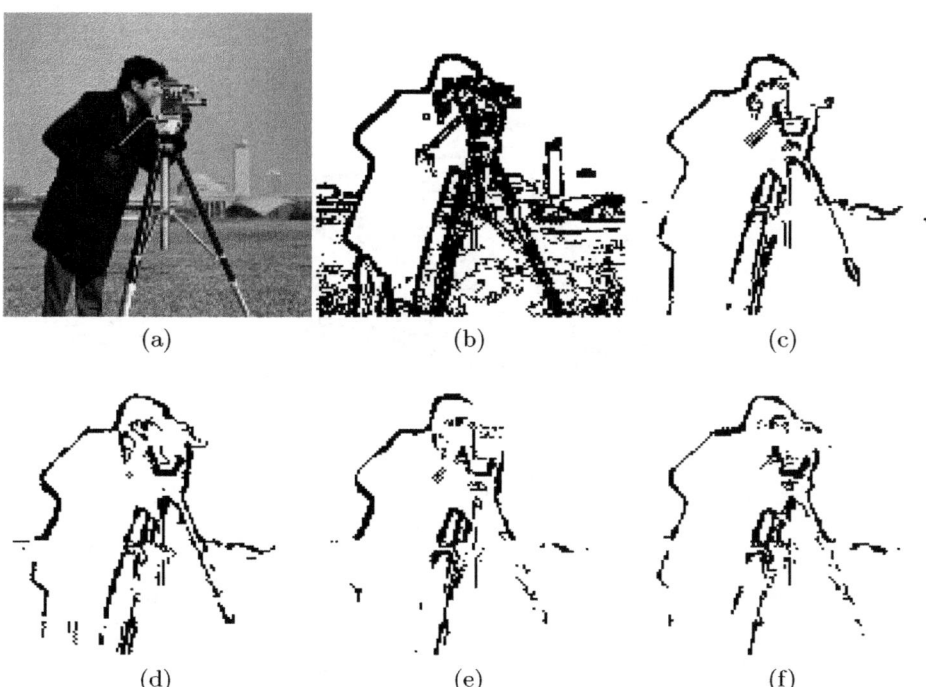

(a)   (b)   (c)

(d)   (e)   (f)

Fig. 4. Functions used in establishing the heuristic information matrix ($f(\cdot)$ in (4)): (a) the original *Camera* image; (b) Nezamabadi-Pour *et al.*'s method [13]; (c)-(f) proposed algorithm with the incorporation of the functions defined in (5), (8)-(10), respectively.

3.2   Experimental Results and Discussions

Experimental results are provided to compare the proposed approach with the state-of-the-art method developed in the literature, e.g., Nezamabadi-Pour *et al.*'s method [13]. To provide a fair comparison, the morphological thinning operation of [13] is neglected, since it is performed as a post-processing to further refine the edge that is extracted by the ACO technique [13]. As seen from Figures 4 and 5, the proposed provides superior performance to that of Nezamabadi-Pour *et al.*'s method [13], in terms of visual image quality. Furthermore, the determination of several parameters are critical to the performance of the proposed approach; this issue will be discussed in detail as follows.

Functions Used in Establishing the Heuristic Information Matrix ($f(\cdot)$ in (4)). To determine the function $f(\cdot)$ in (4), the following three functions could be incorporated into the proposed approach, besides the function (5). All these functions are mathematically expressed as follows and illustrated in Figure 6, respectively.

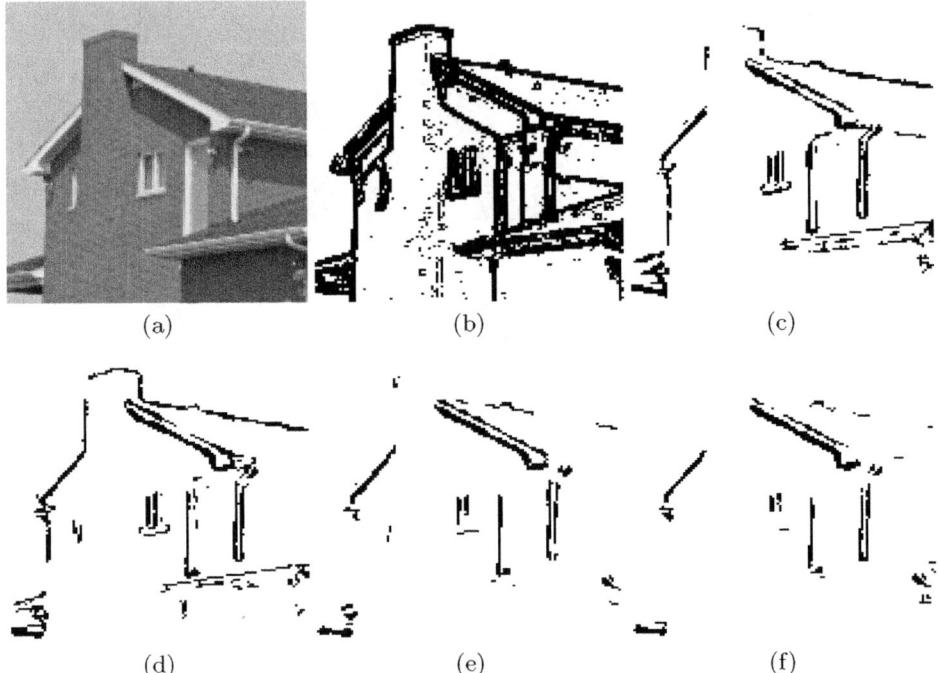

Fig. 5. Functions used in establishing the heuristic information matrix ($f(\cdot)$ in (4)): (a) the original *House* image; (b) Nezamabadi-Pour *et al.*'s method [13]; (c)-(f) proposed algorithm with the incorporation of the functions defined in (5), (8)-(10), respectively

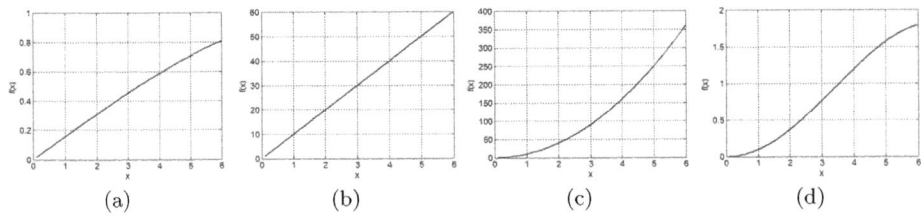

Fig. 6. Various functions ($\lambda = 10$) used for establishing the heuristic information matrix: (a) the function defined in (5); (b) the function defined in (8); (c) the function defined in (9); and (d) the function defined in (10)

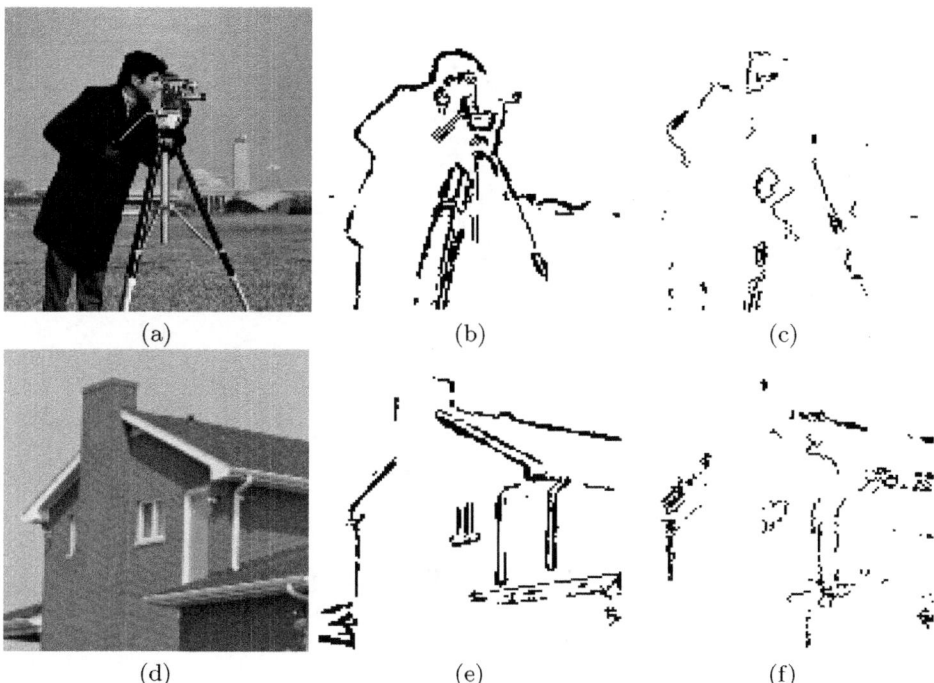

Fig. 7. Weighting factors of the pheromone (α in (1)) and the heuristic information (β in (1)): (a) the original image *Camera*; (b) the proposed algorithm ($\alpha = 10, \beta = 0.01$); (c) the proposed algorithm ($\alpha = 0.01, \beta = 10$); (d) the original image *House*; (e) the proposed algorithm ($\alpha = 10, \beta = 0.01$); and (f) the proposed algorithm ($\alpha = 0.01, \beta = 10$).

$$f(x) = \lambda x, \quad \text{for} \quad x \geq 0, \tag{8}$$

$$f(x) = \lambda x^2, \quad \text{for} \quad x \geq 0, \tag{9}$$

$$f(x) = \begin{cases} \frac{\pi x \sin(\frac{\pi x}{\lambda})}{\lambda} & 0 \leq x \leq \lambda; \\ 0 & \text{else.} \end{cases} \tag{10}$$

The parameter λ in each of above functions (8)-(10) adjusts the functions' respective shapes.

To present how the determination of the heuristic information matrix (i.e., (2)) is crucial to the proposed method, various functions defined in (5), (8)-(10) are individually incorporated into (4) of the proposed approach, and their resulted performances are presented. Figures 4 and 5 present the results of test images *Camera* and *House*, respectively.

Weighting Factors of the Pheromone (α in (1)) and the Heuristic Information (β in (1)). To demonstrate how the weighting factors of the pheromone (i.e., α in (1)) and the heuristic information (i.e., β in (1)) affect the

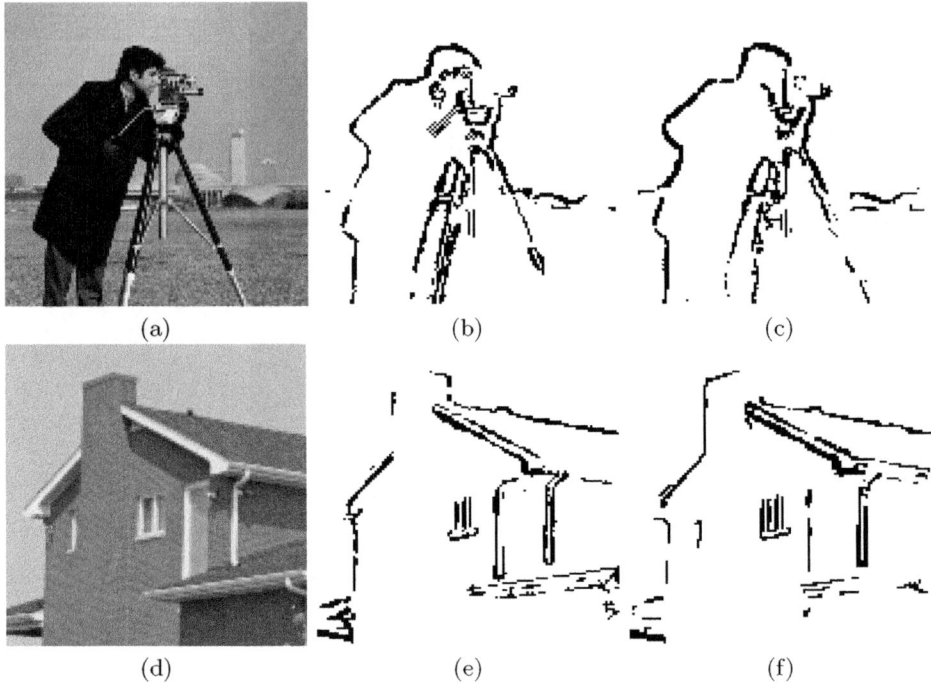

(a)   (b)   (c)

(d)   (e)   (f)

Fig. 8. Permissable range of ant's movement ($\Omega_{(l,m)}$ in (1)): (a) the original image *Camera*; (b)-(c) the proposed algorithm using 8-connectivity neighborhood and 4-connectivity neighborhood, respectively; (d) the original image *House*; (e)-(f) the proposed algorithm using 8-connectivity neighborhood and 4-connectivity neighborhood, respectively.

performance of the proposed algorithm, two experiments are conducted using two parameter setups: i) $\alpha = 10, \beta = 0.01$ and ii) $\alpha = 0.01, \beta = 10$. Their respective results are presented in Figure 7. As seen from the Figure 7, a large α value and a small β value will let ants tend to discover edges that have already been discovered by other ants; on the contrary, a small α value and a large β value will let ants tend to discover edges using stochastic movements.

Permissable Range of Ant's Movement ($\Omega_{(l,m)}$ in (1)). The permissable range of the ant's movement (i.e., $\Omega_{(l,m)}$ in (1)) at the position (l, m) could be either the 4-connectivity neighborhood or the 8-connectivity neighborhood. Both of these two cases are demonstrated in Figure 9 and their respective results are shown in Figure 8. As seen from Figure 9, a large permissable movement range will let ants to move to a far position; consequently, much edge will be discovered by ants. On the other hand, a small permissable movement range will let ants to prefer staying in their current positions; consequently, less edge will be discovered by ants.

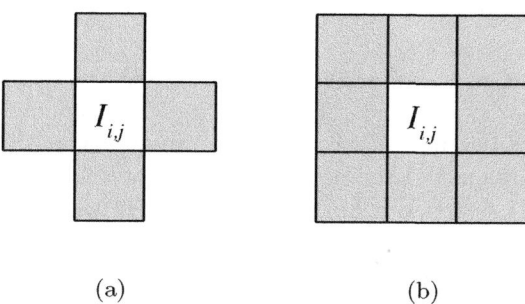

Fig. 9. Various permissable range of the ant's movement (marked as gray regions) at the position $I_{i,j}$: (a) 4-connectivity neighborhood; and (b) 8-connectivity neighborhood

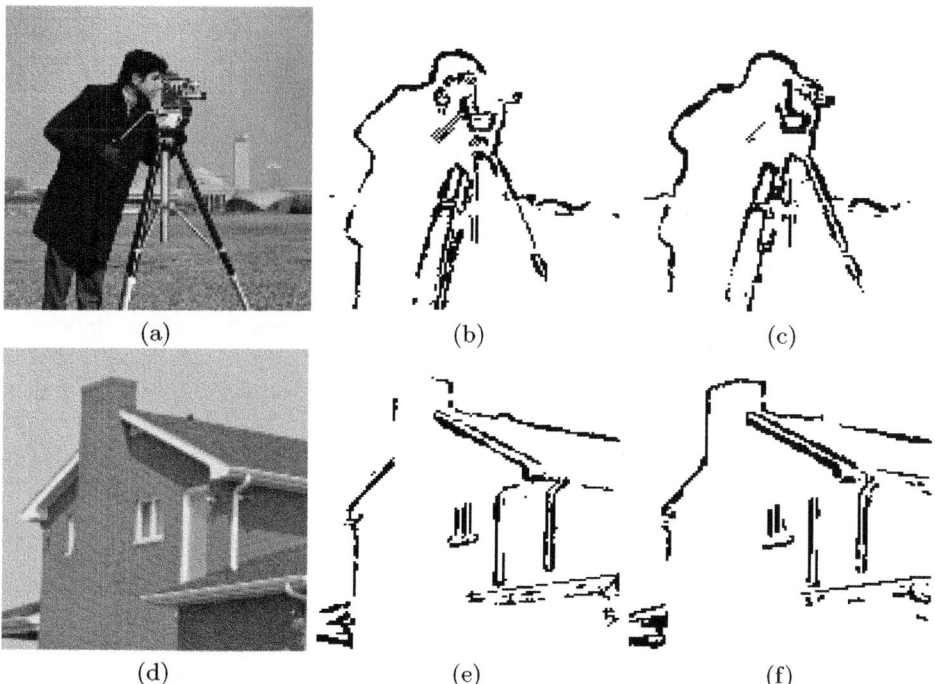

Fig. 10. Influence of evaporation factor (ρ in (6)): (a) the original image *Camera*; (b) the proposed algorithm ($\rho = 0.1$); (c) the proposed algorithm ($\rho = 0.99$); (d) the original image *House*; (e) the proposed algorithm ($\rho = 0.1$); and (f) the proposed algorithm ($\rho = 0.99$)

Influence of Evaporation Factor (ρ in (6)). Evaporation factor plays a key role to determine the performance of the proposed algorithm. To demonstrate this point, experiments are conducted using different evaporation factors and their results are presented in Figure 10.

Computational Cost. Experiments are conducted to compare the computational cost of the proposed algorithm and that of Nezamabadi-Pour *et al.*'s algorithm [13]. Both of the above two algorithms are implemented using the *Matlab* programming language and run on a PC with a Intel Core™ DUO E6400 2.13 GHz CPU and a 1 GB RAM. Furthermore, both of them are implemented for ten times, then their respective average running times are recorded.

The running times of the proposed approach are 64.97 seconds and 63.73 seconds for the test image *Camera* and *House*, respectively. On the other hand, the running time of Nezamabadi-Pour *et al.*'s algorithm [13] are 53.02 seconds and 53.18 seconds for the above two test images, respectively. Therefore, the proposed algorithm yields slight extra computational load, 22.54% and 19.84% for test images *Camera* and *House*, respectively, compared with that of Nezamabadi-Pour *et al.*'s algorithm [13]. However, this extra computational cost is tolerable, since the visual quality of our result is much better than that of Nezamabadi-Pour *et al.*'s algorithm [13]. On the other hand, since the ACO algorithm is inherently suitable to be parallelized, various parallel ACO algorithms [15, 10] can be exploited to further shorten the running time of the proposed algorithm for future research work.

4 Conclusions

In this paper, an ACO-based image edge detection approach has been developed to exploit the pheromone that is established by the ACO technique to determine the edge presented in the image. Fairly extensive simulations have been conducted to demonstrate the performance of the proposed algorithm using different parameters.

There are few issues of the proposed approach need further investigation. First, images are usually corrupted with noises in image acquisition or image communication. The ACO technique has been reported to be fairly robust to handle the edge detection in noisy image cases [1]. Second, the proposed approach exploits the conventional ACO algorithm [3] that updates the pheromone matrix using the initial pheromone value (see (7)). It would be important to investigate whether such update scheme is efficient. Third, since the edge is very critical to determine image's quality, it would be interesting to see how the edge detected by the proposed approach could benefit other image processing applications, such as image denoising [18, 17] and image saliency detection [12].

Acknowledgement. This work was supported by National Natural Science Foundation of China (60972133); Key Project of Chinese Ministry of

Education (210139); SRF for ROCS, SEM; GDSF Team Project (Grant No. 9351064101000003); the Fundamental Research Funds for the Central Universities (x2dxD2105260), SCUT; Fund of Provincial Key Lab. for Computer Information Processing Tech. (KJS0922).

References

1. Aydın, D.: An efficient ant-based edge detector. In: Nguyen, N.T., Kowalczyk, R. (eds.) Transactions on Computational Collective Intelligence I. LNCS, vol. 6220, pp. 39–55. Springer, Heidelberg (2010)
2. Cordon, O., Herrera, F., Stutzle, T.: Special Issue on Ant Colony Optimization: Models and Applications. Mathware and Soft Computing 9 (December 2002)
3. Dorigo, M., Birattari, M., Stutzle, T.: Ant colony optimization. IEEE Computational Intelligence Magazine 1, 28–39 (2006)
4. Dorigo, M., Caro, G.D., Stutzle, T.: Special Issue on Ant Algorithms. Future Generation Computer Systems 16 (June 2000)
5. Dorigo, M., Gambardella, L.M.: Ant colony system: A cooperative learning approach to the traveling salesman problem. IEEE Trans. on Evolutionary Computation 1, 53–66 (1997)
6. Dorigo, M., Gambardella, L.M., Middendorf, M., Stutzle, T.: Special Issue on Ant Colony Optimization. IEEE Transactions on Evolutionary Computation 6 (July 2002)
7. Dorigo, M., Maniezzo, V., Colorni, A.: Ant system: Optimization by a colony of cooperating agents. IEEE Trans. on Systems, Man and Cybernetics, Part B 26, 29–41 (1996)
8. Dorigo, M., Thomas, S.: Ant Colony Optimization. MIT Press, Cambridge (2004)
9. Gonzalez, R.C., Woods, R.E.: Digital image processing. Prentice Hall, Harlow (2007)
10. Janson, S., Merkle, D., Middendorf, M.: Parallel ant colony algorithms. In: Alba, E. (ed.) Parallel Metaheuristics: A New Class of Algorithms. Wiley-Interscience, Hoboken (2005)
11. Lu, D.S., Chen, C.C.: Edge detection improvement by ant colony optimization. Pattern Recognition Letters 29, 416–425 (2008)
12. Ma, L., Tian, J., Yu, W.: Visual saliency detection in image using ant colony optimisation and local phase coherence. Electronics Letters 46, 1066–1068 (2010)
13. Nezamabadi-Pour, H., Saryazdi, S., Rashedi, E.: Edge detection using ant algorithms. Soft Computing 10, 623–628 (2006)
14. Otsu, N.: A threshold selection method from gray level histograms. IEEE Trans. Syst., Man, Cybern. 9, 62–66 (1979)
15. Randall, M., Lewis, A.: A parallel implementation of ant colony optimization. Journal of Parallel and Distributed Computing 62, 1421–1432 (2002)
16. Stutzle, T., Holger, H.: Max-Min ant system. Future Generation Computer Systems 16, 889–914 (2000)
17. Tian, J., Chen, L.: Image despeckling using a non-parametric statistical model of wavelet coefficients. Electronics Letters 6 (2011)

18. Tian, J., Yu, W., Ma, L.: Antshrink: Ant colony optimization for image shrinkage. Pattern Recognition Letters (2010)
19. Tian, J., Yu, W., Xie, S.: An ant colony optimization algorithm for image edge detection. In: Proc. IEEE Congress on Evolutionary Computation, Hongkong, China, pp. 751–756 (June 2008)
20. Zhuang, X.: Edge feature extraction in digital images with the ant colony system. In: Proc. IEEE Int. Conf. on Computational Intelligence for Measurement Systems and Applications, pp. 133–136 (July 2004)

An Iterative Process for Component-Based Software Development Centered on Agents

Yves Wautelet[1], Sodany Kiv[2], and Manuel Kolp[2]

[1] Hogeschool-Universiteit Brussel, Belgium
yves.wautelet@hubrussel.be
[2] Université catholique de Louvain, Belgium
{sodany.kiv,manuel.kolp}@uclouvain.be

Abstract. The use of the component-based approach to develop large-scale information systems has become increasingly prominent over the past decade. However, there is a lack of established frameworks that cover the life cycle of component-based system development. This paper proposes a formalization of the process for component-based software development through the use of the agent paradigm. To this end, components are considered as low-level functional providers integrated into the software project through an agent architecture subject to monitoring - i.e. checking constraints - in order to determine the proper advancement of the software project. The use of agents typically allows a logical independence: the business logic is built separated from components making their integration process more flexible. The component selection is performed on two levels: components are selected on the basis of actors' intentions at the analysis level, and of their functional performances at the runtime level. The process is thus highly iterative and formal constraints are provided to monitor the iterative progression on a management point of view.

1 Introduction

Component-Based System Development (CBSD) has driven a lot of research over the last ten years. CBSD is based on the idea of building new systems by selecting appropriate components and assembling them with well-defined software architecture. It has become a strategic field for building large-scale and complex systems due to its potential benefits that are mainly its reduced costs and shorter development time, while maintaining quality. However, despite the plethora of software project management frameworks that exist for the traditional (developed-from-scratch) system development, there is a lack of established frameworks that cover the full life cycle of CBSD.

In this paper we define on a process for developing component-based software systems using agent-based architectural concepts. The originality of the approach resides in the advantages that:

N.T. Nguyen (Ed.): Transactions on CCI V, LNCS 6910, pp. 41–65, 2011.

- component selection is performed both at analysis and at runtime levels;
- components are considered as low-level functional providers rather than high-level ones such as in classical service oriented architecture, this allows us to design a context specific multi-agent system (MAS) encapsulating the business logic. This lowers the need for component customization and consequently eases their integration.

The proposed process is rooted in requirements-driven iterative development with life cycle milestone constraints adapted to monitor the MAS evolution process. To that extend, we define the concepts required to properly model a MAS exploiting collections of components through an API or any other technical means such as XML or SOAP messages typical in component-based systems. In our process, MAS is built up on analysis using i* ([31]); then, components are selected on the basis of high level functional aspects (represented as agent intentions) using a goal-based analysis based on the NFR (Non Functional Requirements) framework [9]. Components are then competing against each other into the MAS architecture to achieve low level functional requests required by the domain specific agents. Runtime feedbacks feed decisions concerning involvements of components in the next iterations.

The paper brings the following contributions:

- it formalizes an iterative software process to build component based software;
- it proposes a formal model to build up a MAS exploiting software components through agent capabilities. This goes beyond a classical definition of agent concepts by incorporating access and dialogue (thus basic delegation) to (third party) components. The MAS represents an abstraction layer between the modelled organization and the available components so that this formal model constitutes a framework for integrating software components;
- it defines iteration milestone constraints to monitor the progression of the software project. Therefore we refer to the I-Tropos [28] milestones and define specific constraints the overall project has to respect to achieve its iterations;
- finally, as a whole, it attempts to develop a framework where MAS contextual issues, mainly in terms of component integration, are together considered with project management questions. This reinforces the interest of adopting iterative templates such as those proposed in the Unified Process [15,19] or Agile methodologies in MAS and component-based software development.

Moreover, the proposed process is *requirements-driven* in the sense that even if the purpose is the reuse of generic software components, the domain model is logically independent. It is specified without any assumption on the available solutions and the deduced business logic is build up flexibly into the MAS, not by adapting the components themselves. By relegating the functional execution to a lower level, the process has the ability to round-trip between requirements analysis and MAS execution. This approach allows:

- to integrate both functional and non-functional aspects into the components evaluation and selection process;

- to make the components evaluation and selection process continuous during the whole project life cycle;
- to compare components performance on a low-level functional basis in order to select the best performing solution based on cost and QoS (quality of services) ontologies (see Section 3);
- to continually seek for an optimal solution;
- to ease the components integration process by building the business logic outside the components so that it requires less customization;
- to ease the transaction compared to a service approach. Indeed, only a mediator agent is needed to manage transactions and no complex dedicated set of agents should be involved. This also tends to speed up the application execution process;
- to ease the system transition process when facing changing requirements since only the business logic into the MAS has to be adapted.

The paper is structured as follows. Section 2 introduces the software process and the induced architecture. Section 3 defines the MAS conceptual model, the constraints for monitoring components integration using an iterative template and the MAS to-be equilibrium. Section 4 introduces the monitoring of components-based development through milestones from an agent iterative process. Section 5 illustrates the concepts on the basis of a real-world case study. Section 7 overviews related work and finally Section 8 concludes the paper.

2   A Process for Component-Based Software Development

This section firstly defines the two-level software process, and then further discusses its constituting elements granularity and the software architecture.

2.1   Process Definition

As said, *Component-Based Software Development (CBSD)* has become a crucial construction philosophy for building open large-scale and complex software architecture. It mainly consists of developing new software from pre-built components with the potential advantages of adequately managing complexity, reducing development time, increasing productivity and improving quality.

CBSD includes typically four disciplines [6,4]: *Requirement Engineering (RE)*, *Components Evaluation and Selection (CES)*, *Components Mismatches Handling (CMH)*, and *Components Integration and System Evolution* (split into *CI* and *SE* into the rest of this section).

We propose below an engineering process for CBSD taking into account the parts above specified above (see abbreviations within Figure 2). The Software Process Engineering Meta-Model (SPEM, [13]) is an OMG specification of an UML meta-model (and UML profile) used to represent a family of software development processes and their components. Figure 1 represents the icons related to a limited number of the SPEM concepts. Indeed, we focus here on the illustration of the most important process steps rather than an exhaustive illustration.

Fig. 1. Some Relevant SPEM Icons

In Figure 2, we instantiate some of the elements of the generic SPEM to define a custom two-level component-selection process. This instance is proposed in the form of a workflow, the *WorkDefinitions* represent the most important process steps and, as illustrated in the bottom of the figure, the process is highly iterative so that WorkDefinitions are repeated during each of the project iterations with variable effort on each of them. At the end of each iteration, the *Current Milestone Constraints* are evaluated to determine the whole software project achievement. Typically there are four phases in the process: *Setting*, *Blueprinting*, *Building* and *Setuping*, their objective and milestones constraints are extensively depicted in section 4. The process is structured as follows:

- in the *RE* discipline:
  - the *Organizational Analysis* WorkDefinition regroups the activities to build up an organizational model using the i* [31] framework in order to formalize the goals and tasks pursued by the actors involved in the software project;
  - then, the *Goal Formalization* WorkDefinition regroups the activities to perform an NFR goal analysis [9] in order to set up the expected functional and non-functional requirements of the software system;
- in the *CES* discipline:
  - the *Components Selection* WorkDefinition regroups the activities to firstly select the components to integrate based on a comparison between the functional and non-functional attributes of the available components with respect to the identified requirements. Components are thus evaluated at analysis level, i.e. their high-level functional and non-functional aspects are compared to the actors' intentions for eventual integration into the system under development;
- in the *System Design* discipline:
  - the *Multi-Agent System Architectural Design* WorkDefinition regroups the activities to build up the business logic on the basis of the organizational models and encapsulate it into a MAS acting as a wrapper over integrated COTS-components;
- in the *CI* discipline:
  - the *Selected Components Integration* WorkDefinition regroups the activities to properly integrate the selected components within the MAS architecture;
- in the *Runtime Evaluation* discipline:
  - the *Mismatches Identification* WorkDefinition regroups the activities aimed to monitor the competition between integrated components (and arbitrated by a mediator agent) to execute low-level functionalities requested by the MAS agents.

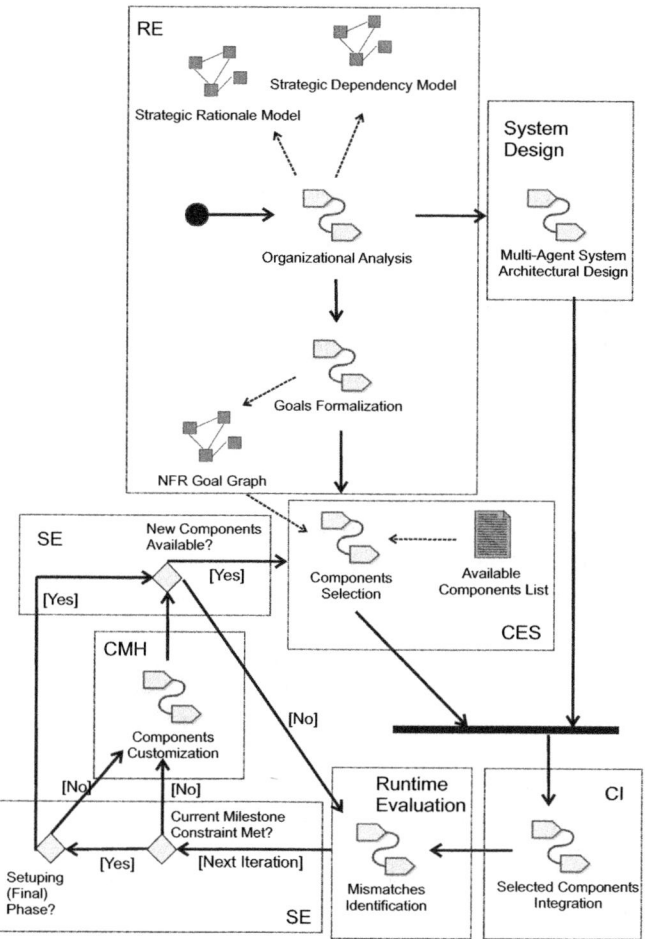

Fig. 2. The Two Level Selection Process

- in the *SE* discipline, is concerned with the evaluation of the project advancement with respect to runtime feedbacks. Indeed, the latter allows analysts to determine if milestones constraints are met and to take further component integration decisions. Typically, the possible actions taken by analysts for the next iteration include:
  - removal of unnecessary (or underperforming) components;
  - customization of existing components to include new capabilities (see section 3 for a formal definition) or higher their level of performance (*CMH* discipline);
  - development of capabilities into a new ad-hoc (i.e. custom) component (*CMH* discipline);
  - integration of newly available components;

- Finally, in the *CMH* discipline:
  - the *Components Customization* WorkDefinition regroups the activities aimed to customize specific existing components to include new capabilities or higher their level of performance or the development of capabilities into a new ad-hoc component.

2.2   Elements Granularity and Software Architecture

Service-oriented development can be distinguished from CBSD based on a series of characteristics such as those analysed in [5] notably in terms of granularity. Typically, [5] points out that operations on services are frequently implemented to encompass more functionality and operate on larger data sets when compared with component-interface design. The tricky question of service granularity has notably been studied in [14] which furnishes a service decomposition based on data, business value and functionality. Without going into that level of details, a service is traditionally considered as a single, discrete business process while components deal with finer grained functionalities. Agent-oriented development processes, notably thoses using the i* modeling framework propose different approaches for defining what a service is. Recent works such as [10], [23], [30] evoke services as a complete business processes and consider goals, tasks, resources (i.e. actors intentions) as a functional decomposition of the service while previously works like [12], [11] refer these actors' intentions as being services. We consider here the position to evoke a service as an entire business process which is also the approach found in logistics or accounting. This paper is nevertheless targeted to components providing functionality at lower level typically the one where agent capabilities reside. Figure 3 depicts in a generic way the supporting software architecture. It distinguishes three levels of granularity referred to as layers:

- the **service layer** i.e., the business process one, is the most coarse grained one. We do not explicitly deal with it in our methodology. This is the layer of the *Graphical User Interface (GUI)* where the services the application offers are composed by user's requests;
- the **actor intentions or goals and tasks layer**, representing its goals or tasks, is the highest we deal with (in the form of a realization path, see Section 3). This is the level of the *Multi-Agent System (MAS)* where the sub-processes (tasks or goals) are resolved following a defined business logic (encapsulated into the MAS) in the form of sequences of capabilities (called resolution paths). The communication with the lower layer is handled by a mediator agent;
- the **capability layer** where software components are, in our architecture, concretely interfaced to the MAS and represents thus the most detailed layer. This is the *Components* level where components advertise their ability to fulfil a capability request directly to the mediator agent and, when this agent orders it, components execute the capability.

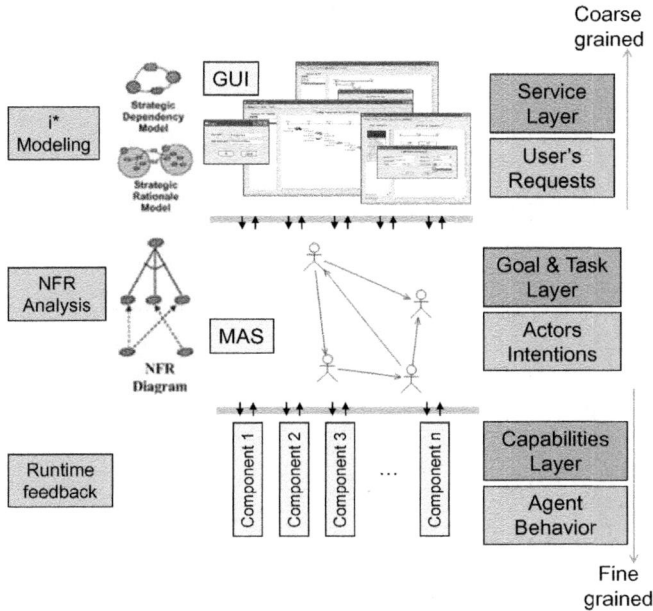

Fig. 3. A framework architecture

3   MAS Conceptual Foundations

We define in this section a conceptual model for the second layer of actor goals and tasks, the highest granularity level we deal with as introduced just above. The model is used to build the MAS while the accompagnied transaction procedures described just after ensure the communication with the capability layer.

Figure 4 depicts the relevant MAS concepts and their dependencies using a UML class diagram. The model is structured as follows: the agent pursues a series of intentions which can be tasks or goals as defined by i* and are then resolved through a series of capabilities by software components under the responsibility of agents in the form of a realization path. A UML sequence diagram can be used to document those realization paths as depicted in Figure 5. The MAS architecture ensures that capabilities' realization are delegated by agents to software components through the use of capability requests. Components are source code packages able to achieve a capability that is part of its offer.

Component. A tuple $\langle \{(cp_i, q_{cp_i}^c), \ldots, (cp_{i+m}, q_{cp_{i+m}}^c)\}, Comp^c \rangle$ is called an component c, where cp_i is a capability. The component advertises to the mediator agent its ability to resolve a capability at defined QoS level and cost $q_{cp_i}^a$. $Comp^c$ is assumed to contain all additional properties of the component irrelevant for the present discussion, yet necessary when integrating the component.

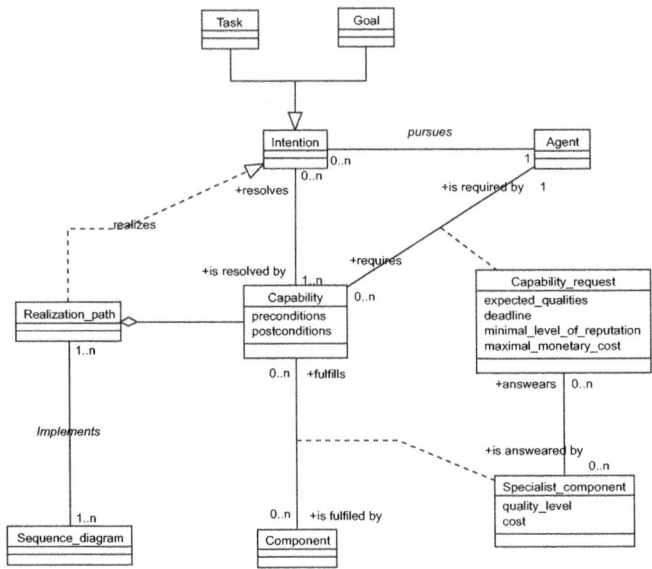

Fig. 4. The MAS Meta-Model

Format and content of $Comp^c$ will depend on the component technologies being used. A *Capability* is part of a *Goal* or *Task* realization (those are generalized as *Intentions* in the UML class diagram). Non-available capabilities must be specifically developed inside the scope of a component.

Specialist Component. $\langle c, cp_i, q_{cp_i}^c, ct_{cp_i}^c \rangle$ associating a capability cp_i to a quality level $q_{cp_i}^c$ at cost $ct_{cp_i}^c$ advertised by component c is a specialist component c_i^{SC}. The component must be capable of performing the capability: $\forall c_i^{SC} = \langle c, cp_i, q_{cp_i}^c, ct_{cp_i}^c \rangle, (cp_i, q_{cp_i}^c, ct_{cp_i}^c) \in c$. $ct_{cp_i}^c$ specifies the cost at which the specialist component c_i^{SC} can realize the capability. Its definition follows a specific cost ontology.

Any component c that can accomplish $m > 1$ capabilities can also be seen as a set of specialist components: $\{c_i^{SC}, \ldots, c_{i+m}^{SC}\}$.

Capability. A capability cp_i is $\langle cp_i^{pre}, \tau_i, cp_i^{post} \rangle$, where cp_i^{pre} describes the capability preconditions, τ_i is a specification (in some language) of how the component is to execute the capability and cp_i^{post} describes the conditions true after the capability is executed. Capabilities belong to the set $\mathbb{CP}$.

The capability is realized by a component under the responsibility of an agent. Agents are issued of the domain model on the exception of a special agent called the *mediator agent*. The latter is in charge of managing the transaction between the domain specific agents and the integrated components.

Mediator. A service mediator agent a_c^{SM} in the multi-agent system is an agent that can execute the transaction procedure: $t_A \in a_c^{SM}$.

The transaction procedure t_A is documented below.

Realization Path. $\langle rp_j^\iota, rp_{cp_j}^c, rp_{cp_j}^a, rpTransit_j, rpState_j \rangle$ is a realization path rp_j, where rp_j^ι provides the details of the functional specification of the realized intention, $(rp_{cp_j}^c, rp_{cp_j}^a)$ defines a sequence diagram where $rp_{cp_j}^c$ represents the series of capabilities required to realize the intention and $rp_{cp_j}^a$ the agents responsible for their realization. The two functions label swimlanes and messages with capability information: $rpTransit_j : rp_{cp_j}^c \longmapsto \mathbb{CP}$ is a partial function returning the capability for a given message in the sequence diagram, while $rpState_j : rp_{cp_j}^a \longmapsto \{cp_i^{pre}\}_{cp_i \in \mathbb{CP}} \cup \{cp_i^{post}\}_{cp_i \in \mathbb{CP}}$ maps each message to a condition from the set of all capability preconditions (i.e., $\{cp_i^{pre}\}_{cp_i \in \mathbb{CP}}$) and postconditions (i.e., $\{cp_i^{post}\}_{cp_i \in \mathbb{CP}}$). The capability specified on a message must have the precondition and postcondition corresponding to conditions given, respectively, on its origin and its destination swimlane. Realization paths belong to the set $\mathbb{RP}$.

Capabilities can thus be understood as a functional decomposition of a "higher level" intention (a task or goal) with the realization path as a success scenario. However in the context of this paper we are mostly focusing on the lowest level functional decomposition.

By conceptualizing the realization path as suggested above, the service is thus mapped onto a sequence diagram SeQ where each lifeline is a step in task/goal realization and a message in SeQ corresponds to the execution of a capability cp_k by a component $c_{k,u}^{SC}$, where u ranges over components that can execute cp_k according to the criteria set in the task/goal through an agent a_k. Each path from the starting agent (e.g., agent $Agent_k$ in Figure 5) to the ending agent (agent $Agent_{k+n}$ in Figure 5) thus corresponds to a sequence of capabilities ensuring the completion of the goal/task within the prescribed quality of service (QoS).

A realization path could be $\langle cp_k, cp_{k+1}, ..., cp_{k+n} \rangle$. The model thus assumes that there are alternative ways for completing the task/goal. The topology of the sequence diagram—i.e., the agent structure and the capabilities associated to messages between the agents—is provided by the designer through the task/goal definition, so that the sequence diagram is a graphical model of the different ways the task/goal can be performed as a sequence of capabilities delegated to components with cost and QoS constraints.

Capability Request. $\hat{cp}_j$ is $\langle Ag^a, cp_j, cp_j^{QoS}, cp_j^D, cp_j^R, cp_j^{cost} \rangle$ is a capability request where:

- Ag^a is the Agent requesting the capability realization by software components i.e. the one responsible for the capability realization.
- cp_j is the capability to provide.

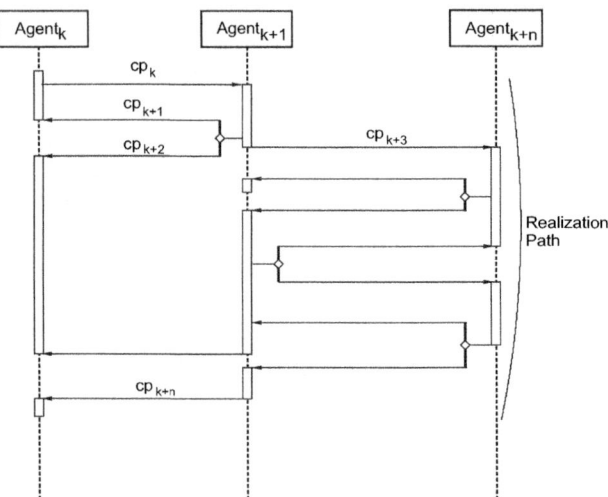

Fig. 5. A series of capabilities as a sequence diagram

- cp_j^{QoS} specifies expected qualities and their required level. Its definition follows a QoS ontology. Whatever the specific QoS ontology, expected qualities are likely to be specified as (at least) $cp_j^{QoS} = \langle (p_1, d_1, v_1, u_1), \ldots, (p_r, d_r, v_r, u_r) \rangle$, where:
  - p_k is the name of the QoS parameter (e.g., connection delay, standards compliance, and so on).
  - d_k gives the type of the parameter (e.g., nominal, ordinal, interval, ratio).
  - v_k is the set of desired values of the parameter, or the constraint $<, \leq, =, \geq, >$ on the value of the parameter.
  - u_k is the unit of the property value.
- cp_j^D is a deadline, specified as a natural.
- cp_j^R specifies minimal levels of reputation over task quality parameters that any component participating in the provision of the given capability must satisfy.
- cp_j^{cost} is the maximal monetary cost the agent requesting the capability is ready to pay to obtain the service.

Capability requests belong to the set $\mathbb{REQ}$.

Transaction. When a capabiltiy request $\hat{cp}_i$ is submitted to the mediator agent with cp_i as capability to provide. Let $W[]$ be the ordered vector containing a weighting factor for all of the aspects of the QoS ontology for the particular business logic, $\forall cp_j \in \mathbb{CP}$ where cp_j meets the functional specification of cp_i, $cp_j^{QoS} = \langle (p_1, d_1, v_1, u_1), \ldots, (p_r, d_r, v_r, u_r) \rangle$, with v_k being the value of the quality parameter: cp_{best} is the capability with $max(W[1]*v_1 + W[2]*v_2 +, \ldots + W[r]*v_r)$ value. The mediator agent a_c^{SM} will delegate the functional execution of the capability request to the component advertising cp_{best}.

4   Monitoring MAS Components with Iterations and Phases

Iterative development for MAS has been studied by different authors, see e.g., [28] for a state-of-the art about MAS iterative processes. This paper specifically focuses on using an **iterative project management** perspective to monitor MAS at runtime. Iterative refinements are provided by agent delegation choices but also by managerial decisions to develop missing (or existing under performing) capabilities. In iterative engineering processes [24] such as the Unified Process, each iteration belongs to one of the usually four or five phases composing the process. We refer in this work to a UP-based agent-oriented process called I-Tropos [28] which consists mainly of an iterative extension of the Tropos methodology [7]. These phases are made of one to more iterations (as many as required to at least meet the phase milestone) used here to depict constraints for evaluating the MAS evolution at runtime; we overview each phase objective below as well as, for each of them, constraints applied to capabilities at runtime.

Setting. The setting phase is concerned with the first sketch of the MAS through identifying the main agents and the capabilities they are responsible for. This phase is mostly concerned with determining the objectives of the software project so that there is a strong focus on analysis disciplines. MAS runtime considerations are largely out of the scope of this phase so that no formal milestone constraint is given for this phase.

Blueprinting. The blueprinting phase is concerned with a first executable version of the MAS with each of the capability requests addressable by at least one of the specialist components over minimal QoS.

The condition for evaluating the MAS state at blueprinting phase milestone is: $\forall \hat{c}p_j \in \mathbb{REQ}$ where cp_j is the capability to provide, $\exists c_i^{SC} \mid cp_j \in c_i^{SC} \wedge q_{cp_i}^c \geq cp_j^{QoS}(v_k)$.

Building. The building phase is concerned with a first executable version of the MAS with each of the capability requests addressable by at least one of the specialist components over minimal QoS and under maximal cost.

The condition for evaluating the MAS state at building phase milestone is: $\forall \hat{c}p_j \in \mathbb{REQ}$ where cp_j is the capability to provide, $\exists c_i^{SC} \mid cp_j \in c_i^{SC} \wedge q_{cp_i}^c \geq cp_j^{QoS}(v_k) \wedge ct_{cp_i}^c \leq cp_j^{cost}$.

Setuping. Even if the MAS is running "at equilibrium" (which means it uses the best possible specialist component available for each of the capability requests) new components can be available onto the market with better performance. This last phase monitors the inclusion of such components and has no formal milestone constraint since it virtually never ends.

5   Case Study: The Translogistic Project

This section introduces the application of our framework onto the development of an e-collaboration platform for outbound logistics (OL). It presents successively the case study domain in some brief details and part of the work realized during the successive project phases. The process is iterative which means that effort is spent on each of the process' WorkDefinitions (see section 2 for a detailed enumeration) at each of the iterations. The relative effort is however variable and more resources are spent on the WorkDefinitions of the RE discipline at the beginning of the project (e.g. during the setting phase) and more on software implementation at the middle of the project (e.g. during the blueprinting and building phases). Due to a lack of space and to be in line with this relative effort balance we will focus on the WorkDefinitions of the RE, CES and System Design disciplines when presenting the setting phase and on the MAS runtime feedbacks when presenting the following ones.

5.1   Outbound Logistics

Outbound logistics (OL) is the process related to the movement and storage of products from the end of the production line to the end user. In the context of this case study we mostly focus on transportation. The actors of the supply chain play different roles in the OL flow. The producer will be a logistic client in its relationship with the raw material supplier, which will be considered as the shipper. The carrier will receive transportation orders from the shipper and will deliver goods to the client, while relying on the infrastructure holder and manager. In its relationship with the intermediary wholesaler, the producer will then play the role of the shipper and the wholesaler will be the client.

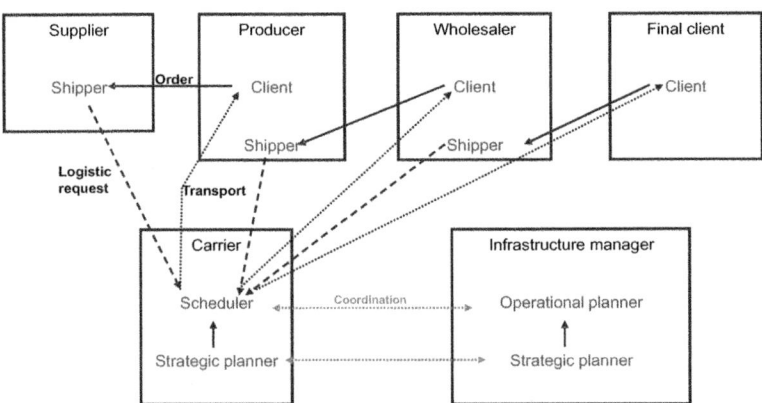

Fig. 6. Material flows in the outbound logistics chain

Figure 6 summarizes the material flows between the actors of the OL chain. The responsibilities corresponding to the different roles are:

- the *Shipper* has received an order from a client, and does a logistic request to a carrier for the delivery of that order.
- the *Carrier* is subdivided into two subroles:
  - the *strategic planner* decides on the services that are offered on the long term, on the use of infrastructure, on the logistic resources to hold and on the client's acceptation conditions.
  - the *scheduler* orders transports to be realized, according to the strategic network and constraints, coordinates with the infrastructure manager and assign logistic requests to those transports such that the delivery requirements are met.
- the *Infrastructure manager* holds the logistic infrastructure and coordinates with the carrier's scheduler to offer the network for the planned transports.
- the *Customer* books the transported merchandises.

The idea underlying the software development is to favour these actors' collaboration. Indeed, collaborative decision will tend to avoid local equilibriums (at actor level) and wastes in the global supply chain optimisation, giving quality expectations to achieve the greatest value that the chain can deliver at lowest cost (see [22,26]). The collaborative application package to be developed is thus composed of a multitude of aspects including the development of applications and databases to allow the effective collaboration and the use of flexible third-party components providing well-identified services. This dual aspect is from primary interest when managing the software project as shown in the rest of this paper.

5.2   Setting

Organizational Analysis. Figure 7 documents an i* diagram issued of organizational modelling. This strategic dependency diagram (*SDD*) depicts the relevant actors and their respective goal, task and resource dependencies.

Those dependencies are further analysed in a strategic rationale diagram (*SRD*) not presented here due to lack of space. It provides a more detailed level of modelling by looking inside actors. A strategic dependency diagram is a graph involving *actors* who have *strategic dependencies* among each other. A dependency describes an "agreement" (called *dependum*) between two actors: the *depender* and the *dependee*. The *depender* is the depending actor, and the *dependee*, the actor who is depended upon. The type of the dependency describes the nature of the agreement. *Goal* dependencies are used to represent delegation of responsibility for fulfilling a goal; *softgoal* dependencies are similar to goal dependencies, but their fulfillment cannot be defined precisely (for instance, the appreciation is subjective, or the fulfillment can occur only to a given extent); *task* dependencies are used in situations where the dependee is required to perform a given activity; and *resource* dependencies require the dependee to provide a resource to the depender. As shown in Figure 7, actors are represented as circles; dependums – goals, softgoals, tasks and resources – are respectively

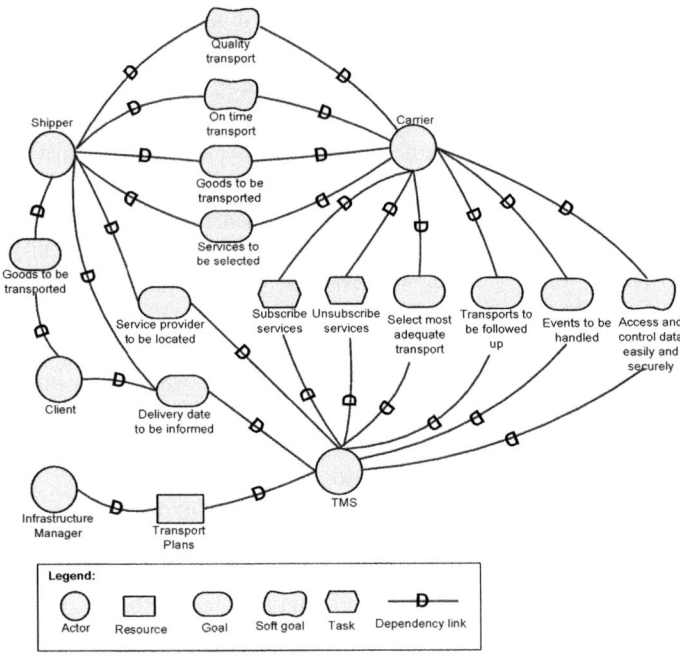

Fig. 7. The i* Strategic Dependency Diagram

represented as ovals, clouds, hexagons and rectangles; and dependencies have the form *depender → dependum → dependee*.

Each outbound logistic actor depicted above (as well as the final client) and the third-party component we want to integrate in the global system are all represented as actors. These diagrams allow to get a first representation of the system to be at high abstraction level.

Goals Formalization. As in Tropos [7], we use the NFR framework [9] to conduct goal analysis and formalization. The NFR framework introduces soft (or NFR) goal contributions to model sufficient/partial positive (respectively ++ and +) or negative (respectively -- and -) to analyse soft (NFR) goals (also called quality or strategic goals) and operational goals in addition to classical AND or OR decomposition links. The analysis allows one to select among alternative operationalized goals as software requirements and qualities are modeled as softgoals, decomposed as more specific and more precise sub-goals contributing positively or negatively to each other and then allowing one to evaluate and select operationalized softgoals.

The NFR goal graph of Figure 8 represents the non-functional aspects that *Transportation Management System* (*TMS*) components should fulfil or at least contribute to. Non-functional requirements include *Security*, *Flexibility* and *Adaptability*. After posing these highest level non-functional requirements as softgoals to satisfy, we tend to refine them into sub-goals through *AND* and

OR decompositions and the interdependencies among the goals are also studied as shown in Figure 8. The NFR *Security* was refined into *Authorization* and *Data encryption*. The NFR *Flexibility* was decomposed into *integrability of data base*, *wrappability of product* and *extensibility of new modules*.The NFR *Flexibility* has a positive influence to the NFR *Adaptability* which has been decomposed into *vendor support, developed in a standard technology, source code openness,* and *configuration*. The *authority to read source code openness* operationalize goal can partly satisfy the *source code openness* goal which can be fully fulfilled by the *authority to modify code* operationalize goal.

Certainly all of the components do not have the same usage cost; for example TMS3 from elcomionero.com is an open source software component while TMS1 from Oracle and TMS2 from SAP are commercial ones. Cost based selection is here considered at runtime with only a maximal cost constraint (as defined in section 4). A larger perspective on the overall process cost is given following a given cost ontology in section 6; to match with the paper focus we will not enter into more "cost ontological" refinements.

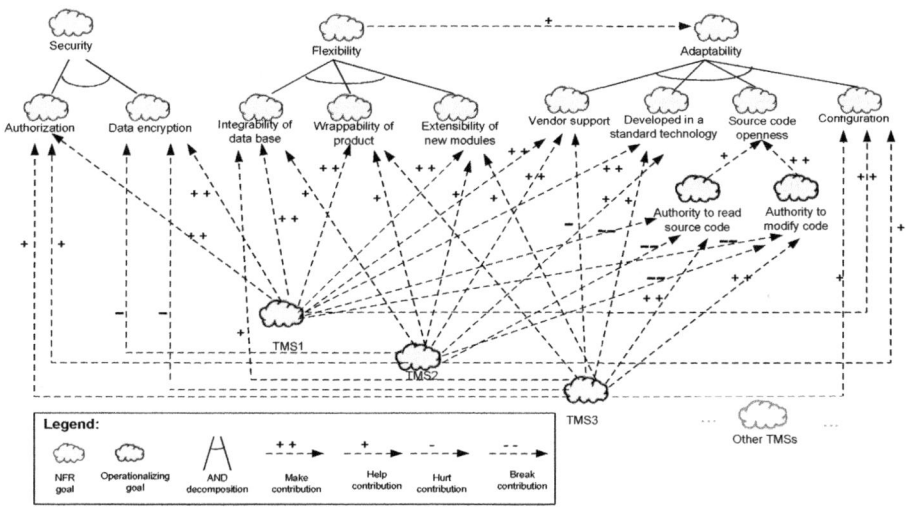

Fig. 8. Analysis of the TMS Components on the Basis of their High-Level Attributes (Analysis Perspective)

Components Selection. The detailed process of looking for, evaluating and selecting available component-based packages is outside the focus of this paper. For illustration in this case study, we suppose that component based packages are selected after short-listing the ones that are available and evaluating the pre-selected ones through the NFR analysis presented above. More details about such a selection process can be found in [7] for selecting organizational architectural styles. The NFR analysis shown previously allowed us, on the basis of the analysis high level considerations to distinguish a hierarchy between the available TMS components, TMS1 is preferred followed by TMS2 and TMS3. Other TMSs are eliminated and they will be not evaluated at runtime. At this stage we do not yet know what their low level functional performances are so that this first selection is only based on high-level functional and non-functional aspects. Runtime feedbacks will provide this information and allow us to iteratively refine this analysis procedure.

MAS Architectural Design. Based on the i* and NFR organizational and goal analysis above, the next step is to define the MAS architecture and specify the characterization of agent behavior typically referring to the sociocentric design of multiagent architecture exposed in [17]. The result is expressed in terms of agents and capabilities requiring resources such as those summarized in Figure 9 for the *Select Most Adequate Transport* goal from Figure 7. Specifically the realization path concept presented above is applied to the goal analysis.

Figure 10 details the sequence diagram documenting the evoked goal's success scenario.

Phase Milestone. The objective of this phase was to overview the life cycle objectives so that the RE, CES and System Design disciplines have (partly) been presented. No formal constraints are associated with this phase so that we can continue with the next process phase (i.e. blueprinting).

5.3   Blueprinting

We only focus here on the *Select Most Adequate Transport* goal, as an illustrative example. The aim of this goal is, for a carrier, to select the offer from the most adequate transport (if he or she has one) to transport the shipper's demand (for a defined amount of merchendise to be transported from a source to a destination under defined constraints as dates, transportation mode, etc).

To select the most adequate transport three main actors of the MAS are involved: the *Shipper*, *Carrier* and *Infrastructure Manager* (agents are the instances of these actors). Capabilities that agents are responsible for and modelled with respect to Section 3 are extensively described in Figure 9. Capabilities realization are delegated to the most adequate specialist component using the procedure described in Section 3.

Phase Milestone. Figure 11 represents a MAS runtime within the Blueprinting phase. It documents the capabilities that are available with QoS over minimal values (A) or not-available (N/A) in each of the integrated TMS components as well as whether they are selected for capability execution at runtime or not (best). The rntime report shows that at the end of the iteration each of the capabilities are not fulfilled under QoS and cost constraints. Indeed, capabilities 6 and 9 are not fulfilled by any of the integrated components so that it cannot fulfill the blueprinting milestone within the constraint expressed in section 4.

N°	Capability	Description	Responsible Agent	Ressource
1	createLogisticRequest()	When the Shipper requires to transport merchandise from a source to a destination (generally to fulfill an order or for internal reasons) it creates a logistic request (which remains an internal concept)	Shipper	logistic_request
2	handleTransportationCall(logistic_request)	The Shipper transmits a Logistic_Request in the form of a Transportation_Call to a Carrier which is is in charge of proposing a planning to realize them (note that the Logistic_Request is an abstract requirement, the Transportation_Call is a Logistic_Request with requested departures and arrival dates/times adressed to a Carrier)	Carrier	logistic_request
3	evaluateTransportationServiceOffer(transportation_call)	The Carrier disposes of a transportation offer in the form of Transportation Services. So it is in charge of evaluating the possible matches between the demand (the transportation call) and its own offer.	Carrier	service
4	relaxConstraints(transportation_call)	The Carrier eventually needs relaxing the constraints to mach transportation offer and demand.	Carrier	transportation_proposal
5	computeRequiredOperations(transportation_proposal)	The Carrier computes the required logistic operations needed to sucessfully achieve the possible transports	Carrier	transportation_proposal
6	evaluateInfrastructureAvailability(transportation_proposal)	The Infrastructure Manager manages a series of ressources to make transportations possible. Ressources are limited and should be booked; on request it answers on disposals.	Infrastructure_Manager	transportation_proposal
7	acceptResolutionSequence(transportation_call_resolution_sequence)	The Shipper is responsible for accepting the transportation call resolution sequence proposal submitted by the Carrier.	Shipper	transportation_call_resolution_sequence
8	handleProposalAcceptance(transportation_call_resolution_sequence)	When the Shipper has accepted the transportation call resolution sequence proposal, the Carrier is in charge of achieving the procedures required to adequately fulfill it.	Carrier	transportation_call_resolution_sequence
9	createTransport(transport_proposal)	The Carrier is in charge of creating the transport so that it will be part of the Carrier and other involved agents future plannings.	Carrier	transport
10	bookRequiredRessources(operation_list)	Required ressources to adequately fulfill the transport are booked at the infrastructure manager	Infrastructure_Manager	operation_list

Fig. 9. *Select Most Adequate Transport*: Capabilities Description

This information is thus provided to analysts that can take a development decision to be achieved in the next iteration so that the MAS can fulfil the milestone constraint. In this particular case the taken decision is the customization of respectively TMS components 1 and 2.

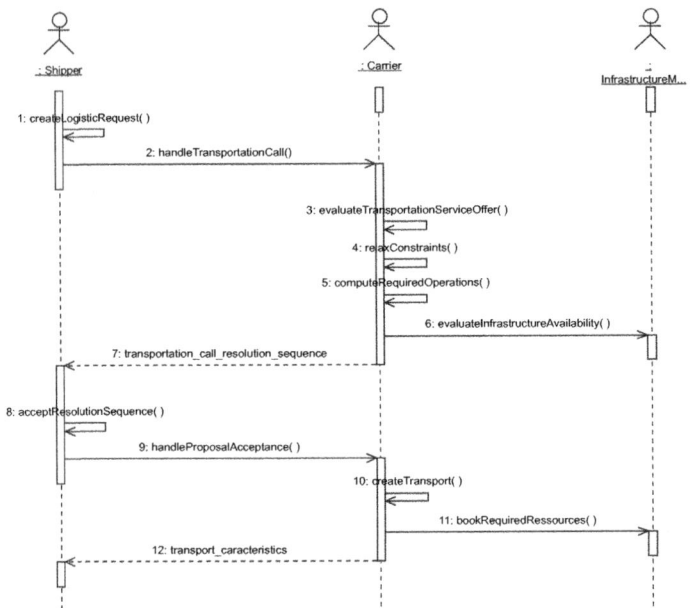

Fig. 10. The resolution path of *Select Most Adequate Transport* goal

5.4 Building

Phase Milestone. Figure 12 resumes a MAS runtime report of the Building phase. It documents the capabilities that are available with QoS over minimal values (A) or non-available (N/A) in each of the integrated TMS components as well as whether they are selected for capability execution at runtime or not (best).

Since we are at the Building phase, each of the capabilities is fulfilled under QoS and cost constraints. The focus of this phase is on minimizing the overall execution cost of the MAS so that the analysts can overview if they can lower it by removing a component from the MAS design. In this particular case they can, for example, overview the possibility of removing TMS3 (see section 6 for more information). In the actual state of definition if the execution is below the maximum defined cost then the milestone constraint is met and the project can move to the Setuping phase. Further work involves refining the cost ontology and consequently refining the cost constraint(s) of the milestone.

5.5 Setuping

Phase Milestone. In line with the definition of section 4, as long as there is no new component integrated into the system, the MAS is at equilibrium.

	Capab. 1	Capab. 2	Capab. 3	Capab. 4	Capab. 5	Capab. 6	Capab. 7	Capab. 8	Capab. 9	Capab. 10
TMS1	best	A	N/A	A	best	N/A	A	A	N/A	best
TMS2	A	best	best	best	A	N/A	A	best	N/A	N/A
TMS3	N/A	N/A	A	N/A	A	N/A	best	N/A	N/A	A

Fig. 11. A MAS Runtime Report at Blueprinting Phase

	Capab. 1	Capab. 2	Capab. 3	Capab. 4	Capab. 5	Capab. 6	Capab. 7	Capab. 8	Capab. 9	Capab. 10
TMS1	best	A	N/A	A	best	A	A	A	N/A	best
TMS2	A	best	best	best	A	N/A	A	best	best	N/A
TMS3	N/A	N/A	A	N/A	A	best	best	N/A	N/A	A

Fig. 12. A MAS Runtime Report at Building Phase

6   A Perspective on the Process Cost

We propose here a mathematical constraint formulation to estimate the overall cost of the software process use within a particular (but general and realistic) cost ontology so that we first clarify some MAS concepts in the specific context of this mathematical formulation. First of all, let us remind that MAS agents emit capability requests; these are "matched" with the components advertised capabilities. We emphasize hereby that advertised capabilities are ranked as a single index suite from 1 to n. In other words and to ease the formulation of the problem, a same capability advertised by two or more different components will get two different index numbers with nothing indicating that they could fulfil a same capability request.

The following indices are defined:

- j for the **components** present into the system;
- m for the **capability requests** of the MAS;
- n for the **advertised capabilities** by the components;
- t for the project **iterations**.

The data available into the MAS is depicted as follows:

- D_n equals 1 if capability n is initially advertised; 0 otherwise;
- C_n is the variable cost of using advertised capability n;
- K_n is the fixed cost for developing capability n;
- B_n^j equals 1 if capability n is advertised or could be advertised if developed by component j; 0 otherwise;
- S^j subscription cost for 1 period for using component j;
- N_m^t amount of capability requests m - for a same specific capability - in period t;
- A_n^m equals 1 if advertised capability n fulfils capability request m; 0 otherwise.

The model variables are:

- x_n^t (continuous) represents the number of units of advertised capability n executed in period t;
- y_j^t (binary) equals 1 if subscription is paid to component j in period t;
- z_n^t (binary) equals 1 if advertised capability n is developed in period t;

The mathematical formulation of the problem is as follows:

$$\text{Min} \sum_{j,t} y_j^t \, S^j + \sum_{n,t} x_n^t \, C_n + \sum_{n,t} z_n^t \, K_n \tag{1}$$

$$\forall \text{n},t: \sum_n x_n^t \, A_n^m \geq N_m^t \tag{2}$$

$$\forall \text{n},t: x_n^t \leq M(D_n + \sum_{1 \leq s \leq t} z_n^s) \tag{3}$$

$$\forall \text{n},t: x_n^t \leq M \sum_j y_j^t \, B_n^j \tag{4}$$

$$x \geq 0, y, z \in \{0, 1\}$$

The objective (1) minimizes the overall MAS cost (we assume only capabilities over minimal QoS are advertised). The supported cost is divided into 3 components:

- the overall **subscription cost** represented by the sum of all the subscriptions paid for any of the used components at any periods;
- the variable costs paid for consumptions of any of the used capabilities at any period;
- the overall **capability development cost** represented by the sum of all the capabilities development costs at any periods;

Constraint (2) ensures that the requirement for capability m in period t is met. It states that the number of units of advertised capabilities n, which fulfils the capability m, executed in period t is sufficient.

Constraint (3) authorizes the execution of advertised capability n only if it is developed. The capability is developed in period t if it was initially developed, which is indicated by D_n, or if it was developed in a previous or in the current period, which is indicated by the sum over the corresponding z variables. M is a large number.

Constraint (4) authorizes the execution of advertised capability n only if subscription is paid to the component j owning the advertised capability n.

7   Related Work

A number of component-based software development methods have been proposed in the literature. We first overview the need for multiple-components in a single software development as well as the importance of the functional aspects on a low level basis, then we will evaluate the literature on the particular aspect of iterative development in CBSD.

Historically, [18] has been the first methodology proposed for component selection, more specifically COTS (Commercial Off The Shelf) components. It notably distinguishes three phases: searching, screening and evaluation. It notably provides some specific techniques for those phases and has served as a first basis for the development of other methods. In the same way, STACE (Social-Technical Approach to COTS Evaluation) [20] has been the first to emphasize the importance of social and organizational issues to components selection process as well as the other non-technical factors such as the relationship with the vendor. These two first methodologies remains nevertheless limited and do not support the complex process of requirements analysis balanced with component features limitations.

[27] highlights the fact that components are designed to meet the needs of a marketplace rather than satisfying the requirements of a particular organization. Consequently, there is no single component satisfying them all and can be realized by the use of multiple components. This statement is fundamental in our approach where we consider components as low level functional service providers rather than entirely packaged solutions.

Moreover a series of proposed component-based software development methods consider the focus on non-functional requirements more important than on functional ones since the latests are already present (see for example in [3]). We will overview here some methodologies focused on non-functional aspects, more specifically:

- [1] proposes the CRE (COTS based on Requirements Engineering) model for the components selection. The CRE model focuses on non-functional requirements to assist the processes of evaluation and selection of components. The CRE model adopts the NFR framework proposed in [9] for acquiring the user non-functional requirements;
- [25] proposes the REACT (REquirement-ArChiTecture) approach for the components selection. The innovation, implemented in REACT, was to apply i* SD models to model software architectures in terms of actors dependencies to achieve goals, satisfy soft goals, consume resources and undertake tasks. The i* SD models are derived from existing use cases to represent the architecture of the system. The components are then selected to be plugged into the system architecture as instances of models actors.
- [29] proposes FaMOS-C, a service-oriented FrAMework fOr maS modeling and Component selection. This approach emphasizes the importance of the functional and non-functional requirements of the system under development for identifying and selecting the compoent software components and provides a practical model supporting its application. The NFR analysis is however performed at higher level than in the approach presented in this paper.

We do not minimize the importance of non-functional requirements but state the prior aspect of a component remains its functional one in order to best satisfy user requirements. Moreover, by nature, our approach focuses on low-level functionalities so that part of non-functional requirements can easily be taken into account at upper level and the other part is passed on the advertised QoS. Indeed, we use a classical software development process where non-functional requirements are identified during analysis disciplines and can be taken into account when developing interfaces to the MAS. The later serves as an abstraction layer to the low level functionalities (called the capabilities). Our approach is more flexible and development-oriented. Indeed, CRE, REACT and FAMOS-C distinguish a set of high level functional and non-functional requirements and evaluates them at the light of those modelled for a specific project for an adequate selection. Finally, one can believe that we adopt all the market available components without adequate analysis. This approach is however present (as evoked in Section 4) but not completely documented in the paper since the focus is on the MAS and its integration into an agent iterative process such as I-Tropos. [16] documents this two levels (macro-level goals and micro-level capabilities) analysis framework and applies it on the same case study.

With respect to iterative development in CBSD, PORE (Procurement-Oriented Requirements) [21] is a template-based approach for evaluating components in an iterative manner. Following [2], its model distinguishes four goals:

- acquiring information from stakeholders;
- analysing the information to determine if it is complete and correct;
- making the decision about product requirement compliance if the acquired information is sufficient;
- selecting one or more candidate components.

The study of the existing components functional aspects as well as the "traditional" requirements engineering do constitute parallel activities with, moreover, an iterative process for acquiring requirements and evaluating the available components. The idea is to progressively reject products that do not meet user requirements. This approach is also present in our process where components are also progressively rejected but on a two level basis. At first, they are selected on the basis of their high level functional aspects depicted in a goal model and second they are selected dynamically at runtime on the basis of their ability to resolve the required capabilities. They can be rejected at any time in the project lifecycle if they are comparatively not enough performing (on the basis of cost and QoS constraints) and not indispensable (see case study in Section 5). The idea of a progressive rejection is thus also present but goes further by evaluating execution possibilities on a low level basis and consuming the cheapest solution offered by components. The selection process is thus not only based on a functional evaluation but also on cost and QoS constraints at runtime.

Finally, CARE (COTS-Aware Requirements Engineering) [8] proposes to create a *Digital Library System* for storing component specifications. This means that they define a goal-oriented process for describing and selecting components from a technical view. For any identified component, they capture its functional specification in the form of hard and softgoals and further define their specification. Then, they are stored and maintained in a knowledge base called the Digital Library System. On the basis of the component descriptions, a research can determine which product(s) can be useful. Some of the CARE ideas are also present in the process described in this paper. Among them we find the comparison of functional features of the components and the idea of using a series of components to fulfil defined goals in a classical software engineering process. Once again, we consider, in the approach presented in this paper, functional specifications on the lowest level in order to have an implementation where real-time functional calls can be ordered to components at runtime. We consequently do not point to a global components library but rather a selection in the development process of potential components candidates competing at runtime within the developed MAS.

8   Conclusion

Software reuse can lead to reduced costs through CBSD if components are adequately selected and their integration can be done flexibly. Since they are generically developed, components can hardly meet the organization expectations and user requirements at once. Moreover, some components are better performing than others on particular functions and practitioners need methods to evaluate, customize and combine them for proper integration. In that perspective, we have defined in this paper a methodology for CBSD centred on agents in Section 2. A conceptual model defines, in Section 3 a set of concepts to build the context specific MAS and constraints to monitor its iterative evolution properly in Section 4. Section 5 proposes an illustration based on a real-world case study.

The MAS architecture is designed to be centric in the development methodology and bridge, in the form of an abstraction layer, the traditional organizational analysis i* and NFR – describing the required behaviour of software components – with the functional aspects they offer. Even if, by nature, one could be tempted to apply a technology driven process in CBSD, a requirements-driven approach is preferable since the developed system based on components has to adequately fit the target organization. In that perspective, using models is from primary interest. The MAS is built from the domain model (i.e., the i*/NFR models); agents are in charge of capabilities which are realized through delegation to software components so that the business logic is encapsulated into the ad-hoc MAS to-be. Components are considered here to be flexible source code packages that communicate through an API to execute specified functionalities at defined costs. They are also supposed to be customizable at evaluable cost.

Outside this vertical dimension, the process proposed here also offers an horizontal (iterative) one in which a series of constraints applied to the MAS architecture ensures a proper follow-up of the project life cycle.

The MAS conceptual model can still be subject to more evolutions notably in terms of adaptive intelligence. Moreover, the software project management perspective could be larger with the adoption of complete risk, quality and time disciplines at managerial level. Also, the constraints depicted for the process milestones are not a fixed set but can be subject to more evolutions in order to incorporate other aspects determining the software project evolution. Constraints on requirements can for example easily be integrated. Finally, on an empirical basis more case studies into different application domains could enhance the framework to a higher level of maturity.

References

1. Alves, C., Castro, J., Alencar, F.: Requirements engineering for cots selection. In: The Third Workshop on Requirements Engineering, Rio de Janeiro, Brazil (2000)
2. Ayala, C.: Systematic construction of goal-oriented cots taxonomies. PhD Thesis (2008)
3. Beus-Dukic, L., Bøegh, J.: COTS software quality evaluation. In: Erdogmus, H., Weng, T. (eds.) ICCBSS 2003. LNCS, vol. 2580, pp. 72–80. Springer, Heidelberg (2003)
4. Boehm, B.W., Port, D., Yang, Y., Bhuta, J.: Not all CBS are created equally: COTS-intensive project types. In: Erdogmus, H., Weng, T. (eds.) ICCBSS 2003. LNCS, vol. 2580, pp. 36–50. Springer, Heidelberg (2003)
5. Brown, A., Johnston, S., Kelly, K.: Using service-oriented architecture and component-based development to build web service applications. White paper, IBM Corporation (2003)
6. Boehm, B.W., Abts, C., Clark, E.B.: Cocots: a cots software integration cost model: model overview and preliminary data findings. In: The 11th ESCOM Conference, Munich, Geremany, pp. 325–333 (2000)
7. Castro, J., Kolp, M., Mylopoulos, J.: Towards requirements-driven information systems engineering: the tropos project. Inf. Syst. 27(6), 365–389 (2002)
8. Chung, L., Cooper, K.: Defining goals in a cots-aware requirements engineering approach. System Engineering 7(1), 61–83 (2002)
9. Chung, L., Nixon, B., Yu, E., Mylopoulos, J.: Non-functional requirements in software engineering. Kluwer Academic Publishing, Dordrecht (2000)
10. Estrada, H., Rebollar, A.M., Pastor, Ó., Mylopoulos, J.: An empirical evaluation of the i* framework in a model-based software generation environment. In: Martinez, F.H., Pohl, K. (eds.) CAiSE 2006. LNCS, vol. 4001, pp. 513–527. Springer, Heidelberg (2006)
11. Giorgini, P., Massacci, F., Mylopoulos, J., Zannone, N.: Modeling security requirements through ownership, permission and delegation. In: RE, pp. 167–176 (2005)
12. Giorgini, P., Massacci, F., Mylopoulos, J., Zannone, N.: Requirements engineering for trust management: model, methodology, and reasoning. Int. J. Inf. Sec. 5(4), 257–274 (2006)
13. Object Management Group. Software process engineering metamodel. version 2.0. Technical report (2008)
14. Haesen, R., Snoeck, M., Lemahieu, W., Poelmans, S.: On the definition of service granularity and its architectural impact. In: Bellahsène, Z., Léonard, M. (eds.) CAiSE 2008. LNCS, vol. 5074, pp. 375–389. Springer, Heidelberg (2008)
15. IBM. The rational unified process. Rational Software Corporation, Version 2003.06.00.65 (2003)
16. Kiv, S., Wautelet, Y., Kolp, M.: A process for cots-selection and mismatches handling - a goal-driven approach. In: Filipe, J., Fred, A.L.N., Sharp, B. (eds.) ICAART (1), pp. 98–106. INSTICC Press (2010)
17. Kolp, M., Wautelet, Y., Faulkner, S.: Social-centric design of multi-agent architectures. In: Yu, E., Giorgini, P., Maiden, N., Mylopoulos, J. (eds.) Social Modeling for Requirements Engineering. MIT Press, Cambridge (2011)

18. Kontio, J.: A cots selection method and experiences of its use. In: Proceedings of the 20th Annual Software Engineering Workshop, Maryland (1995)
19. Kruchten, P.: The rational unified process: An introduction. Addison-Wesley, Longman (2003)
20. Kunda, D., Brooks, L.: Applying social-technical approach for cots selection. In: Proceeding of the 4th UKAIS Conference, University of York (1999)
21. Maiden, N.A.M., Kim, H., Ncube, C.: Rethinking process guidance for selecting software components. In: Palazzi, B., Gravel, A. (eds.) ICCBSS 2002. LNCS, vol. 2255, pp. 151–164. Springer, Heidelberg (2002)
22. Pache, G., Spalanzani, A.: La gestion des chanes logistiques multi-acteurs: perspectives stratgiques. Presses Universitaires de Grenoble, PUG (2007)
23. Pastor, O., Estrada, H., Martínez, A.: The strengths and weaknesses of the i* framework: an experimental evaluation. In: Giorgini, P., Maiden, N., Mylopoulos, J. (eds.) Social Modeling for Requirements Engineering. Cooperative Information Systems series. MIT Press, Cambridge (2011)
24. Royce, W.: Software project management: a unified framework. Addison-Wesley, Reading (1998)
25. Sai, V., Franch, X., Maiden, N.A.M.: Driving component selection through actor-oriented models and use cases. In: Kazman, R., Port, D. (eds.) ICCBSS 2004. LNCS, vol. 2959, pp. 63–73. Springer, Heidelberg (2004)
26. Samii, A.K.: Stratgie logistique, supply chain management: Fondements - méthodes - applications, Dunod (2004)
27. Tran, V., Liu, D.-B., Hummel, B.: Component-based systems development: challenges and lessons learned. In: International Workshop on Software Technology and Engineering Practice, p. 452 (1997)
28. Wautelet, Y.: A goal-driven project management framework for multi-agent software development: The case of i-tropos. PhD thesis, Université catholique de Louvain, Louvain School of Management (LSM), Louvain-La-Neuve, Belgium (August 2008)
29. Wautelet, Y., Achbany, Y., Kiv, S., Kolp, M.: A service-oriented framework for component-based software development: An i* driven approach. In: Filipe, J., Cordeiro, J. (eds.) ICEIS. LNBIP, vol. 24, pp. 551–563. Springer, Heidelberg (2009)
30. Wautelet, Y., Achbany, Y., Kolp, M.: A service-oriented framework for mas modeling. In: Cordeiro, J., Filipe, J. (eds.) ICEIS (3-1), pp. 120–128 (2008)
31. Yu, E.: Social Modeling for Requirements Engineering. MIT Press, Cambridge (2011)

Cellular Gene Expression Programming Classifier Learning

Joanna Jędrzejowicz[1] and Piotr Jędrzejowicz[2]

[1] Institute of Informatics, Gdańsk University,
Wita Stwosza 57, 80-952 Gdańsk, Poland
jj@inf.ug.edu.pl
[2] Department of Information Systems, Gdynia Maritime University,
Morska 83, 81-225 Gdynia, Poland
pj@am.gdynia.pl

Abstract. In this paper we propose integrating two collective computational intelligence techniques: gene expression programming and cellular evolutionary algorithms with a view to induce expression trees, which, subsequently, serve as weak classifiers. From these classifiers stronger ensemble classifiers are constructed using majority-voting and boosting techniques. The paper includes the discussion of the validating experiment result confirming high quality of the proposed ensemble classifiers.

Keywords: gene expression programming, cellular evolutionary algorithm, ensemble classifiers.

1 Introduction

Gene expression programming introduced by Ferreira [6] is an automatic programming approach. In GEP computer programs are represented as linear character strings of fixed-length called chromosomes which, in the subsequent fitness evaluation, can be expressed as expression trees of different sizes and shapes. The approach has flexibility and power to explore the entire search space, which comes from the separation of genotype and phenotype. As it has been observed by Ferreira [7] GEP can be used to design decision trees, with the advantage that all the decisions concerning the growth of the tree are made by the algorithm itself without any human input, that is, the growth of the tree is totally determined and refined by evolution.

Several experiments with gene expression programming for classification tasks were presented in [11], [12]. In this paper, following [13], gene expression programming is strengthened by the paradigm of cellular evolutionary algorithms - the population of genes is structured by using the concept of neighbourhood. Individuals can only interact with their closest neighbours in the population. For an introducion to cellular evolutionary algorithms see [1].

The paper is organized as follows. In section 2 classifiers induced by gene expression programming are proposed and discussed. In section 3 two classification

N.T. Nguyen (Ed.): Transactions on CCI V, LNCS 6910, pp. 66–83, 2011.

algorithms based on gene expression programming and cellular evolutionary algorithms are introduced. In section 4 the results of validating experiment are shown. Finally, section 5 contains conclusions.

2   Using Cellular Gene Expression Programming to Induce Classifiers

Consider data classification problem. In what follows C is the set of categorical classes which are denoted $1, \ldots, |C|$. We assume that the learning algorithm is provided with the training set $TD = \{< \boldsymbol{d}, c > \mid \boldsymbol{d} \in D, c \in C\} \subset D \times C$, where D is the space of attribute vectors $\boldsymbol{d} = (w_1^d, \ldots, w_n^d)$ with w_i^d being symbolic or numeric values. The learning algorithm is used to find the best possible approximation $\bar{f}$ of the unknown function f such that $f(\boldsymbol{d}) = c$. Then $\bar{f}$ is a classifier which can be applied to find the class $c = \bar{f}(\boldsymbol{d})$ for any $\boldsymbol{d} \in D$. As usual when applying GEP methodology, the algorithm uses a population of chromosomes, selects them according to fitness and introduces genetic variation using several genetic operators. Each chromosome is composed of a single gene (chromosome and gene mean the same in what follows) divided into two parts as in the original head-tail method [6]. The size of the head (h) is determined by the user with the suggested size not less than the number of attributes in the dataset. The size of the tail (t) is computed as $t = h(n - 1) + 1$ where n is the largest arity found in the function set. In the computational experiments the functions are: logical AND, OR, XOR, NOR and NOT. Thus $n = 2$ and the size of the gene is $h + t = 2h + 1$. The terminal set contains triples $(op, attrib, const)$ where op is one of relational operators $<, \leq, >, \geq, =, \neq$, $attrib$ is the attribute number, and finally $const$ is a value belonging to the domain of the attribute $attrib$. As usual in GEP, the tail part of a gene always contains terminals and head can have both, terminals and functions. Observe that in this model each gene is syntactically correct and corresponds to a valid expression. Each attribute can appear once, many times or not at all. This allows to define flexible characteristics like for example $(attribute1 > 0.57)$ AND $(attribute1 < 0.80)$. On the other hand, it can also introduce inconsistencies like for example $(attribute1 > 0.57)$ AND $(attribute1 < 0.40)$. This does not cause problems since a decision subtree corresponding to such a subexpression would evaluate it to $false$. Besides, when studying the structure of the best classifiers in our experiments the above inconsistencies did not appear.

The expression of genes is done in exactly the same manner as in all GEP systems. Consider the chromosome C with head=6, defined below.

0	1	2	3	4	5	6	7	8	9
OR	AND	AND	$(>,1,0)$	$(=,2,5)$	$(>,1,2)$	$(<,1,10)$	$(>,3,0)$	$(<,3,5)$	$\cdots$

The start position (position 0) in the chromosome corresponds to the root of the expression tree (OR, in the example). Then, below each function branches are attached and there are as many of them as the arity of the function - 2 in our case.

The following symbols in the chromosome are attached to the branches on a given level. The process is complete when each branch is completed with a terminal. The number of symbols from the chromosome to form the expression tree is denoted as the termination point. For the discussed example, the termination point is 7.

Tradidionally, GEP algorithms work on a single population of genes. Here, the benefits of structuring the population by defining neighbourhoods are explored. Individuals are arranged on a torus-like grid of dimension $xmax \times ymax$. Each point of the grid has a neighbourhood that overlaps the neighbourhood of nearby individuals; all the neighbourhoods have the same size and identical shape. The boundary individuals of the grid are connected to the individuals located in the opposite borders in the same row/column, depending on the case. This results in toroidal grid and all the individuals have exactly the same number of neighbours. In the experiments the two most commonly used neighbourhoods were applied:

- L5, or NEWS neighbourhood - 4 nearest neighbours in a given axial (north, east, west, south) direction,
- C9, or Moore neighbourhood - 8 neighbours in horizontal, vertical and diagonal direction.

Table 1. Two neighbourhoods

The algorithm for learning the best classifier using cellular GEP works as follows. Suppose that a training dataset is given and each row in the dataset has a correct label representing the class. In the initial step the minimal and maximal value of each attribute is calculated and a random population of genes placed on the grid is generated. For each gene the symbols in the head part are randomly selected from the set of functions AND, OR, NOT, XOR, NOR and the set of terminals of type $(op, attrib, const)$, where the value of $const$ is in the range of $attrib$. The symbols in the tail part are all terminals.

To introduce variation in the population the following genetic operators are used:

- mutation,
- transposition of insertion sequence elements (IS transposition),

– root transposition (RIS transposition),
– one-point recombination,
– two-point recombination.

Mutation can occur anywhere in the chromosome. We consider one-point mutation which means that with a probability, called mutation rate, one symbol in a chromosome is changed. In case of a functional symbol it is replaced by another randomly selected function, otherwise for $g = (op, attrib, const)$ a random relational operator op', an attribute $attrib'$ and a constant $const'$ in the range of $attrib'$ are selected. Note that mutation can change the respective expression tree since a function of one argument may be mutated into a function of two arguments, or vice versa.

Transposition stands for moving part of a chromosome to another location. Here we consider two kinds of transposable elements. In case of transposition of insertion sequence (IS) three values are randomly chosen: a position in the chromosome (start of IS), the length of the sequence and the target site in the **head** - a bond between two positions. For example consider the chromosome C defined above. Suppose that IS is defined as: start position=6, length=2, target=0. Then a cut is made in the bond defined by the target site (in the example between symbol 0 and 1), and the insertion sequence (the symbols from positions 6 and 7) is copied into the site of the insertion. The sequence downstream from the copied IS element loses, at the end of the head, as many symbols as the length of the transposon. The resulting chromosome is shown below:

0	1	2	3	4	5	6	7	8	9
OR	$(<, 1, 10)$	$(>, 3, 0)$	AND	AND	$(>, 1, 0)$	$(<, 1, 10)$	$(>, 3, 0)$	$(<, 3, 5)$	$\cdots$

Observe that since the target site is in the head, the newly created individual is always syntactically correct though it can reshape the tree quite dramatically as in the above case. The termination point is 3 for the new chromosome.

In case of root transposition, a position in the head is randomly selected, the first function following this position is chosen - it is the start of the RIS element. If no function is found then no change is performed. The length of the insertion sequence is chosen. The insertion sequence is copied at the root position and at the same time the last symbols of the head (as many as RIS length) are deleted. For the chromosome C defined before and RIS sequence starting with the function AND at the position 2, of length 2 the resulting chromosome is defined as:

0	1	2	3	4	5	6	7	8	9
AND	$(>, 1, 0)$	OR	AND	AND	$(>, 1, 0)$	$(<, 1, 10)$	$(>, 3, 0)$	$(<, 3, 5)$	$\cdots$

Again the change has quite an effect since the termination point is now 9.

For both kinds of recombination two parent chromosomes P_1, P_2 are randomly chosen and two new child chromosomes C_1, C_2 are formed. In case of one-point recombination one position is randomly generated and both parent chromosomes are split by this position into two parts. Child chromosomes C_1 (respectively, C_2) is formed as containing the first part from P_1 (respectively, P_2) and the second part from P_2 (and P_1). In two-point recombination two positions are randomly chosen and the symbols between recombination positions are exchanged between two parent chromosomes forming two new child chromosomes. Observe that again, in both cases, the newly formed chromosomes are syntactically correct no matter whether the recombination positions were taken from the head or tail.

During GEP learning, the individuals are selected and copied into the next generation based on their fitness and the roulette wheel sampling with elitism which guarantees the survival and cloning of the best gene in the next generation. More details of applied GEP learning can be found in [11].

Genetic operations may only take place in a small neighbourhood (either L5 or C9) of each individual. What is more, the reproductive cycle is applied to all the individuals synchronously, that is the population for the next generation is created at the same time for all individuals on the grid.

In order to compare the quality of genes used as classifiers two measures are introduced. Suppose that the learning dataset TR and a class $cl \in C$ are fixed. The first measure counts the rows which are classified incorrectly. For a gene g

$$nF^{cl}(g) = \sum_{rw \in TR,\ g(rw)\ is\ true} sg(\text{rw is from class} \neq cl)$$

where

$$sg(\varphi) = \begin{cases} 1 & \text{if } \varphi \text{ is true} \\ 0 & \text{otherwise} \end{cases}$$

The second measure is defined as:

$$nT^{cl}(g) = \sum_{rw \in TR,\ g(rw)\ is\ true} sg(\text{rw is from class } cl)$$

Obviously, for two genes the one with the higher nT^{cl} is better and respectively for the measure nF^{cl} - the lower the better. Using the above measures, fitness of a gene g is defined as:

$$fitness^{cl}(g) = nT^{cl}(g) - nF^{cl}(g)$$

The algorithm of cGEP learning is shown as Algorithm 1.

3   Learning Algorithms

Below two learning algorithms, called cGEP-mv and cGEP-ada, are described.

Algorithm 1. Algorithm cGEP learning

Require: class cl, training data, integer NG, integer $noInd$, integer $xmax$, $ymax$
1: create the grid of size $xmax \times ymax$ with a random population Pop
2: **for** $i = 1$ to NG **do**
3:     express genes as expression trees,
4:     calculate fitness of each gene,
5:     keep best gene
6:     **for all** $g \in Pop$ **do**
7:         nghbrs←CalculateNeighourhood(g)
8:         offspring1←One-pointRecomb(g, nghbrs)
9:         offspring2←Two-pointRecomb(g, nghbrs)
10:        $gNew \leftarrow$ the better fitted of two offsprings
11:        mutation($gNew$)
12:        IStransposition($gNew$)
13:        RIStransposition($gNew$)
14:        Replacement($postion(g)$, $AuxiliaryPop$, $gNew$)
15:    **end for**
16:    $Pop \leftarrow AuxiliaryPop$
17: **end for**
18: **return** $noInd$ best genes from Pop

3.1   Algorithm cGEP-mv

Learning takes place in two steps, shown as Algorithms 2 and Algorithm 3. Firstly, for each class (separately) the population of genes best fitting the class is found. During this step, in each generation the algorithm cGEP is applied and using the domination relation (defined below) best individuals are copied to next generation. The objective of the second step, called meta learning, is to select subsets of informative genes from the population defined in the first step in order to obtain high classification accuracy.

Definition 1. *We say that gene g_1 dominates gene g_2 in class cl if $nT^{cl}(g_1) > nT^{cl}(g_2)$ and $nF^{cl}(g_1) < nF^{cl}(g_2)$.*

The relation of domination is irreflexive, antisymmetric and transitive.

Definition 2. *We say that gene g is not dominated in the population pop iff no gene from pop dominates g.*

In the process of meta-learning genetic algorithms are applied in order to select a subset of genes obtained in the process of learning and resulting in the population of $|C| \times sizeBest$ genes. Now individuals are defined as matrices of type $MG = \{0, 1\}^{|C| \times sizeBest}$ which correspond to the distribution of genes from *population_best*. For the matrix $mg \in MG$ the set $\{i : mg[cl, i] = 1\}$ picks up genes from *population_best^{cl}* which are meaningful for the class cl. To define fitness of an individual mg, we assume the majority vote is performed to classify

---

Algorithm 2. Algorithm cGEP-mv, first step

Require: training data with correct labels representing $|C|$ classes, integer $sizePop$,
   integer $sizeBest$
Ensure: population of $sizeBest$ genes for each class
1: **for all** $cl \in C$ **do**
2:     $population\_best^{cl} \leftarrow \phi$
3:     **repeat**
4:         call algorithm cGEP for class cl to generate pop
5:         add to $population\_best^{cl}$ those genes from population pop which are not dominated in $population\_best^{cl}$
6:     **until** $population\_best^{cl}$ contains at least $sizeBest$ elements
7: **end for**

---

each data row and the number of correct answers is counted. Let $r = (\boldsymbol{x}, y)$ be
a data row

$$which_i^{cl}(mg, \boldsymbol{x}) = \begin{cases} 1 & \text{if } mg[cl, i] = 1 \text{ and} \\ & population\_best^{cl}(i) \text{ is true for } \boldsymbol{x} \\ 0 & \text{otherwise} \end{cases}$$

$$mv(mg, \boldsymbol{x}) = \max_{cl}(\sum_{i=1}^{sizeBest} which_i^{cl}(mg, \boldsymbol{x}))$$

and, finally

$$fitness(mg) = \frac{|r :\ mv(mg, \boldsymbol{x}) = y|}{|dataset|}$$

Standard genetic operators: mutation and crossover are applied to find one matrix mg best fitting the given dataset. This matrix is then used in testing where again, the majority vote is applied.

Algorithm 3. Algorithm cGEP-mv second step (meta-learning)

Require: training data with correct labels representing $|C|$ classes, integer $noIter$,
   population of $sizeBest$ genes for each class,
Ensure: best metagene mg
1: create random population $popMet$ of metagenes
2: **for** $i = 1$ to $noIter$ **do**
3:     calculate fitness of each metagene from $popMet$
4:     using roulette rule choose the metagenes for the next step,
5:     mutation,
6:     crossover,
7: **end for**
8: **return** the best metagene mg

Algorithm 4. Algorithm cGEP-mv

Require: training data with correct labels representing $|C|$ classes, integer $sizePop$,
    integer $sizeBest$, testing data TS
Ensure: qc quality of the majority vote classifier
 1: apply Algorithm 2 to define $population\_best$
 2: apply Algorithm 3 to find metagene mg
 3: $qc \leftarrow 0$ {test mg for testing data TS}
 4: **for all** $(x, y) \in TS$ **do**
 5:    **if** $mv(mg, x) = y$ **then**
 6:        $qc \leftarrow qc + 1$
 7:    **end if**
 8: **end for**
 9: $qc \leftarrow qc/|TS|$
10: **return** qc

3.2   Algorithm cGEP-ada

As suggested in [16] a weak classifier can be considerably improved by *boosting*.
The general idea is to create an ensemble of classifiers by resampling the training
dataset and creating a classifier for each sample. In each step the most informative training data is provided - for example those for which the previous classifier
misclassified. Then an ensemble of generated classifiers together with an intelligent combination rule proves often to be a more efficient approach. Freund and
Schapiro [8] suggested a refinement of a boosting algorithm called AdaBoost. For
a predefined number of iterations T, the following procedures are performed. In
the tth step, according to the current distribution - which is uniform in the first
iteration, a sample is drawn from the dataset. The best classifier C_t is found for
the sample and using the whole dataset the error of the current classification is
calculated. The distribution is updated so that the weights of those instances
that are correctly classified by the current classifier C_t are reduced by the factor
depending on the error, and the weights of misclassified instances are unchanged.
Once T classifiers are generated 'weighted majority voting' is used to classify the
test set. The idea is to promote those classifiers that have shown good performance during training - they are rewarded with a higher weight than the others.
The details are given in Algorithm 5, where cGEP is used as a weak classifier
and AdaBoost methodology is applied.

It can be observed that in each iteration t the distribution weights of those
instances that were correctly classified are reduced by a factor β_t and the weights
of the misclassified instances stay unchanged. After the normalization the weights
of instances misclassified are raised and they add up to $1/2$, and the weights of
the correctly classified instances are lowered and they also add up to $1/2$. What
is more, since it is required that the weak classifier has an error less than $1/2$, it
is guaranteed to correctly classify at least one previously misclassified instance.
In the ensemble decision those classifiers which produced small error and β_t is
close to zero, have a large voting role since $1/\beta_t$ and logarithm of $1/\beta_t$ are large.

Algorithm 5. Algorithm cGEP-ada

Require: training data TD of size N, test dataset TS, integer T, integer $M \leq N$ - size of the selected dataset

Ensure: qc quality of the AdaBoost classifier.

1: initialize the distribution $D_1(i) = \frac{1}{N}, i = 1, \ldots, N$
2: **for** $t = 1$ to TT **do**
3:     for the current distribution D_t select a training dataset $S_t \subset TD$ of size M,
4:     call Algorithm cGEP for the dataset S_t, receive the classifier C_t
5:     using the majority voting for C_t calculate the error $\epsilon_t = \sum_{C_t(\mathbf{x}_i) \neq y_i} D_t(i)$
6:     **if** $\epsilon_t > 0.5$ **then**
7:         abort
8:     **else**
9:         $\beta_t = \epsilon_t / (1 - \epsilon_t)$
10:    **end if**
       { update the distribution}
11:    **for** $i = 1$ to N **do**
12:        **if** $C_t(x_i) = y_i$ **then**
13:            $D_t(i) \leftarrow D_t(i) \times \beta_t$
14:        **end if**
15:        normalize the distribution $D_{t+1}(i) = D_t(i)/Z_t, \ Z_t = \sum_i D_t(i)$
16:    **end for**
17: **end for**
    {test the ensemble classifier $C_1, C_2, \ldots, C_T$ in the test dataset TS}
18: $qc \leftarrow 0$
19: **for all** $(\boldsymbol{x}, y) \in TS$ **do**
20:    $V_i = \sum_{C_t(\mathbf{x})=i} \log(1/\beta_t), \ i = 1, \ldots, |C|$
21:    $c \leftarrow argmax_{1 \leq j \leq |C|} V_j$
22:    **if** $c = y$ **then**
23:        $qc \leftarrow qc + 1$
24:    **end if**
25: **end for**
26: $qc \leftarrow qc/|TS|$
27: **return** qc

---

4   Computational Experiment Results

To evaluate the proposed approach computational experiment has been carried out. The experiment involved the following 2-classes datasets from the UCI Machine Learning Repository [2]: Wisconsin Breast Cancer (WBC), Diabetes, Sonar, Australian Credit (ACredit), German Credit (GCredit), Cleveland Heart (Heart), Hepatitis and Ionosphere. Basic characteristics of these sets are shown in Table 2.

Table 2. Datasets used in the computational experiment

name	data type	attribute type	no. instances	no. attributes
WBC	multivariate	integer	699	11
Diabetes	multivariate, time-series	categorical, integer	768	9
Sonar	multivariate	real	208	61
ACredit	multivariate	categorical, integer, real	690	15
GCredit	multivariate	categorical, integer	1000	21
Heart	multivariate	categorical, real	303	14
Hepatitis	multivariate	categorical, integer, real	155	20
Ionosphere	multivariate	integer, real	351	35

In the reported experiment the following classification tools have been used: Cellular GEP with majority voting (cGEP-mv) and Cellular GEP with adaboost (cGEP-ada) described in details in the previous sections versus 16 well-known classifiers from WEKA Environment for Knowledge Analysis v. 3.7.0 [20] including Naïve Bayes, Bayes Net, Logistic Regression, Radial Basis Function Network, AdaBoost, Support Vectors Machine, Ensemble Selection, Bagging, Classification via Clustering, Random Committee, Stacking, Rotation Forest, Decision Table, FT Tree, Random Forest and C4.5.

Computations involving cGEP-mv have been run with the following arbitrary parameter settings: xmax = ymax = 15; target population size 80; percentage of the non-dominated expression trees taking part in the majority voting 70%; number of iterations in Cellular GEP 250; probability of mutation 0.5, RIS transposition 0.2, IS transposition 0.2, 1-point recombination 0.2 and 2-point recombination 0.2. Computations involving CGEP-ada have been run with the following arbitrary parameter settings: xmax = ymax = 10; number of the Adaboost iterations 5; number of iterations in Cellular GEP 30; number of repetitions in the class learning 50. The remaining settings are identical as in case of cGEP-mv. In all WEKA classifiers the default parameter settings have been used.

Tables 3, 4, 5, 6 and 7 show computation results averaged over 10 repetitions of the 10-cross-validation scheme. Performance measures include classifier accuracy shown in Table 3, the area under the ROC curve shown in Table 4, value of the F-measure shown in Table 5 and values of the precision and recall shown in Tables 6 and 7, respectively. Accuracy is understood as a percentage of the right class predictions over the whole test dataset. An area under the receiver operating characteristic (ROC) curve calculated as the Wilcoxon-Mann-Whitney statistic, measures discrimination, that is, the ability of the classifier to correctly classify "positive" and "negative" instances. The F-measure can be interpreted as a weighted average of the precision and recall, where a score reaches its best value at 1 and worst at 0. Finally, the precision for a class is the number of true positives divided by the total number of elements labeled as belonging to the positive class (i.e. the sum of true positives and false positives, which are items incorrectly labeled as belonging to the class). Recall in this context is defined as the number of true positives divided by the total number of elements that actually belong to the positive class (i.e. the sum of true positives and false negatives). For the detailed description of the above measures see, for example, [5].

Table 3. Comparison of the classifier accuracy (%)

no.	classifier	WBC	Diab.	Sonar	ACr.	GCr.	Heart	Hep.	Ion.
1	Stacking	65,52	65,10	53,36	55,51	70,00	55,56	79,35	64,10
2	Class. via clustering	95,71	64,84	54,32	74,06	56,60	77,04	74,19	70,94
3	Naive Bayes	95,99	76,30	67,78	77,68	75,40	83,70	84,51	82,62
4	SVM	96,99	77,34	75,96	84,92	75,10	84,07	85,16	88,60
5	Logistic	96,56	77,21	73,08	85,22	75,20	83,70	82,58	88,89
6	Decision Table	95,28	71,22	69,23	83,48	71,00	84,81	76,13	89,46
7	Bayes Net	97,14	74,35	80,28	86,23	75,50	81,11	83,22	89,46
8	FT	96,99	77,34	79,81	85,51	68,30	82,96	81,29	90,31
9	Ensemble Selection	94,42	74,61	75,48	84,93	73,10	80,00	81,29	90,59
10	AdaBoost M1	94,85	74,34	71,63	84,64	69,50	80,00	82,58	90,88
11	Bagging	95,56	74,61	77,40	85,07	74,40	79,26	84,52	90,88
12	cGEP-ada	95,86	**77,21**	**81,24**	**86,52**	**77,37**	**83,84**	**87,13**	**91,35**
13	C4.5	94,56	73,82	71,15	86,09	70,50	76,66	83,87	91,45
14	cGEP-mv	**95,58**	**76,99**	**80,79**	**87,39**	**76,27**	**80,24**	**86,46**	**91,73**
15	RBF Network	95,85	75,39	72,11	79,71	74,00	84,07	85,80	92,31
16	Random Committee	95,99	73,95	84,13	83,48	73,90	80,37	84,52	92,59
17	Random Forest	96,13	73,82	80,77	85,07	72,50	78,15	82,58	92,87
18	Rotation Forest	96,99	76,69	84,13	87,25	74,80	80,74	82,58	93,73

Table 4. Comparison of the area under the ROC curve

no.	classifier	WBC	Diab.	Sonar	ACr.	GCr	Heart	Hep.	Ion.
1	Stacking	0,496	0,497	0,485	0,494	0,500	0,500	0,467	0,485
2	Class. via clustering	0,949	0,605	0,543	0,749	0,524	0,772	0,803	0,715
3	Naive Bayes	0,986	0,819	0,800	0,876	0,787	0,898	0,860	0,925
4	SVM	0,968	0,720	0,758	0,856	0,671	0,837	0,756	0,853
5	Logistic	0,993	0,832	0,763	0,904	0,785	0,900	0,802	0,870
6	Decision Table	0,987	0,773	0,763	0,909	0,723	0,877	0,763	0,895
7	Bayes Net	**0,992**	0,806	0,877	0,921	0,780	0,902	0,882	0,948
8	FT	0,975	0,763	0,846	0,883	0,662	0,857	0,754	0,896
9	Ensemble Selection	0,987	0,806	0,824	0,906	0,745	0,852	0,733	0,940
10	AdaBoost M1	0,989	0,801	0,841	0,929	0,723	0,878	0,851	0,944
11	Bagging	0,987	0,817	0,873	0,915	0,776	0,875	0,821	0,934
12	cGEP-ada	**0.978**	**0.826**	**0.845**	**0.893**	**0.877**	**0.843**	0,798	**0,969**
13	C4.5	0,955	0,751	0,743	0,887	0,639	0,744	0,708	0,892
14	cGEP-mv	**0.980**	**0.811**	**0.911**	**0.890**	**0.823**	**0.880**	**0.921**	**0,982**
15	RBF Network	0,986	0,783	0,809	0,854	0,753	0,893	0,835	0,939
16	Random Committee	0,987	0,785	0,912	0,900	0,761	0,866	0,848	0,976
17	Random Forest	0,988	0,779	0,912	0,914	0,748	0,854	0,835	0,956
18	Rotation Forest	0,986	0,810	0,925	0,921	0,757	0,883	0,826	0,967

Table 5. Comparison of the F-measure values

no.	classifier	WBC	Diab.	Sonar	ACr.	GCr	Heart	Hep.	Ion.
1	Stacking	0,519	0,513	0,371	0,396	0,576	0,384	0,702	0,501
2	Class. via clust.	0,957	0,645	0,544	0,741	0,579	0,795	0,766	0,715
3	Naive Bayes	0,96	0,76	0,673	0,769	0,746	0,835	0,848	0,829
4	SVM	0,959	0,763	0,759	0,85	0,741	0,841	0,849	0,883
5	Logistic	0,966	0,765	0,731	0,852	0,744	0,844	0,818	0,887
6	Decision Table	0,953	0,708	0,692	0,835	0,679	0,762	0,757	0,893
7	Bayes Net	0,972	0,742	0,802	0,861	0,749	0,835	0,837	0,894
8	FT	0,97	0,768	0,798	0,855	0,684	0,824	0,812	0,902
9	Ensemble Sel.	0,944	0,742	0,754	0,85	0,714	0,827	0,78	0,906
10	AdaBoost M1	0,948	0,738	0,716	0,846	0,665	0,821	0,823	0,906
11	Bagging	0,956	0,742	0,771	0,851	0,732	0,821	0,816	0,908
12	cGEP-ada	**0,943**	**0,831**	**0,825**	**0,852**	**0,846**	**0,817**	**0,917**	**0,934**
13	C4.5	0,946	0,736	0,712	0,861	0,692	0,774	0,825	0,913
14	cGEP-mv	**0,933**	**0,838**	**0,806**	**0,862**	**0,839**	**0,754**	**0,915**	**0,936**
15	RBF Network	0,959	0,746	0,721	0,793	0,728	0,838	0,854	0,923
16	Random Comm.	0,96	0,734	0,841	0,835	0,724	0,791	0,837	0,926
17	Random Forest	0,961	0,731	0,808	0,851	0,707	0,813	0,8	0,929
18	Rotation Forest	0,96	0,758	0,841	0,873	0,739	0,821	0,820	0,937

Table 6. Comparison of the precision values

no.	classifier	WBC	Diab.	Sonar	ACr.	GCr	Heart	Hep.	Ion.
1	Stacking	0,429	0,424	0,285	0,308	0,49	0,297	0,63	0,411
2	Class. via clust.	0,957	0,643	0,546	0,757	0,6	0,795	0,858	0,733
3	Naive Bayes	0,962	0,759	0,704	0,793	0,743	0,835	0,853	0,842
4	SVM	0,96	0,769	0,759	0,861	0,738	0,843	0,847	0,891
5	Logistic	0,966	0,767	0,731	0,854	0,741	0,846	0,814	0,889
6	Decision Table	0,953	0,706	0,692	0,836	0,68	0,762	0,753	0,896
7	Bayes Net	0,972	0,741	0,805	0,864	0,746	0,835	0,845	0,894
8	FT	0,971	0,768	0,798	0,855	0,685	0,825	0,811	0,903
9	Ensemble Sel.	0,945	0,74	0,755	0,855	0,712	0,831	0,786	0,906
10	AdaBoost M1	0,948	0,737	0,716	0,847	0,661	0,822	0,82	0,915
11	Bagging	0,956	0,741	0,781	0,853	0,73	0,822	0,844	0,909
12	cGEP-ada	**0,947**	**0,86**	**0,793**	**0,88**	**0,892**	**0,804**	**0,93**	**0,943**
13	C4.5	0,946	0,735	0,713	0,861	0,687	0,776	0,825	0,915
14	cGEP-mv	**0,919**	**0,908**	**0,782**	**0,893**	**0,88**	**0,681**	**0,92**	**0,968**
15	RBF Network	0,96	0,747	0,729	0,806	0,726	0,838	0,852	0,924
16	Random Comm.	0,96	0,733	0,841	0,835	0,722	0,792	0,834	0,926
17	Random Forest	0,962	0,73	0,813	0,851	0,705	0,819	0,806	0,929
18	Rotation Forest	0,96	0,761	0,843	0,873	0,736	0,822	0,817	0,937

Table 7. Comparison of the recall values

no.	classifier	WBC	Diab.	Sonar	ACr.	GCr	Heart	Hep.	Ion.
1	Stacking	0,655	0,651	0,534	0,555	0,7	0,545	0,794	0,641
2	Class. via clust.	0,957	0,648	0,543	0,741	0,566	0,795	0,742	0,709
3	Naive Bayes	0,96	0,763	0,678	0,777	0,754	0,835	0,845	0,826
4	SVM	0,959	0,712	0,76	0,849	0,751	0,842	0,852	0,886
5	Logistic	0,966	0,772	0,731	0,852	0,752	0,845	0,826	0,889
6	Decision Table	0,953	0,773	0,692	0,835	0,71	0,762	0,761	0,895
7	Bayes Net	0,971	0,743	0,803	0,862	0,755	0,835	0,832	0,895
8	FT	0,97	0,773	0,798	0,855	0,683	0,825	0,813	0,903
9	Ensemble Sel.	0,944	0,746	0,755	0,849	0,731	0,828	0,813	0,906
10	AdaBoost M1	0,948	0,743	0,716	0,846	0,695	0,822	0,826	0,909
11	Bagging	0,956	0,746	0,784	0,851	0,744	0,822	0,845	0,909
12	cGEP-ada	**0,938**	**0,804**	**0,859**	**0,826**	**0,806**	**0,83**	**0,9**	**0,924**
13	C4.5	0,946	0,738	0,712	0,861	0,705	0,776	0,839	0,915
14	cGEP-mv	**0,948**	**0,779**	**0,832**	**0,832**	**0,802**	**0,844**	**0,91**	**0,907**
15	RBF Network	0,959	0,754	0,721	0,797	0,74	0,838	0,858	0,923
16	Random Comm.	0,96	0,74	0,841	0,835	0,739	0,792	0,845	0,926
17	Random Forest	0,961	0,738	0,808	0,851	0,725	0,815	0,826	0,929
18	Rotation Forest	0,96	0,768	0,841	0,872	0,748	0,822	0,826	0,937

To evaluate more deeply the performance of cGEP-mv and cGEP-ada the Friedman's non-parametric test using ranks of the data has been applied. For each of the performance measures including classification accuracy, ROC area, F-measure, precision and recall the following hypotheses were tested:

- Null Hypothesis H0: All of the 18 population distribution functions are identical.
- Alternative Hypothesis H1: At least one of the populations tends to yield larger observations than at least one of the other populations.

Analysis of the experiment results shows that in each of the considered cases the null hypothesis should be rejected at the significance level of 0,05. The average Friedmans ranks for the classification accuracies, ROC areas, F-measures, precisions and recalls are shown in Fig. 1 - 5, respectively. The highest rank was given 1 point and the lowest - 18 points.

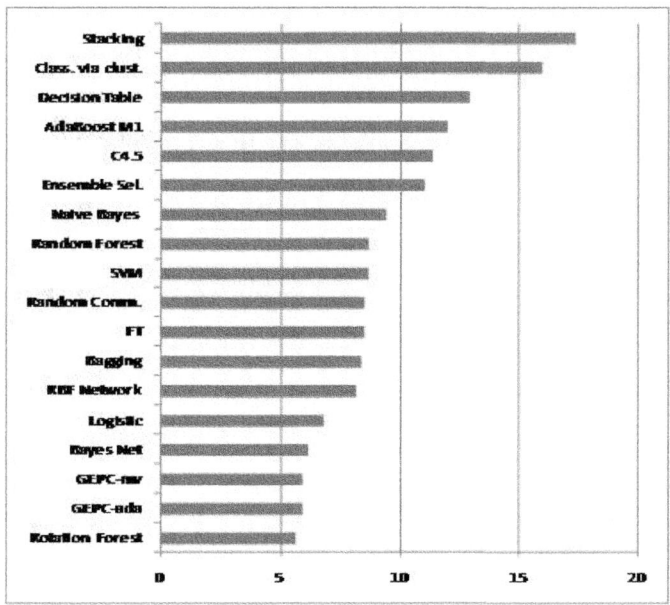

Fig. 1. The average Friedmans ranks for the classification accuracy of different classifiers

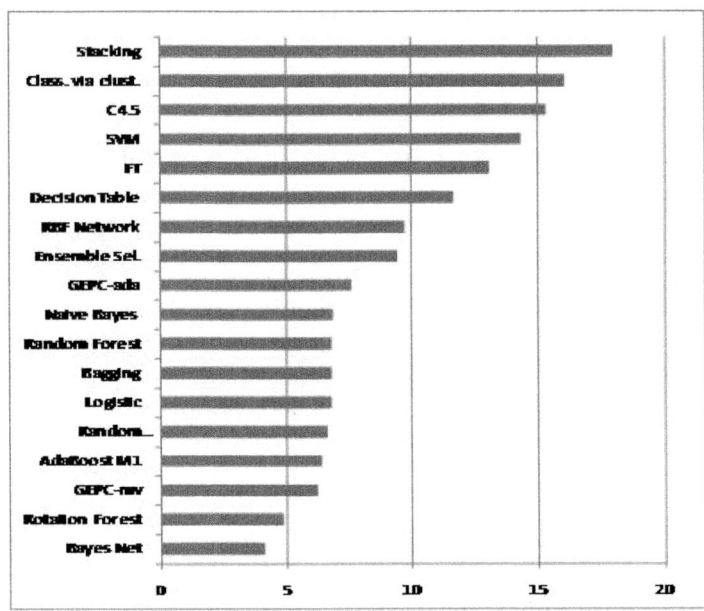

Fig. 2. The average Friedmans ranks for the ROC area of different classifiers

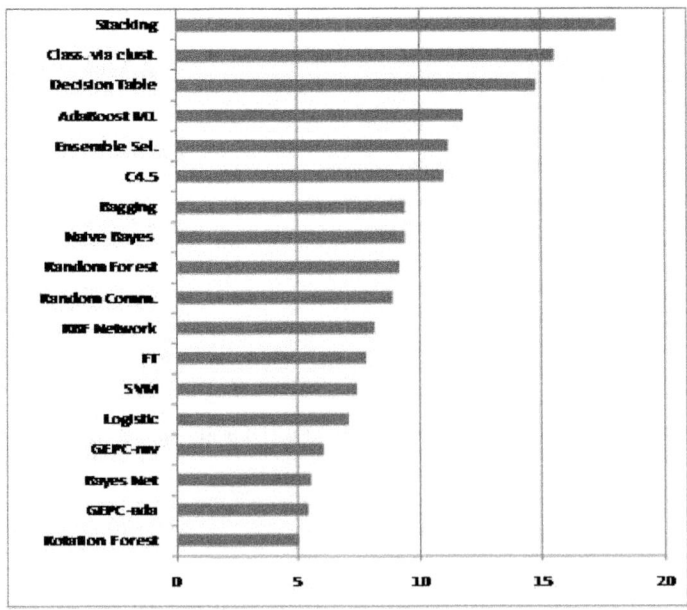

Fig. 3. The average Friedmans ranks for the F-measure of different classifiers

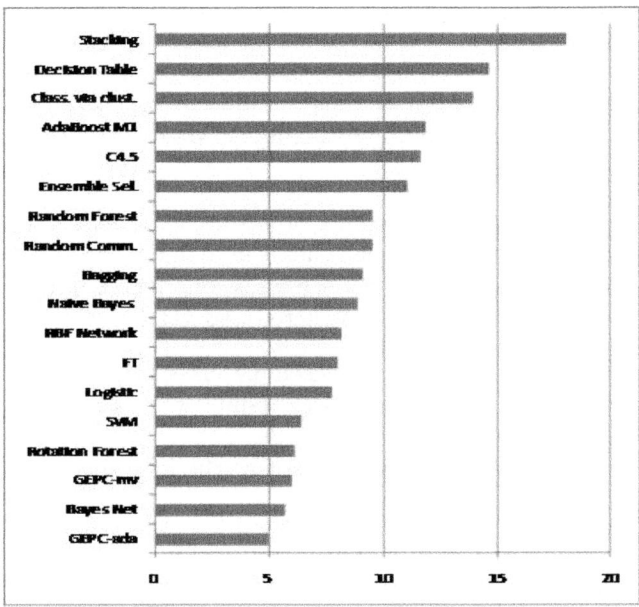

Fig. 4. The average Friedmans ranks for the precision of different classifiers

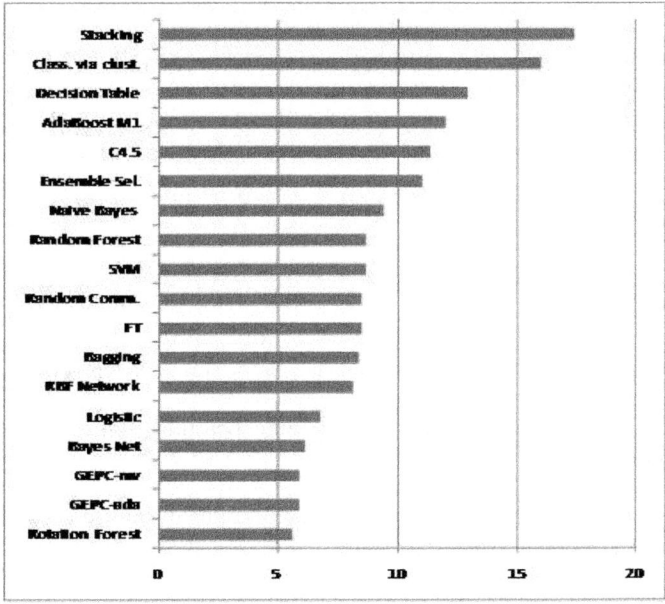

Fig. 5. The average Friedmans ranks for the recall of different classifiers

5   Conclusions

The paper proposes an approach based on integrating gene expression programming with cellular genetic programming to induce expression trees. The induced trees are used to construct ensemble classifiers. Main contribution of the paper can be summarized as follows:

 - Class specific cellular GEP learning procedure is proposed and implemented
 - Non-dominance relation between genes is used in the process of gene selection
 - Two ensemble classifiers based on expression trees induced using cellular GEP learning procedure are constructed and validated.

The resulting cellular GEP-induced ensemble classifiers were validated experimentally using several datasets and the results were compared with those of other well established classification methods.

Validation experiment results allow to draw the following conclusions:

 - In terms of all major performance metrics including the classification accuracy, the area under the ROC curve both, F-measure precision nad recall, both - cGEP-mv and cGEP-ada perform very well and are competitive in comparison with a majority of other approaches,
 - Both algorithms (cGEP-mv and cGEP-ada) are consistent assuring high quality classification results when applied to different datasets.

Presented experiment results confirm that next generation collective computational intelligence techniques like gene expression programming and cellular evolutionary algorithms, when applied to the field of machine learning, can be of help in producing excellent quality results through exploiting their collaborative and synergetic features. The proposed family of ensemble classifiers constructed from expression trees stands out as a convincing example showing effectiveness of the combinatorial effort of integrating collaborative data technologies for computational intelligence.

References

1. Alba, E., Dorronsoro, B.: Cellular Genetic Algorithms. Springer Science, New York (2008)
2. Asuncion, A., Newman, D.J.: UCI Machine Learning Repository. University of California, School of Information and Computer Science (2007), http://www.ics.uci.edu/~mlearn/MLRepository.html
3. Bi, Y., Guan, J., Bell, D.: The combination of multiple classifiers using an evidential reasoning approach. Artif. Intell. 172, 1731–1751 (2008)
4. Centeno, P., Lawrence, N.D.: Optimising Kernel Parameters and Regularisation Coefficients for Non-linear Discriminant Analysis. Journal of Machine Learning Research 7, 455–491 (2006)
5. Fawcett, T.: ROC Graphs: Notes and Practical Considerations for Researchers, HP Labs Tech Report HPL-2003-4, Palo Alto, Ca (2003)

6. Ferreira, C.: Gene Expression Programming: a New Adaptive Algorithm for Solving Problems. Complex Systems 13(2), 87–129 (2001)
7. Ferreira, C.: Gene Expression Programming. Studies in Computational Intell. 21, 337–380 (2006)
8. Freund, Y., Schapire, R.E.: Decision-theoretic generalization of on-line learning and application to boosting. Journal of Computer and System Science 55, 119–139 (1997)
9. FT Datasets, http://www.grappa.univ-lille3.fr/torre/Recherche/Experiments/Results/tables.php
10. Ishibuchi, H., Nojima, Y.: Analysis of Interpretability-accuracy Tradeoff of Fuzzy Systems by Multiobjective Fuzzy Genetics-based Machine Learning. Intern. Journal of Approximate Reasoning 44, 4–31 (2007)
11. Jędrzejowicz, J., Jędrzejowicz, P.: GEP-induced expression trees as weak classifiers. In: Perner, P. (ed.) ICDM 2008. LNCS (LNAI), vol. 5077, pp. 129–141. Springer, Heidelberg (2008)
12. Jędrzejowicz, J., Jędrzejowicz, P.: A family of GEP-induced ensemble classifiers. In: Nguyen, N.T., Kowalczyk, R., Chen, S.-M. (eds.) ICCCI 2009. LNCS, vol. 5796, pp. 641–652. Springer, Heidelberg (2009)
13. Jędrzejowicz, J., Jędrzejowicz, P.: Cellular GEP-induced classifiers. In: Pan, J.-S., Chen, S.-M., Nguyen, N.T. (eds.) ICCCI 2010. LNCS, vol. 6421, pp. 343–352. Springer, Heidelberg (2010)
14. Krętowski, M.: A memetic algorithm for global induction of decision trees. In: Geffert, V., Karhumäki, J., Bertoni, A., Preneel, B., Návrat, P., Bieliková, M. (eds.) SOFSEM 2008. LNCS, vol. 4910, pp. 531–540. Springer, Heidelberg (2008)
15. Polikar, R.: Ensemble Based Systems in Decision Making. IEEE Circuits and Systems Magazine 3, 22–43 (2006)
16. Schapire, R.E., Freund, Y., Bartlett, P., Lee, W.S.: Boosting the margin: A new explanation for the effectiveness of voting methods. The Annals of Statistics 26(5), 1651–1686 (1998)
17. Shafer, G.: A Mathematical Theory of Evidence. Princeton University Press, Princeton (1976)
18. Torre, F.: Boosting Correct Least General Generalizations, Technical Report GRApp A-0104, Grenoble (2004)
19. Weinert, W.R., Lopes, H.S.: GEPCLASS: A classification rule discovery tool using gene expression programming. In: Li, X., Zaïane, O.R., Li, Z.-h. (eds.) ADMA 2006. LNCS (LNAI), vol. 4093, pp. 871–880. Springer, Heidelberg (2006)
20. Witten, I.H., Frank, E.: Data Mining: Practical machine learning tools and techniques, 2nd edn. Morgan Kaufmann, San Francisco (2005)
21. Zhou, C., Xiao, W., Tirpak, T.M., Nelson, P.C.: Evolving Accurate and Compact Classification Rules with Gene Expression Programming. IEEE Transactions on Evolutionary Computation 7(6), 519–531 (2003)

A Situation-Aware Computational Trust Model for Selecting Partners

Joana Urbano, Ana Paula Rocha, and Eugénio Oliveira

LIACC – Laboratory for Artificial Intelligence and Computer Science
Faculdade de Engenharia da Universidade do Porto – DEI
Rua Dr. Roberto Frias, 4200-465, Porto, Portugal
{joana.urbano,arocha,eco}@fe.up.pt
http://www.fe.up.pt

Abstract. Trust estimation is a fundamental process in several multi-agent systems domains, from social networks to electronic business scenarios. However, the majority of current computational trust systems is still too simplistic and is not situation-aware, jeopardizing the accuracy of the predicted trustworthiness values of agents. In this paper, we address the inclusion of context in the trust management process. We first overview recently proposed situation-aware trust models, all based on the predefinition of similarity measures between situations. Then, we present our computational trust model, and we focus on Contextual Fitness, a component of the model that adds a contextual dimensional to existing trust aggregation engines. This is a dynamic and incremental technique that extracts tendencies of behavior from the agents in evaluation and that does not imply the predefinition of similarity measures between contexts. Finally, we evaluate our trust model and compare it with other trust approaches in an agent-based, open market trading simulation scenario. The results obtained show that our dynamic and incremental technique outperforms the other approaches in open and dynamic environments. By analyzing examples derived from the experiments, we show why our technique get better results than situation-aware trust models that are based on predefined similarity measures.

Keywords: computational trust systems, dynamics of trust, situation-aware trust, multi-agent systems.

1 Introduction

Computational trust systems are systems that collect information, such as evaluation of direct experiences, reputation, recommendations or certificates, about agents (e.g. representing individuals or organizations) and that computes the trustworthiness of these agents based on the collected information. In this document, we envision trust as the confidence that an evaluator agent has on the capabilities and the willingness of another agent (the trustee) in fulfilling some kind of task in a given context.

N.T. Nguyen (Ed.): Transactions on CCI V, LNCS 6910, pp. 84–105, 2011.

Trust management is in these days a fundamental research topic in agent-based and multi-agent systems, and its appliance concerns decision making processes in almost all electronic forms of commerce and social relationship. In this context, several trust and reputation models have been proposed to represent and aggregate social evaluations into trustworthiness scores (see [1] for an overview). However, the majority of these models are based on simple aggregation engines that do not differentiate between situations and therefore use all available evidences about an agent to compute its trustworthiness, independently of the context of the current assessment, potentially jeopardizing the accuracy of the estimated trust value.

In order to address this limitation, some models have been recently proposed that bring situation into the trust loop [2][3][4][5][6][7]. Some of them rely on the existence of taxonomies that allow defining a situation, and all of them use predefined domain-specific similarity metrics. Our belief is that these systems are more adequate to environments where the evidences about the agents in evaluation are abundant and where there is a relative stability concerning the context definition. However, there are real world scenarios where these assumptions are not guaranteed. For example, in e-sourcing activities performed in open and global markets, it is expected that agents risk new partnerships outside the embedded set on known acquaintances, which, consequently, reduces the availability of direct evaluations of the potential partners in the several distinct contexts that can be considered. In such harsh scenarios, we need different and more dynamic types of trust models that are able to reasoning even when the available evidences about the agents in evaluation are scarce, contextual and heterogeneous.

In this paper, we address the development of trust models that are adequate to these scenarios. First, we present our situation-aware trust model that is based in three fundamental characteristics:

- The inclusion in the aggregation procedure of important properties of the dynamics of trust, as addressed in research areas related to social sciences and psychology;
- The dynamic detection of tendencies of agents' behavior in the presence of different situations;
- The ability to infer the trustworthiness of agents even when the available trust evidences are scarce.

Then, we set up a multi-agent simulation environment where textile client agents seek for optimal deals by selecting from a range of suppliers with different behaviors. We are interested in evaluating the benefits of using our own trust proposal for the selection of partners in open and global scenarios and to compare it with other trust approaches. Also, we intend to evaluate how the different trust methods can support the exploration of new potential partners in such a way that the risk associated to trading with strangers is decreased by the method. A final achievement of the work presented in this paper is the development of a simulation environment that can be used to support important studies about parochialism and trust that are being done in the social sciences area [8] [9].

This paper is structured as follows: Section 2 briefly introduces situation-aware trust and overviews the most significant computational situation-aware trust models existing to date. Section 3 presents our own contextual trust model, and presents the scenario and notation used in this paper. Section 4 evaluates our approach and compares it with other computational trust models, in the open market scenario defined. Finally, Section 5 concludes the paper and refers future work.

2   Situation-Aware Trust

There are several definitions of trust in the literature, and most of them refer context as a dimension to take into consideration in the trust assessment process. For instance, in one of the earliest research on computational trust, Marsh (1994) considers situational trust as "the amount of trust an agent has in another in a given situation", and gives a helpful example: "I may trust my brother to drive me to the airport, I most certainly would not trust him to fly the plane" [10]. Another well known definition of trust, from the economics area, is given by Dasgupta, where trust reflects the expectation on the activities of an entity when it reacts on a given context [11]. In the same line of thought, Dimitrakos defines trust as a measurable belief that a given entity has on the competence of the trustee entity in behaving in a dependably way, in a given period of time, within a given context and relative to a specific task [12].

Therefore, the need for some kind of computational situation-aware trust seems evident. In one hand, it is realistic to assume that not all the past evidences are equally relevant to future interactions, as it is common sense that a given entity might behave differently in different contexts, as shown by Marsh definition above. It is the same to say that the trust aggregator algorithm shall not take all positive evidences concerning the car driving ability of the author's brother when assessing his ability to drive an airplane.

This same reasoning further extends to reputation models based on transitivity graphs, much used in recommendation systems. In fact, although existing models of reputation are generally based on the transitivity of trust, some authors consider that trust is not transitive [13]. In this context, Tavakolifard (2009) suggests a theoretically approach that incorporates a situational dimension into graph-based reputation models [14].

There are other theoretically benefits that can derive from the consideration of context into computational trust models. One of these benefits is the bootstrapping of unanticipated situations, where missing information from a given target agent can be inferred from similar situations (e.g. "A person trusting Bob as a good car mechanic will not automatically trust him also in undertaking heart surgeries (. . .) [but] he probably could be quite good in repairing motorcycles" [2]); the other is the management of newcomers, where the use of similarities between both agents and situations can generate an approximate estimate for the initial trustworthiness value of the newcomer. Finally, Neisse et al. consider that the consideration of context may allow the reduction of the complexity of management of trust relationships [7].

2.1   Overview on Situation-Aware Models

Although the need for contextual trust has been identified several years ago, only recently there started to appear practical approaches of situation-aware trust models. However, the majority of them is based on ontologies or taxonomies and implies the predefinition of domain-based similarity measures of situations or roles.

The first example we analyze is defined in the domain of message-based communications. In this work, the authors propose to use rules based on the explicit context of messages in order to determine the trustworthiness of these messages [15]. In order to capture the message content and the context-dependent trust relations, the authors extend a trust ontology proposed by Golbeck et al. [16] in order to include the notion of context-sensitivity trust in messages. However, the authors do not address important questions, such as how the context is extracted from messages and how to compute the context-sensitive factor that allows determining the overall trustworthiness of a message.

Another example of such a model is the Context Management Framework (CMF) model, where trust relations in one domain are used to infer trust relations in similar domains [2][14][17]. The model uses case-base reasoning techniques to estimate trust in unanticipated situations, by retrieving the most similar cases from a case base. In this approach, the authors use a trust-based ontology ([18]) to specify situations and they measure the similarity between situations using a relational similarity model based on the SimRank algorithm [19]. A major drawback of this approach resides in the weak assumption made by this algorithm about the similarity between different objects, as even signaled by the authors ([2]) which prevent the model to adequately scale to more complex representations of contexts.

The CMF model drinks from the collaborative filtering research area that use taxonomy-based similarity measures for recommendation purposes. There, the similarity between users is normally derived from the items or classes of items they tend to share (also known as co rating behavior). A recent extension on this topic is cross-domain recommendation. In this context, a recent work [20] proposes a model that allows users that share similar items or social connections to provide recommendations chains on items on other domains. This model uses Web taxonomies made available by service providers. In order to allow measuring the similarity of users that do not have rated the same items, the model first computes class classifications from the individual classifications of items of the class, and then computes the similarity between users taking into account the resulting similarities of users in each class. This model implies, however, that subtleties between items within classes cannot be taken into account because of the generalization process it assumes.

The next model also uses an ontology for describing situations, or concepts (e.g. business orders) [3]. In this approach, the expected behavior of an agent on a given situation is represented as a conditional probability distribution function (PDF) over the possible observations given the possible agreements. As in the previous model, a concrete experience about a commitment can be used to update the expectation of behavior over semantically close commitments, allowing for faster bootstrapping of unanticipated situations. Although the authors state that the PDF is initialized using background knowledge on the other agents, the model suffers from the a priori information limitation of conditional probability distributions. Also, the authors do not present an evaluation of the model, which prevents a further understanding of its potential benefits.

A related approach by Hermoso and Billhardt dynamically builds a taxonomy of organizational roles from trust information maintained by the agents, using clustering techniques [4]. When evaluating the trustworthiness of a target agent, the evaluator uses the direct experiences it has with the agent and weights them according to the similarity between the role assumed by the agent in the specific experience and the role of the current situation.

Finally, another approach in the area of social browsing [21] allows the representation of context based on personal ontologies of Web collaborators and provide context mapping methods.

Although the use of taxonomies and ontologies is increasing in the Web, both in social networks and e-business activities, the main limitation associated with the above referred models is the necessity to predefine adequate similarity measures for all possible situations in assessment before such situations are even presented to the evaluator. This is a domain specific, hard tuning process that may be a challenge in dynamic environments with complex representations of contexts.

A somewhat different approach is presented in the Context Space and Reference Contexts model [5][22][23]. This approach defines the context space as a Q-dimensional metric space, with one dimension per each represented situation feature, and places $n < Q$ reference contexts (either regularly or adaptively) over the context space. There exist as many context spaces as agents in evaluation. Then, every time a new trust evidence is generated for a given agent, the trustworthiness at each one of the reference contexts of the agent's context space is updated with the outcome of the evidence, weighted by the similarity between the reference context and the context of the new evidence. This interesting model is, however, also dependent on predefined measures of similarity between contextual attributes. Also, the consideration of multiple dimensions can lead to an exponential number of reference contexts that each evaluator needs to keep for every agent, jeopardizing the scalability of the model to complex contextual scenarios. Another limitation of this model is that it can only be used complementary to traditional trust systems that aggregate evidences using weighted means approaches.

Finally, there is a related approach [6] to the previous model that differentiates from it on the definition of the context space, where each dimension of the context space is now a function of many context attributes, instead of one sole attribute. However, all limitations pinpointed above for the previous model are still present in this approach.

The situation-aware trust model we propose in this paper distinguishes from the above models by performing online evaluation of the trust evidences, as it is able to dynamically extract tendencies of the (probably changing over time) behavior of the trustee, on a given specific situation. This means that our approach does not rely on a priori definition of similarity measures. It is our firm belief that such a model is more adequate to detect subtleties between two similar contexts and then to perform better in open and dynamic environments than the models we overviewed above. In Section 4, we present the results of the experiments we have performed that strongly support our belief.

3   The Proposed Trust System

We developed a trust method envisioning its use in future semi-automatic and open business-to-business markets, taking into special consideration the exigent requirements of such environments. Namely, we are concerned with the performance of the method when the trust evidences available about a given agent are scarce and heterogeneous, and when the activity of the agents under evaluation can span through different situations and contexts. The current implementation of our system that encompasses the proposed method is composed of two different components, as depicted in Figure 1:

- The aggregator component, which is responsible for aggregating the available trust evidences of an agent into a trustworthiness score for this agent. Several trust engines that are defined in the literature can be used (cf. [1]), although we are particularly interested on engines that model the dynamics of trust, as they appear to perform better than the traditional statistical approaches [24][25][26];
- The Contextual Fitness component, which tunes the outcome of the aggregating step by taking into consideration the specificities of the current business opportunity and the adequacy of the agent in evaluation to the specific situation under assessment.

The idea beyond this extension is that if the trust system detects that an agent has some kind of handicap related to the current necessity, the overall trustworthiness of the agent for this necessity will be zero; otherwise, the trustworthiness score is the value computed by the aggregator component. One good characteristic of this approach is that it can be used with any conventional trust aggregation engine, being it based on statistical, probabilistic or heuristic-based models. Before we describe the Contextual Fitness component in more detail, we first introduce the notation and the scenario used all over this paper.

3.1   Scenario and Notation

The scenario used in this paper situates on the automation of the procurement processes of business-to-business relations in the textile industry. Ideally, the development of adequate agreement technologies would allow opening the space of business opportunities, where agents would have the means and the confidence knowledge to search for good business opportunities outside their limited sphere of breeding relations. However, the fear of risking unknown partners is one of

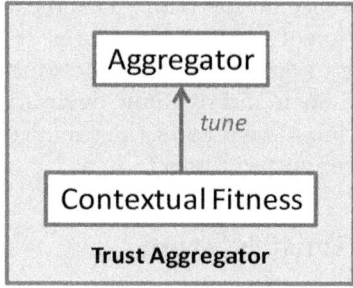

Fig. 1. The current implementation of our trust system

the biggest barriers to trade in a truly open market environment. Taking our subcontracting scenario in the textile industry as an example, the client part of the relation can be deceived by the provider part in several different ways [27]:

- A delay in delivery, which affects all the supply chain;
- The quality received, as specified by affordability, safety and degree of uniqueness parameters;
- The quantity received (too much or too less);
- The violation of intellectual property rights;
- Ethical problems;
- Other problems, such as price rise and legislative changes.

Without some kind of a trust mechanism, it is reasonable to conclude that business partners would preferentially adopt parochial environments in detriment to more aggressive exploration of deals outside the space of already known partner relationships. For instance, in the fashion retail industry, clients often rely on knowledge available through textile fairs and textile agents to make the bridge between brands and the trustable and reliable textile suppliers. However, even with this form of trust guarantees, the space of available suppliers is relatively small and it is strongly supported on the expected behavior of the partner, rather than on the potential real utility of the business transaction.

In our scenario, business clients in the textile industry try to select the best suppliers of textile fabric. For this, they announce their business needs and wait for proposals from the suppliers. The need is announced through a call for proposals (CFP) and concerns the delivery of some quantity of a fabric due in some delivery time. An example of such a need is the following: (fabric = cotton, quantity = 900000 meters, delivery time = 15 days). In this context, we define $at \in AT$ as the description of the need, i.e. an instance of the space AT of all possible combinations of attribute-value pairs that describe the need (good, product or service).

Then, after issuing the CFP, the client agent selects the best proposal based on the evaluation of the trustworthiness of each proponent supplier, for the situation announced in the need, taking as input contracts the suppliers have established in the past and their respective outcome.

This way, we define $trust_{ac}(as) \in [0,1]$ as the trustworthiness value of a trustee agent as, in the eye of the evaluator agent ac, as computed by a traditional trust aggregator engine; and *adequacy trust* $ad_{ac}(as, at) \in [0,1]$ as a binary operator for situation-awareness purposes, where $ac \in AC$ is an agent from the set AC of client agents and $as \in AS$ is an agent from the set AS of supplier agents.

Therefore, the trustworthiness value of agent as as seen by agent ac in the specific context at is given by the following equation:

$$trust_{ac}(as, at) = trust_{ac}(as) * ad_{ac}(as, at) \tag{1}$$

This is the same as to say that, in a given moment, an agent may be qualified as trustworthy in a specific situation and as untrustworthy in a (maybe slightly) different situation.

Finally, a contractual evidence is represented by the tuple $\langle\ ac, as, at, t, o\rangle$, where t is the timestamp of the transaction that occurred between client agent ac and supplier agent as and $o \in \{true, false\}$ is the outcome of this transaction. Here, a *true* outcome means that agent as has succeeded in providing the good in the contractual terms and a *false* outcome means that as has violated the contract. Therefore, in our scenario, each supplier agent as has a history of its past contractual evidences.

3.2   The Contextual Fitness Component

The Contextual Fitness component is based on an online, incremental and flexible technique of extraction of behavior tendencies that we have developed. We have been testing different methods for extracting these tendencies from the historical set of agents' evidences, such as the use of the increase in frequency metric, as explained in [28]. Our current version, introduced in [29], uses the information gain metric. This is a metric used in the machine learning area (such as in the simple decision tree learning algorithm ID3 [30]) for classification purposes. It is typically used as an offline process, implying that the training and testing phases occur before the actual classification of new instances is performed.

The information gain metric is based on the entropy concept of information theory, and is defined as following:

$$Gain(S, A) \equiv Entropy(S) - \sum v \in Values(A) \frac{|s_v|}{|S|} Entropy(s_v), \tag{2}$$

where $Gain(S, A)$ is the information gain of attribute A relative to a collection of samples S, $Values(A)$ is the set of all possible values for attribute A, and s_v is the subset of S for which attribute A has value v [30].

In our approach, we use this metric in a novel way, as it is used to dynamically learn a decision tree from the history of evidences of a given agent as, *every time* a client agent needs to verify the adequacy of as proposal to its current business need. In fact, we use all the evidences available about the supplier to build the decision tree, which normally consists of a dataset with some dozens of evidences, if that much. This means that no training or testing phases are performed. After that, the failure tendencies of the agent in evaluation are extracted from the rules pointing to *false* outcomes. Figure 2 depicts a decision tree that was learned for a given supplier in a specific experiment we have run (we use the Weka API [31] in our simulations).

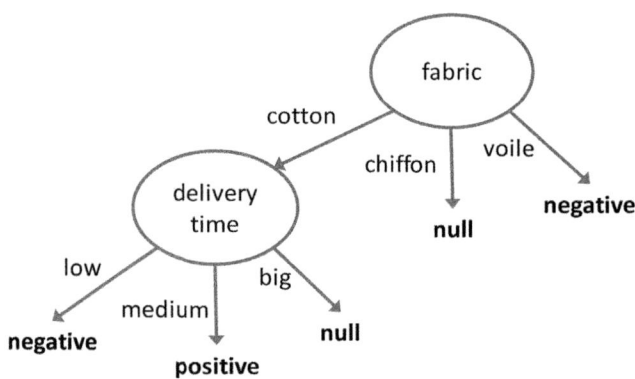

Fig. 2. Decision tree generated in our simulations

Concerning the tree above, our algorithm was able to identify that, at the time of this particular assessment, the supplier showed the failure tendencies (fabric = cotton, $*$, dtime = low) and (fabric = voile, $*$, $*$). Therefore, the trustworthiness value $trust_{ac}(as, at)$ of agent as, as given by Equation 1, would be zero if situation at matched any of the failure tendencies derived from the learned decision tree. Otherwise, the trustworthiness value of the target agent for the considered situation would be given by the $trust_{ac}(as)$ component of Equation 1.

For now, we are only exploring the *false* branch of the generated trees, which means that currently Contextual Fitness is a binary operator. However, we leave for future work the extraction of the *true* and *null* branches of the trees, in order to further distinguish between positive tendencies and uncertainty.

4   Experiments

We set up a multi-agent simulation scenario where business clients in the textile industry try to select the best suppliers of textile fabric, i.e. the ones that would maximize the utility of the clients. At every round of the simulation, each client issues a call for proposals (CFP) specifying a business need. This need is established randomly for each agent at setup time and is an instance $at \in AT$, as described in section 3.1. The clients keep their needs constant in all the experiment rounds. Moreover, all values of possible quantities and delivery times are fuzzified in the categorical values depicted in Table 1.

After issuing the CFP, every client selects the more adequate proposal for the current need based only on the trustworthiness value of all the proposals received, as computed by the trust model used by the client. In these experiments, we use three different trust models, including our situation-aware approach, in order to evaluate and compare the ability of each model in supporting better selection decisions.

Moreover, most of the suppliers that exist in our market have different handicaps on performing some particular aspect of a business transaction. For example, some suppliers tend to fail to deliver fabric in short delivery times, while others might fail to deliver high quantities of any fabric type. The aim of these experiments is to evaluate how effective are different trust models and correspondent aggregation techniques in detecting and acting upon these handicaps, in order to better assist the partners' selection decision. It is assumed that every supplier is able to provide any different type of fabric.

In this paper, we run the experiments with three different populations of suppliers, as described in the following sections. In the next section, we describe the generic configuration common to all the experiments.

4.1   Generic Configuration

Table 1 presents the configuration parameters that are common to all experiments.

Table 1. Configuration of the experiments

Parameter	Value
Fabrics	Chiffon, Cotton, Voile
Quantities	Low, Medium, High
Delivery Time	Low, Medium, Big
# buyers	20
# of sellers	50
Seller stocks	4 contracts per round
Types of sellers	Uniform distribution over the types considered in population (described later on)
# rounds	60
# runs per experiment	15

Trust Models Evaluated. This section introduces the trust models evaluated in these experiments. The first model is the SA approach, which represents *SinAlpha* [25], a traditional, situation-less trust aggregation system that we have developed which uses properties of the dynamics of trust. In previous work [26], we thorough compared *SinAlpha* to a traditional statistical aggregation engine that uses weighted means by recency and we have shown that *SinAlpha* outperforms this model. In the present paper, we use the SA model in order to compare the behavior of both non situation and situation-aware approaches in open contextual environments.

The second model is the CS approach [5][22][23], which goes one step further traditional trust models by considering contextual aspects of the business in assessment. As we mentioned before in Section 2.1, it is a situation-aware technique that defines a context space as a multidimensional metric space with one dimension per each represented situation feature. It is able to estimate the trustworthiness values of agents in unanticipated situations using the similarity between different situations. We chose this approach to represent situation-aware trust models that use domain specific, predefined similarity metrics to predict unanticipated situations.

Concerning our implementation of this model in current experiments, we placed the reference contexts regularly over the combinations of all possible values of the contractual attributes. The distance function we used for attribute fabric is given in Equation 3. As can be observed, the distance is minimum (zero) if both contexts c_1 and c_2 have the same fabric and maximum (one) otherwise.

$$d^{fabric}(c_1, c_2) = \begin{cases} 0, \text{ if } fabric_1 = fabric_2, \\ 1, \text{ if } fabric_1 \neq fabric_2. \end{cases} \tag{3}$$

For the remaining attributes considered in the experiments (quantity and delivery time), the distance function is given in Equation 4.

$$d^{attr}(c_1, c_2) = |ln(attr_1) - ln(attr_2)|. \tag{4}$$

In the equation above, considering first the attribute *quantity*, $attr_i$ takes the value of 1, 3 or 5, depending on the value of the quantity is *low*, *medium* or *high*, respectively. In the same way, for attribute *delivery time*, $attr_i$ takes the value of 1, 3 or 5 for values of *low*, *medium* or *big*. The total distance between the two contexts is a weighted means of the three distances calculated above, with all dimensions equally weighted. Finally, the weight used to evaluate the relevance of a context c_1 accordingly to its similarity with context c_2 is given in Equation 5. All the remaining formulas needed to compute the trustworthiness scores of agents were implemented accordingly to one of the authors' paper [5].

$$w_i = e^{-d(c_1, c_2)}. \tag{5}$$

The last model to be evaluated is CF, our trust model that uses the Contextual Fitness technique described in section 3. In the experiments, we used SA as the aggregator component of the trust system (Figure 1). As with happens with the CS approach defined in the previous point, CF is a situation-aware trust model. It was designed to fit well to non parochial open market scenarios, where the available trust evidences for a particular partner agent might be scarce.

Populations of Suppliers. Table 1 characterizes the different types of suppliers used in the experiments.

All suppliers used in the experiments, excepting *RBad* agents, have a given handicap related to one or more contractual dimensions. For example, a supplier initialized with the *HQT* behavior (standing for 'Handicap in Quantity') has a

Table 2. Characterization of the populations of suppliers

Supplier	Prob. Success	PopA	PopB	PopC
HFab, HQt, HDt, HFabQt, HFabDt, HQtDt	0.05 (handicap) 0.95 (otherwise)	100%	66.7%	
I-HFab, I-HQt, I-HDt, I-HFabQt, I-HFabDt, I-HQtDt				100%
RBad	0.50		33.3%	

handicap in providing high quantities of any fabric; this way, if it is selected to a business transaction that involves the delivery of high quantities of fabric, it has a probability of 95% of failing the contract. In any other transaction that the supplier is involved, it has a probability of 5% of failing the contract. Besides HQT, we used five other types of behavior that represent five other different types of handicap: on a given fabric (*HFAB*), on low delivery times (*HDT*), on high quantities of a given fabric (*HFABQT*), on low delivery times for a given fabric (*HFABDT*), and on high quantities to be delivered in low delivery times (*HQTDT*). As happens in the example before, a supplier has a probability of 95% of violating a contract if the current CFP matches the supplier's handicap, and 95% of probability of succeeding the contract otherwise.

Handicapped suppliers with name starting with '*I-*' are similar to the handicapped suppliers just described, excepting the fact that, with a probability of 66.6%, they change their handicap when they reach half of the total number of the rounds.

Finally, suppliers of type *RBad* have a probability of failing a contract of 50%, independently of the context of the contract established with the client.

Evaluation Metrics. We use three different metrics in order to evaluate how client agents tend to behave in terms of selection of partners – and how good is their decision on that – when using each one of the trust approaches in evaluation in scenarios that might involve scarcity of trust evidences. The first metric is the *average total utility* got by all clients in all rounds, given by the ratio of the number of successful contracts got by all clients in one round over the total number of contracts established in the round, averaged over all rounds of the experiments. The second metric is the *average utility per round*, which measures the same ratio but on a per round basis. Finally, the third metric is the *average number of different suppliers per round*, which measures how many distinct suppliers are selected by all the negotiating clients at every round, averaged over all rounds of the experiments.

4.2 Experiments with Population A

We started our experiments with a population of distinct handicapped suppliers, as can be observed from Table 2. These suppliers normally tend to fail in very specific situations (e.g. low delivery times), but perform well in all other situations. Therefore, a good trust model should be able to detect the situations where these agents fail and to prevent their selection (only) in these specific situations.

Results. Figure 3 shows the average utility achieved by all clients in all rounds, with the results of population A being presented in the leftmost plot.

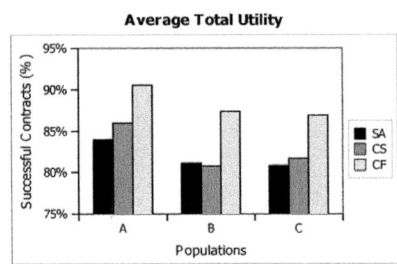

Fig. 3. Average total utility for populations A, B and C

As can be observed from the graph, both situation-aware approaches out-perform SA in population A: SA fulfils in average 83.95% of the established contracts (with standard deviation of 2.87%), where CS succeeds in 86.01% of the contracts (sd. 4.73%) and CF gets the best results by succeeding in 90.57% of the contracts (sd. 1.34%).

The average utility per round and the average number of different suppliers selected per round are presented in Figure 4. As can be seen at the right graph, clients that use the CF approach start, since the first rounds, exploring a larger number of different suppliers than clients that use the other approaches, and they keep showing this behavior all over the rounds. The described behavior of the trust approaches seems to be related with the utility that clients achieve using these approaches, as suggested in the Figure (*left*). We observe that the most exploratory approach, CF, is the one that gets higher utility, at every round.

Another important result obtained with CF is that, after some quick learning at the first rounds, the number of succeeded contracts with this method is very close to the maximum of 19 (out of possible 20) contracts that can succeed per round, i.e. to the 95% probabilistic limit imposed in population A.

4.3   Experiments with Population B

In the second set of experiments, we wanted to verify if the promising good re-sults of the CF model would maintain in an environment with fewer trustworthy suppliers. Therefore, we introduced population B, where one third of the avail-able suppliers have erratic, non contextual behavior, succeeding only 50% of the contracts they enter, irrespective of the context of the contract (cf. Table 2).

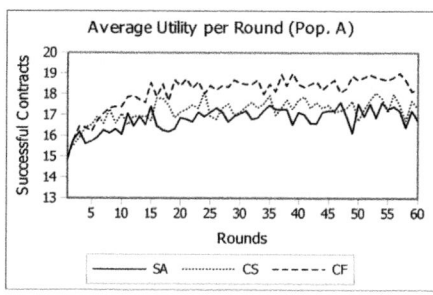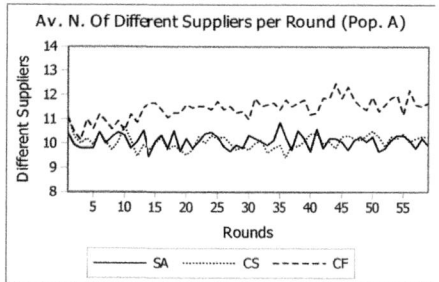

Fig. 4. Results per round for Population A

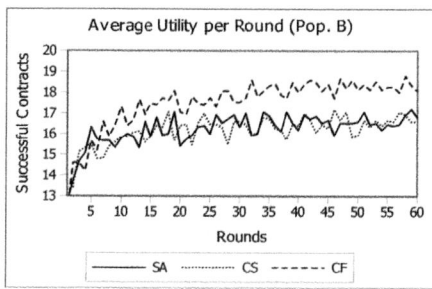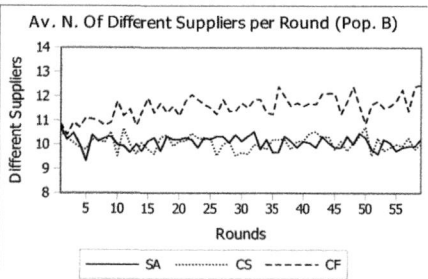

Fig. 5. Results per round for Population B

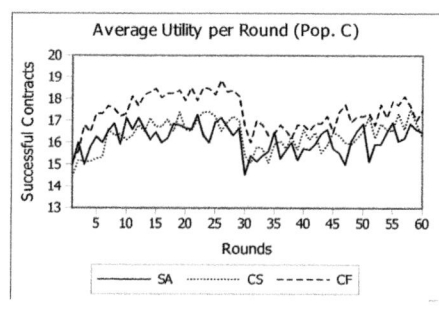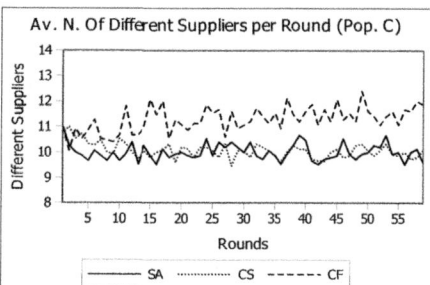

Fig. 6. Results per round for Population C

Results. Figure 3 (*central plot*) presents the results for population B concerning the average total utility achieved by the trust models in evaluation. As can be observed, there is a general decrease in utility for all approaches when compared to population A, as it would be expected, once the set of potential trustworthy suppliers is reduced in one third. In these experiments, SA clients succeeded in 81.08% of the contracts (sd. 2.03%), while CS was successful 80.73% of the times (sd. 4.38%) and CF succeeded 87.38% of the times (sd. 2.15%). In these experiments, the CS approach was significantly more penalized by the introduction of the *RBad* suppliers than the other two approaches, and its performance was as low as the performance of the situation-less approach.

Figure 5 plots the average utility per round (*left*) and the average number of different suppliers selected per round (*right*) for the three trust models in evaluation, for population B. The effect of introducing the *RBad* suppliers is visible in the very first rounds of the experiments, with all trust approaches obtaining less utility than in similar rounds of the experiments with population A. However, as happened in population A, we also observe here that the more exploratory behavior of CF allows clients using this approach to achieve higher utility associated with the choice of suppliers.

4.4   Experiments with Population C

In the last set of experiments, we wanted to evaluate how each trust model in evaluation reacts to a dynamic change of behavior in the suppliers' population. This way, we used the handicapped suppliers of population A, but they have now a 66.6% chance of changing their handicap at round 30 (half of the rounds considered in the experiments).

Results. The results for population C are shown in Figure 3 (*right*) and Figure 6. SA got 80.78% (sd. 4.23%) of average total utility and was the approach that had less suffered from the change in handicaps, as compared to the results obtained with population A. CS got 81.66% (sd. 2.63%) of utility and it was the approach more penalized by the reversal in the behavior of suppliers. Finally, CF still outperforms the other two approaches, obtaining 86.93% (sd. 2.32%) of utility, but it was slightly more penalized in relative terms by the change of the behavior of the suppliers than the traditional approach.

4.5   Discussion

We start the discussion of the results analyzing the relation between the average number of different suppliers selected per round and the average utility achieved per round, for each trust model evaluated. At a first sight, we could expect that an approach that explores more partners in the scenario described would have a smaller number of succeed contracts, at least in the first rounds of suppliers' exploration, where the partners are rather unknown. However, the results show that the CF approach does not perform worse than the remaining representative approaches at this first exploration phase and performs significantly better than the others in the remaining steps of the experiments. This happens due to the CF capability to extracting tendencies of behavior even in the presence of a reduced number of available trust evidences, and to its capacity of doing that in an incremental and dynamic way. This way, when a client makes a bad decision concerning the exploration of a new supplier, the consideration of this new evidence (and corresponding *false* outcome) in a subsequent assessment will update the extracted tendency of failure of the supplier and approximate it to the true handicap of the supplier.

On the contrary, the SA approach tends to select the agents that have the highest values of trustworthiness until that date. As handicapped suppliers have the same probability of succeeding outside the context of their handicap, there is a strong chance that the first partners to be selected are the ones that incrementally increase their trustworthiness in the eye of the evaluator. This parochial strategy results in the undesirable behavior of keep choosing the same suppliers that occasionally fail the contracts for which they have a handicap for the current CFP, not giving a chance to explore other suppliers. In a way, this reflects what succeeds is real life subcontracting in the textile industry.

Concerning the situation-aware CS approach, we observe that it sensitively outperforms the SA approach in populations where all suppliers have some sort of handicap (A and C). This is due to the fact that the CS client reasons based not only on the global trustworthiness of the agent in assessment, but also on the behavior of the supplier in the context of current CFP. On the other hand, the introduction of one third of suppliers that fulfill or violate contracts regardless of the context of those contracts appear to reduce the effectiveness of this trust model based on reference contexts. Moreover, we can see from Figures 4, 5 and 6 that CS also behaves in a conservative way when selecting new partners, being outperformed by CF in terms of utility since the first rounds of the simulation. This is due to the fact that, although CS is a situation-aware technique, it functions in a rather different way than CF. In order to better understand the differences between CS and CF, we present next two examples taken from the experiments we have run.

In the first example we use the past contractual evidences of supplier *as* as depicted in Table 3. For the sake of readability, only the *at* and the *o* elements of the contractual evidence tuple (cf. Section 3.1) are presented in the table.

Table 3. Contractual evidences of supplier *as* (simplified)

evd #	at	o
1	voile, low, medium	true
2	chiffon, low, low	true
3	chiffon, high, medium	false
4	voile, medium, medium	true
5	cotton, low, low	true
6	cotton, medium, big	true
7	voile, low, low	true

Now, suppose the current business need of a client is the instance at_x : (*fabric = chiffon, quantity = high, dtime = medium*), and that the client needs to evaluate the proposal made by *as*. Using the CS approach, we verify that the context space of *as* is composed of 27 (3^3) reference contexts, and only seven of them directly correspond to the contexts of the past contractual evidences of the agent in evaluation. Let us also name the reference context corresponding to at_x as rc_x. Processing the first two evidences, they are located at distances $d_{1,x}$ and $d_{2,x}$ from rc_x, and then rc_x is updated one evidence at a time with the value of its outcome (*true*) weighted by a function of the distance, as given in Equation 5. This means that the trustworthiness of the supplier at rc_x is increased proportionally to the similarity between the reference context and the context of the evidence. The third evidence coincides with at_x and therefore the weight w_x of the evidence is maximum for rc_x, lowering the trustworthiness value of *as* at rc_x in a significant way as the outcome of this evidence is *false*. Finally, the processing of the last four evidences of the supplier, all positive, raise again the trustworthiness value at rc_x, even if attenuated by the distance of the context of each evidence to the context of rc_x. However, due to the scarcity of evidences about supplier *as*, its final trustworthiness score (strongly supported by the rc_x value) is still positive, and therefore bigger than the trustworthiness values of all other suppliers that have not yet been explored. This explains why, in these conditions, the approach has a tendency to select, from the set of the more fitted suppliers, the ones that have been involved in more contracts to date, acting in a rather parochial way. From our analysis, we can conclude that the interesting characteristic of bootstrapping of the CS approach can also be somewhat disappointing in open and dynamic environments where the available evidences for every agent can be scarce.

Now, let us look how our CF approach would behave in the same situation of example number one. Taking all available evidences of supplier *as* as depicted in Table 3, the Contextual Fitness technique would be able to extract the failure tendency (*, quantity = high, *). Applying Equation 1, the global trustworthiness of supplier *as* would be zero for current need at_x, as a failure match was detected, which means that the chances of this supplier being selected for current CFP would be low, allowing for the selection of a more adequate proposal, or even the exploration of a new partner.

At this point, it is necessary to say that a match between a supplier's handicap and the current situation in assessment does not exclude the supplier from the selection process, it just lowers it trustworthiness to zero. In the absence of better alternatives, the supplier can always be selected by the client to do business together.

We are now in conditions to analyze the second example. Table 4 illustrates an excerpt of the past contractual evidences of supplier *as* obtained from another set of experiments we have run using the CS model. In these experiments, supplier *as* is handicapped on low delivery times, which means that it has a high probability of failure in satisfying any (*, *, dtime = low) need.

Table 4. Contractual evidences of supplier *as* (simplified)

evd #	at	o
1	voile, medium, big	true
2	chiffon, high, big	true
3	cotton, low, low	false
4	cotton, medium, big	true
5	chiffon, high, big	true
6	cotton, high, medium	false
7	voile, high, low	false
8	voile, medium, low	false
9	chiffon, medium, big	true
10	voile, low, big	true
11	chiffon, high, big	true
12	voile, medium, big	true
13	chiffon, low, low	false
14	voile, medium, big	true
15	voile, high, low	false

As can be observed from the table above, supplier *as* keeps being selected by clients that use the CS approach for business transactions for which it is not fitted due to its handicap on low delivery times. The problem here concerns the use of predefined similarity distances amongst contexts by the CS approach.

For instance, let us imagine that there is a new contractual evidence with at_{16} : (*fabric = cotton, quantity = low, dtime = medium*) and $o_{16} = true$; also, let us focus on two specific reference contexts: rc_y, which matches at_y : (*fabric = cotton, quantity = low, dtime = low*), and rc_z, corresponding to at_z : (*fabric = voile, quantity = low, dtime = medium*). Using the values considered in Section 4 and equations 3 and 4, we verify that at_{16} is close enough from the reference context rc_y and consequently the trustworthiness of the supplier at rc_y would increase in a significant way with the consideration of this new evidence, regardless its handicap on low delivery times. On the other hand, the same new *true* evidence would increase the reference context rc_z in a less significant way, even though it corresponds to a context for which the supplier does not present a handicap. Figure 7 illustrates this scenario.

This example shows the limitations associated to situation-aware trust models that rely on predefined measures of similarity in defining how similar or different two contexts must be. More concretely, an agent that shows a good behavior in a context might fail in a *very similar* context and succeed in more *distant* contexts. Our study of the CS model in the proposed scenario gives us the strong belief that, even dedicating a team of experts to tune the distance functions, the use of predefined similarity functions, even those based on taxonomy-based similarity, can fail in adequately detecting the contextual subtleties exposed in this last example. Moreover, in the specific case of the CS approach, this hard tuning effort can be even compromised with the addition of more contextual dimensions.

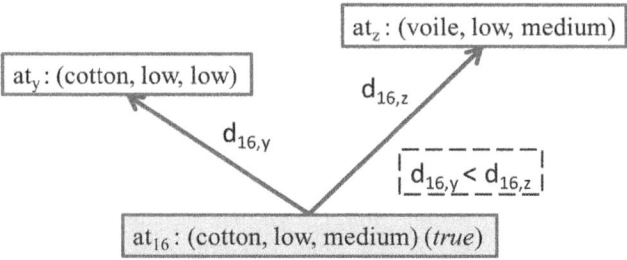

Fig. 7. Distances between a new evidence and two distinct reference contexts

For the sake of comparison, the application of our CF approach to the same scenario (cf. Table 3) after the third evidence would generate the tendency (fabric = cotton, $*$, $*$). In this case, CF would not be able to detect the true handicap of the supplier with the three available evidences and would even lower the probability of the supplier being selected to any contract involving *cotton*, which does not integrate its handicap. Using CF after the sixth evidence, our trust model would generate the tendencies ($*$, $*$, dtime = low) and ($*$, $*$, dtime = medium). In one hand, the CF client would have a high probability of wrongly missing the opportunity of transacting with this supplier in contracts stipulating *medium* delivery times. On the other hand, it would also have a high probability of not choosing the supplier in transactions that involve low delivery times (the supplier's handicap), avoiding all the unsuccessful contracts that derived from the choices done by the CS clients.

In this last example we observed that CF can be sometimes too restrictive, by overfitting the existing evidences. For instance, with only six evidences, the trust approach detects the true handicap of the supplier but adds a new, nonexistent failure tendency concerning medium quantities. We used population B in order to see if this characteristic would prevent the CF approach of doing good deals. By adding one third of bad suppliers, the choice space of the trust approaches reduced substantially and the utility of CF clients could be seriously jeopardized due to this overfitting-based generation of failure tendencies. However, the results obtained have shown that CF was less penalized than CS in this harsh scenario. Once again, the ability of the approach in dynamically rectifying the extracted tendencies every time there is a new evidence has shown to be a positive characteristic of the approach.

Finally, there are cases where the CF approach is not able to extract any failure tendency. This happens, for example, in the presence of RBad suppliers, which have quite an erratic and context less behavior. In these cases, our trust approach assesses the trustworthiness of the agent in evaluation taking into consideration only the value computed by the aggregator component (Equation 1). In the experiments, we used the same aggregator as the SA approach, which embeds the asymmetry property that confers more strength to negative outcomes and less strength to positive outcomes. Although both CF and SA performed better than CS in the presence of *RBad* suppliers, we need further work in order to support our belief about the benefits of separating the aggregation part from the situational part of trust models.

5   Conclusions and Future Work

In this paper, we stated our strong belief that open and dynamic environments, such as global marketplaces where business agents risk new partnership seeking to increase their profit, need robust and situation-aware trust systems that better assist the selection of partners' decision. Then, we presented Contextual Fitness, our innovative situation-aware technique that can be used with any trust aggregation system and that is based on the dynamic extraction of tendencies of behavior of the agents in assessment. This is a different approach from the existing situation-aware trust models that rely on the predefinition of distance metrics to evaluate the similarity between contexts. We evaluated our approach and compared it with both a situation-less and a situation-aware approach that predefines the notion of similarity between contexts. The results have shown that our approach is more adequate than the other two in supporting the process of selection of partners when the candidate partners present some characteristic behavior (even if the behavior changes at some point of the agents' life) and when the evidences available about them are scarce. The results have also shown that the capacity of CF in rapidly correcting a bad decision supported by the incremental extraction of behavior tendencies allows the agents to be more exploratory without jeopardizing their overall utility.

As future work, we intend to further develop the method for extraction of behavior tendencies in order to allow the use of heterogeneous trust evidences. We also intend to further test the trust approach with different populations and different number of contextual dimensions.

Acknowledgments. This research is funded by FCT (Fundação para a Ciência e a Tecnologia) project PTDC/EIA-EIA/104420/2008. The first author enjoys a PhD grant with reference SFRH/BD/39070/2007 from FCT.

References

1. Sabater, J., Paolucci, M.: On Representation and Aggregation of Social Evaluations, in Computational Trust and Reputation Models. Int. J. Approx. Reasoning (2007)
2. Tavakolifard, M.: Situation-aware Trust Management, pp. 413–416 (2009)
3. Fabregues, A., Madrenas-Ciurana, J.: SRM: a tool for supplier performance. In: AAMAS 2009, pp. 1375–1376 (2009)
4. Hermoso, R., Billhardt, H., Ossowski, S.: Dynamic evolution of role taxonomies through multidimensional clustering in multiagent organizations. In: Yang, J.-J., Yokoo, M., Ito, T., Jin, Z., Scerri, P. (eds.) PRIMA 2009. LNCS, vol. 5925, pp. 587–594. Springer, Heidelberg (2009)

5. Rehak, M., Gregor, M., Pechoucek, M.: Multidimensional context representations for situational trust. In: DIS 2006: Proceedings of IEEE Workshop on Distributed Intelligent Systems: Collective Intelligence and Its Applications, pp. 315–320, 383–388 (2006)
6. Nguyen, C., Camp, O.: Using Context Information to Improve Computation of Trust in Ad Hoc Networks. In: 2008 IEEE International Conference on Wireless & Mobile Computing, Networking & Communication (2008)
7. Neisse, R., Wegdam, M., van Sinderen, M., Lenzini, G.: Trust management model and architecture for context-aware service platforms. In: Chung, S. (ed.) OTM 2007, Part II. LNCS, vol. 4804, pp. 1803–1820. Springer, Heidelberg (2007)
8. Stolle, D.: In Trust in Society. In: Cook, K.S. (ed.) Russell Sage Foundation, pp. 202–244 (2001)
9. Macy, M.W., Sato, Y.: Trust, Cooperation, and Market Formation in the U.S. and Japan. Proceedings of the National Academy of Sciences of the United States of America 99(10)(suppl. 3) , 7214–7220 (2002)
10. Marsh, S.P.: Formalising Trust as a Computational Concept. PhD Thesis, University of Stirling (1994)
11. Dasgupta, P.: Trust as a Commodity. In: Gambeta, D. (ed.) Making and Breaking Cooperative Relations, Basil Blackwell (1990)
12. Dimitrakos, T.: System Models, e-Risk and e-Trust. Towards Bridging the Gap? In: Towards the E-Society: E-Business, E-Commerce, and E-Government, Kluwer, Dordrecht (2001)
13. Christianson, B., Harbison, W.S.: Why isn't trust transitive? In: Proceedings of the International Workshop on Security Protocols, London, UK, pp. 171–176 (1997)
14. Tavakolifard, M., Herrmann, P., Ozturk, P.: Analogical trust reasoning. In: Trust Management III, ch. 10, pp. 149–163 (2009)
15. Toivonen, S., Denker, G.: The Impact of Context on the Trustworthiness of Communication: An Ontological Approach. In: Proceedings of the ISWC Workshop on Trust, Security, and Reputation on the Semantic Web (2004)
16. Golbeck, J., Parsia, B., Hendler, J.: Trust networks on the semantic web. In: Klusch, M., Omicini, A., Ossowski, S., Laamanen, H. (eds.) CIA 2003. LNCS (LNAI), vol. 2782, pp. 238–249. Springer, Heidelberg (2003)
17. Tavakolifard, M., Knapskog, S.J., Herrmann, P.: Trust transferability among similar contexts. In: 4th ACM Symposium on QoS and Security for Wireless and Mobile Networks, New York, USA, pp. 91–97 (2008)
18. Strang, T., Linnhoff-Popien, C., Frank, K.: CoOL: A context ontology language to enable contextual interoperability. In: Stefani, J.-B., Demeure, I., Zhang, J. (eds.) DAIS 2003. LNCS, vol. 2893, pp. 236–247. Springer, Heidelberg (2003)
19. Jeh, G., Widom, J.: SimRank: a measure of structural-context similarity. In: Eighth ACM SIGKDD International Conference on Knowledge Discovery and Data Mining, pp. 538–543. ACM Press, New York (2002)
20. Nakatsuji, M., Fujiwara, Y., Tanaka, A., Uchiyama, T., Ishida, T.: Recommendations Over Domain Specific User Graphs. In: 19th European Conference on Artificial Intelligence (ECAI 2010), Lisbon, Portugal (2010)
21. Jung, J.J.: Ontology-based context synchronization for ad hoc social collaborations. Knowledge-Based Systems 21(7), 573–580 (2008)
22. Rehák, M., Pěchouček, M.: Trust modeling with context representation and generalized identities. In: Klusch, M., Hindriks, K.V., Papazoglou, M.P., Sterling, L. (eds.) CIA 2007. LNCS (LNAI), vol. 4676, pp. 298–312. Springer, Heidelberg (2007)

23. Rehák, M., Pěchouček, M., Grill, M., Bartos, K.: Trust-based classifier combination for network anomaly detection. In: Klusch, M., Pěchouček, M., Polleres, A. (eds.) CIA 2008. LNCS (LNAI), vol. 5180, pp. 116–130. Springer, Heidelberg (2008)
24. Jonker, C.M., Treur, J.: Formal analysis of models for the dynamics of trust based on experiences. In: Garijo, F.J., Boman, M. (eds.) MAAMAW 1999. LNCS, vol. 1647, pp. 221–231. Springer, Heidelberg (1999)
25. Urbano, J., Rocha, A.P., Oliveira, E.: Computing confidence values: Does trust dynamics matter? In: Lopes, L.S., Lau, N., Mariano, P., Rocha, L.M. (eds.) EPIA 2009. LNCS, vol. 5816, pp. 520–531. Springer, Heidelberg (2009)
26. Danek, A., Urbano, J., Rocha, A.P., Oliveira, E.: Engaging the dynamics of trust in computational trust and reputation systems. In: Jędrzejowicz, P., Nguyen, N.T., Howlet, R.J., Jain, L.C. (eds.) KES-AMSTA 2010. LNCS, vol. 6070, pp. 22–31. Springer, Heidelberg (2010)
27. Thurman, R.: Purchasing contracts in the textile industry: how can purchasing contracts decrease subcontracting risks and reclamations in a textile industry company?, Tampereen ammattikorkeakoulu, Thesis Report (2007)
28. Urbano, J., Rocha, A.P., Oliveira, E.: Trust estimation using contextual fitness. In: Jędrzejowicz, P., Nguyen, N.T., Howlet, R.J., Jain, L.C. (eds.) KES-AMSTA 2010. LNCS, vol. 6070, pp. 42–51. Springer, Heidelberg (2010)
29. Urbano, J., Rocha, A.P., Oliveira, E.: Trustworthiness Tendency Incremental Extraction Using Information Gain. In: IEEE/WIC/ACM International Conference on Web Intelligence and Intelligent Agent Technology, wi-iat 2010, vol. 2, pp. 411–414 (2010)
30. Quinlan, J.R.: Induction of Decision Trees. Machine Learning 1(1), 81–106 (1986)
31. Hall, M., Frank, E., Holmes, G., Pfahringer, B., Reutemann, P., Witten, I.H.: The WEKA Data Mining Software: An Update. SIGKDD Explorations 11(1) (2009)

Using the Perseus System
for Modelling Epistemic Interactions

Magdalena Kacprzak[1], Piotr Kulicki[2], Robert Trypuz[2],
Katarzyna Budzynska[3], Paweł Garbacz[2], Marek Lechniak[2],
and Paweł Rembelski[1]

[1] Polish-Japanese Institute of Information Technology, Warsaw, Poland
[2] John Paul II Catholic University of Lublin, Poland
[3] Cardinal Stefan Wyszynski University in Warsaw, Poland
http://www.l3g.pl, http://perseus.ovh.org/

Abstract. The aim of the paper is to apply the software tool Perseus to modelling epistemic interactions. We focus on the issue of agents' knowledge acquisition, using a logical puzzle in which agents increase their knowledge about the hats they wear. In the paper, first we present a model of epistemic interactions, which allows us to resolve the hats puzzle. Then, the model is used to build the problem's specification for the Perseus system. Finally, we show how the hats puzzle can be solved and analysed in a detailed way with the use of a parametric verification method executed by Perseus.

Keywords: knowledge representation, dynamic epistemic logic, multi agent systems.

1 Introduction

One of the most important issues when considering agents and multi agent systems is an agent's state of belief and its dynamics in interaction with other agents. The research on the subject was conducted within dynamic doxastic logic, belief revision theory, public announcement logic or argumentation theory (see for example [1,2,3,4]). In [5,6,7], a general model of epistemic interactions is built, as one of the options, and applied to the example of logical puzzles concerning agents knowledge. In [8,9], on the other hand, a theoretical model for persuasive actions of arbitrary agents and its implementation in the Perseus system is presented.

The paper is an extended version of [10]. The new elements occurring in the present paper are: the study of the transition from the ontological description of the scenario to the epistemological facts concerning agents possible states of beliefs, presentation of the architecture of the final puzzle solving system, additional examples, and some more information about other works related to our results. The main subject of it is to connect those two approaches. The fundament, that makes such a connection possible, is a claim that *the formal structure of the process of persuasion is similar to the structure of information*

N.T. Nguyen (Ed.): Transactions on CCI V, LNCS 6910, pp. 106–123, 2011.
© Springer-Verlag Berlin Heidelberg 2011

acquisition of an agent, towards whom the persuasion is presented (see e.g. [11] for the justification of the relation between the processes of persuasion and beliefs change). It enables to use the Perseus system to analyse not only persuasion, but also other epistemic interactions, including knowledge acquisition from an other agent's behaviour.

While building the general model of epistemic interactions (especially in [7]) we explored the details of founding epistemic attitudes of agents on their ontological features. We introduced the notion of epistemic capacities of an agent understood as the feature of an agent defining the kind of information that he or she have access to. As a result, we construct epistemic attitudes (the way in which agents incorporate information) on the foundation of their epistemic capacities. Applying these results in the context of the Perseus system we obtain a possibility of automated generation of its input model. Usually such a model have to be created explicitely and *manually* which is a very laborous process and that fact strongly limits the possibility of application of Perseus and other model verifiers to the real life problems.

We test our ideas on logical puzzles following B. Russell [12], who wrote that: "A logical theory may be tested by its capacity for dealing with puzzles, and it is a wholesome plan, in thinking about logic, to stock the mind with as many puzzles as possible, since these serve much the same purpose as is served by experiments in physical science." As a working example we shall use the following hats puzzle: *Alice, Bob and Charlie sit in a row in such a way that Alice can see Bob and Charlie, Bob can see Charlie and Charlie can see nobody. They are shown five hats, three of which are red and two are black. While the light is off, each of them receives one of the hats to put on the head. When the light is back on, they are asked whether they know what the colours of their hats are. Alice answers that she doesn't know. Then Bob answers that he doesn't know either. Finally Charlie says that he knows the colour of his hat. What colour is Charlie's hat?*

In section 2 Perseus system is described, in section 3 the general model for epistemic interactions is introduced, in section 4 the puzzle is solved in the model, in section 5 transition of the problem description into Perseus is defined and finally in section 6 a solution for the hats puzzle in Perseus is discussed.

2   The Perseus System

The Perseus system is a software designed for an automatic many-sided analysis of persuasive multi-agent systems. It allows for investigations into the change of beliefs and behaviour under the influence of persuasive actions. As a formal base we use $\mathcal{AG}_n$ logic [8]. Now we shall shortly describe its syntax and semantics.

Let $Agt = \{1, \ldots, n\}$ be a set of names of *agents*, V_0 be a set of *propositional variables*, and Π_0 a set of *program variables*. Further, let ; denote the sequential composition operator. It enables to compose *schemes of programs* defined as the finite sequences of program variables: $a_1; \ldots; a_k$. The set of all schemes of programs we denote by Π. Program variables can be interpreted as atomic actions and schemes of programs as an arbitrary composed behaviour.

The set of all *well-formed expressions* of $\mathcal{AG}_n$ is given by the following Backus-Naur form (BNF): $\alpha ::= p \mid \neg\alpha \mid \alpha \vee \alpha \mid M_i^d \alpha \mid \Diamond(i : P)\alpha$, where $p \in V_0$, $d \in \mathbb{N}$, $P \in \Pi$, $i \in Agt$. Other Boolean connectives are defined in the standard way. We also use the abbreviations: $M!_i^d\alpha$ where $M!_i^0\alpha \Leftrightarrow \neg M_i^0\alpha$, $M!_i^d\alpha \Leftrightarrow M_i^{d-1}\alpha \wedge \neg M_i^d\alpha$, if $d > 0$ and $M!_i^{d_1,d_2}\alpha$ for $M!_i^{d_1}\alpha \wedge M!_i^{d_2}(\alpha \vee \neg\alpha)$.

$\mathcal{AG}_n$ logic allows for expressing uncertainty of an agent about a given thesis and a change of this uncertainty caused by specific actions. In order to reason about uncertainty we use the formula $M!_i^{d_1,d_2}\alpha$ which says that agent i considers d_2 doxastic alternatives (i.e. visions of a current global state) and d_1 of them satisfy the condition α. Intuitively it means that the agent i believes with degree $\frac{d_1}{d_2}$ that α holds. For reasoning about the change of uncertainty the formula $\Diamond(i : P)\alpha$ is used. It says that after executing a sequence of (persuasive) actions P by agent i the condition α may hold.

Definition 1. *Let Agt be a finite set of names of agents. By a semantic model we mean a Kripke structure $\mathcal{M} = (S, RB, I, v)$ where*

- *S is a non-empty set of states (the universe of the structure),*
- *RB is a doxastic function which assigns a binary relation to every agent, $RB : Agt \longrightarrow 2^{S \times S}$,*
- *I is an interpretation of the program variables, $I : \Pi_0 \longrightarrow (Agt \longrightarrow 2^{S \times S})$,*
- *v is a valuation function, $v : S \longrightarrow \{\mathbf{0}, \mathbf{1}\}^{V_0}$.*

Function I can be extended in a simple way to define interpretation I_Π of any program scheme: $I_\Pi(a)(i) = I(a)(i)$ for $a \in \Pi_0$ and $i \in Agt$, $I_\Pi(P_1; P_2)(i) = I_\Pi(P_1)(i) \circ I_\Pi(P_2)(i) = \{(s, s') \in S \times S : \exists_{s'' \in S} ((s, s'') \in I_\Pi(P_1)(i)$ and $(s'', s') \in I_\Pi(P_2)(i))\}$ for $P_1, P_2 \in \Pi$ and $i \in Agt$.

For a given structure $\mathcal{M} = (S, RB, I, v)$ and a given state $s \in S$ the Boolean value of the formula α is denoted by $\mathcal{M}, s \models \alpha$ and is defined inductively as follows:

$$\begin{aligned}
\mathcal{M}, s \models p \quad &\text{iff} \quad v(s)(p) = \mathbf{1}, \text{ for } p \in V_0, \\
\mathcal{M}, s \models \neg\alpha \quad &\text{iff} \quad \mathcal{M}, s \not\models \alpha, \\
\mathcal{M}, s \models \alpha \vee \beta \quad &\text{iff} \quad \mathcal{M}, s \models \alpha \text{ or } \mathcal{M}, s \models \beta, \\
\mathcal{M}, s \models M_i^d\alpha \quad &\text{iff} \quad |\{s' \in S : (s, s') \in RB(i) \text{ and } \mathcal{M}, s' \models \alpha\}| > d, d \in \mathbb{N}, \\
\mathcal{M}, s \models \Diamond(i : P)\alpha \quad &\text{iff} \quad \exists_{s' \in S} ((s, s') \in I_\Pi(P)(i) \text{ and } \mathcal{M}, s' \models \alpha).
\end{aligned}$$

We say that α is true in model $\mathcal{M}$ at state s if $\mathcal{M}, s \models \alpha$.

Given a semantic model $\mathcal{M} = (S, RB, I, v)$, the Perseus system analyses its properties. In this case, the system input data, i.e. the *input question*, is a triple $(\mathcal{M}, s, \phi)$, where $\mathcal{M}$ is a model, s is a state of model $\mathcal{M}$ and ϕ is the *input expression*. The input expression is defined by the following BNF form:

$$\phi ::= \omega \mid \neg\phi \mid \phi \vee \phi \mid M!_i^{d_1,d_2}\phi \mid \Diamond(i : P)\phi \mid M!_i^{?,?}\omega \mid \Diamond(i :?)\,\omega \mid M!_?^{d_1,d_2}\omega \mid \Diamond(? : P)\,\omega,$$

where $\omega ::= p \mid \neg\omega \mid \omega \vee \omega \mid M!_i^{d_1,d_2}\omega \mid \Diamond(i : P)\,\omega$, and $p \in V_0, d_1, d_2 \in \mathbb{N}, P \in \Pi$, $i \in Agt$. Therefore the language of extended $\mathcal{AG}_n$ logic is a sublanguage of the Perseus system input expressions. The system accepts two types of the input expressions:

- *unknown free expressions*, where grammar productions
$M!_i^{?,?}\omega \mid \Diamond\,(i:?)\,\omega \mid M!_?^{d_1,d_2}\omega \mid \Diamond\,(?:P)\,\omega$ are not allowed,
- *one-unknown expression*, where only one of the grammar productions
$M!_i^{?,?}\omega \mid \Diamond\,(i:?)\,\omega \mid M!_?^{d_1,d_2}\omega \mid \Diamond\,(?:P)\,\omega$ is allowed .

This grammar allows Perseus to look for answers to questions about diverse properties of systems under consideration and, in consequence, allows to analyze these systems in an automatic way. In particular, questions can concern

- agents - is there an agent who can influence somebody's beliefs?, who can do it?, who can achieve a success?
- beliefs and degrees of beliefs - does an agent believe a thesis?, what is a degree of his uncertainty about this thesis?
- results of actions - whether a degree of agent's belief can change after execution of a given action or sequence of actions?, which actions should be executed in order to convince an agent that a thesis is true?

Next, the Perseus system executes a *parametric verification* of an input question, i.e. tests if (both unknown free and one-unknown expressions) and when (only one-unknown expressions) the expression ϕ becomes a formula of extended $\mathcal{AG}_n$ logic ϕ^* such, that $\mathcal{M}, s \models \phi^*$ holds (see Fig. 1).

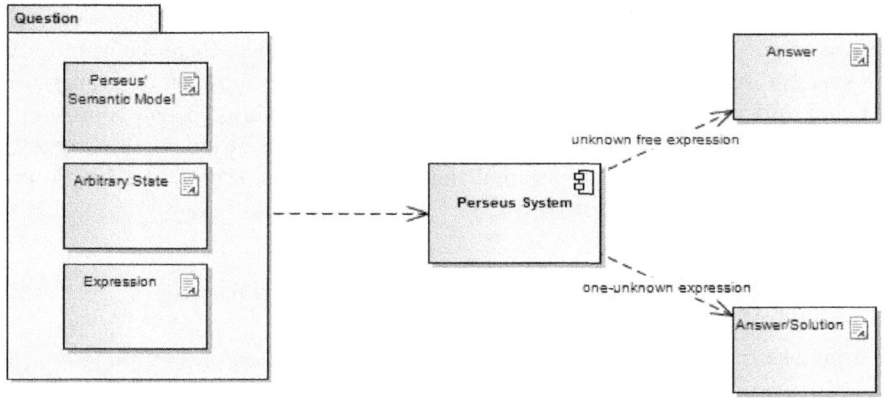

Fig. 1. The idea of the Perseus system

In the case of unknown free expressions $\phi^* = \phi$, i.e a standard model verification is done. In the other case formula ϕ^* is obtained from ϕ by swapping all ? symbols into appropriate values either from set $\{0, 1, \ldots |S|\}$ or Agt or Π. Finally the system output data, i.e the *output answer*, is given. The output answer is *true* if $\mathcal{M}, s \models \phi^*$ and *false* in the other case. As soon as the output answer is determined, the *solution set* X for the one-unknown expression is presented, e.g. $X \subseteq \{0, 1, \ldots |S|\} \times \{0, 1, \ldots |S|\}$, for an expression ϕ with one unknown of the $M!_i^{?_1,?_2}\omega$ type.

In order to find the answer to the input question $(\mathcal{M}, s, \phi)$, Perseus executes the syntax analysis of the expression ϕ. The analysis is based on the standard descent recursive method. As a result a syntax tree of ϕ is created. All inner nodes of such a tree represent either the Boolean operators or $\mathcal{AG}_n$ logic modalities while all outer nodes stand for either propositional variables or an unknown. The solution for an arbitrary unknown is reached in the following way:

- if an unknown type is $M!_i^{?_1,?_2}\omega$, then the counting method is applied, i.e. all states, which are reachable via doxastic relation of the agent i, and in which thesis ω is satisfied or refuted respectively, are counted,
- if an unknown type is $M!_?^{d_1,d_2}\omega$ or $\Diamond\,(?:P)\,\omega$, then for every agent $i \in Agt$ the property respectively $\mathcal{M}, s \models M!_i^{d_1,d_2}\omega$ or $\mathcal{M}, s \models \Diamond\,(i:P)\,\omega$ is tested,
- if an unknown type is $\Diamond\,(i:?)\,\omega$, then a nondeterministic finite automaton, which represents all possible argumentation $P \in \Pi$ such that $\mathcal{M}, s \models \Diamond\,(i:P)\,\omega$ holds, is created.

If an unknown is a nested type, i.e. it is a part of a thesis of extended $\mathcal{AG}_n$ logic operator, then its *solution set is bounded* by the outer modality/modalities. For example, if we consider an input question $\left(\mathcal{M}, s, M!_j^{1,2}\Diamond\,(i:P)\,M!_i^{?,?}\omega\right)$, then solution of the unknown $M!_i^{?,?}\omega$ is reduced firstly by the operator $\Diamond$ and secondly by the operator $M!$. The detailed description of a solution bounding problem is presented in [9].

As we stated at the beginning of this section, the intended application for the Perseus system is to investigate persuasion. However, the formalism underlying the system is more general. Since it includes the representation of agents' states of belief and their changes caused by other agents' actions, it can represent any phenomena that concern such a change. One of them is knowledge aquisition. To capture them we need to assume that all beliefs are true and all actions can be interpreted as equivalent to truthful announcements.

3   General Model for Epistemic Interactions

Our general model for epistemic interactions has two main components: ontological and epistemological. The *ontological part* represents a world that our knowledge concerns. The *epistemological part* represents the phenomenon of the knowledge in its static and dynamic aspects. Additionally, we introduce the *time-like component*, which is used for organising all kinds of changes, for instance by distributing the agents' behaviours over the set of moments.

Ontological layer. Ontological layer of the model is made up of situations. They may have any ontic structure. Thus, there are situations "in which" certain objects possess certain properties or situations "in which" certain objects participate in certain relations or processes, etc. Every situation is a collection of elementary situations. A situation is *elementary* if no other situation is part of it. For instance *that Alice has a red hat* would be an elementary situation and *that both Alice and Bob have red hats* would not be an elementary situation.

Let *ElemSit* be a set of elementary situations. In what follows, we will represent situations as sets of elementary situations: $\emptyset \notin Sit \subseteq \wp(ElemSit)$. Maximal situations occupy a privileged position in the model and are called possible worlds:

$$X \in PossWorld \triangleq X \in Sit \wedge \forall Y(X \subset Y \rightarrow Y \notin Sit). \qquad (1)$$

Time layer. Let $Time = (t_1, t_2, \dots)$ be a sequence of moments. Thus we assume that moments are linearly ordered. We make no additional assumptions about time.

Epistemological layer. The *actual epistemic state* of an agent at a given moment will be represented by a subset of *PossWorld*: $epist(i, t_n) \subseteq PossWorld$. Any such state collectively represents both the agent's knowledge and his ignorance. Due to its actual epistemic state, which is represented by set $epist(i, t_n)$, and for every $X \in Sit$, agent i may be described (at t_n) according to the following three aspects:

Definition 2. *Agent i knows at moment t_n that situation X holds (written: $K_{i,t_n}(X)$) iff $X \subseteq \bigcap epist(i, t_n)$.*

Definition 3. *Agent i knows at moment t_n that situation X does not hold (written: $\overline{K}_{i,t_n}(X)$) iff $X \cap (\bigcup epist(i, t_n)) = \emptyset$.*

Definition 4. *Agent i does not have any knowledge at moment t_n about situation X iff $\neg K_{i,t_n}(X) \wedge \neg \overline{K}_{i,t_n}(X)$.*

However, the puzzles we are dealing with do not presuppose that we know the actual epistemic state of a given agent. Thus, we extend the notion of actual epistemic state to the notion of possible epistemic states. A *possible epistemic state* of an agent represents a body of knowledge (resp. of ignorance) that the agent may exhibit given the ontic situation and epistemic capabilities of the agent. In our case, the possible epistemic states are determined by the relation of seeing, other agents' announcements and the agent's deductive capabilities.

A possible epistemic state of an agent at a given moment will be represented by the set $epist_k(i, t_n) \subseteq Sit$. Then, the definitions of 2–4 can be easily amended to describe the agent's knowledge (resp. of ignorance) in the possible epistemic states. For instance definition 2 is transformed into the one below:

Definition 5. *Agent i knows in a possible epistemic state X that (ontic) situation Y holds (written : $K_{epist_k(i,t_n)}(Y)$) iff $Y \subseteq \bigcap X$.*

We will use the following auxiliary notions: $Epist(i, t_n)$ – the set of all possible epistemic states of agent i at t_n; $Epist(t_n)$ – the set of sets of possible epistemic states of all agents at t_n; $Epist$ – the set of sets of all possible epistemic states of all agents (from Agt) at all moments (from $Time$).

For any $i \in Agt$ and t_n "$\sim_{i,t_n}$" will represent the relation of epistemological indiscernibility, for agent i in time moment t_n. The relation is an equivalence relation. As the notion of knowledge itself, it is relative to time. It is an assumption of our approach that possible epistemic states coincide with the abstraction classes of the epistemological indiscernibility relation:

$$Epist(i, t_n) = PossWorld/ \sim_{i,t_n} \tag{2}$$

Changes of epistemic states. We assume that all changes of epistemic states are caused by the behaviour of agents, in particular by their utterances, by means of which they expose their (current) epistemic states and not by their inference processes. A number of rules that govern the dynamics of epistemic states can be defined. In the hats puzzle the only rule that sets the epistemic states in motion is the following one: If agent i says that he does not know that X holds, in an epistemic state $epist_k(i, t_n)$ i knows that X holds, then after the aforementioned utterance this state (i.e. $epist_k(i, t_n)$) is effectively impossible, i.e. we remove its elements from all possible epistemic states of all agents. Formally,

Rule 1. *If (i says that)* $\neg K_{i,t_n}(X)$ *and* $Y \in Epist(i, t_n)$ *and* $K_Y(X)$, *then for every* $i' \in Agt$, $Epist(i', t_{n+1}) = \delta_0(Epist(i', t_n), Y)$, *where*

Definition 6. δ_0 *maps* $Epist \times \bigcup\bigcup Epist$ *into* $Epist$ *and satisfies the following condition:*

$$\delta_0(Epist(i, t_n), X) = \begin{cases} Epist(i, t_n)\backslash\{Z\}, & \text{if } Z \in Epist(i, t_n) \text{ and} \\ & Z \subseteq X \\ (Epist(i, t_n)\backslash\{Z\}) \cup \{Z\backslash X\}, & \text{if } Z \in Epist(i, t_n) \text{ and} \\ & X \cap Z \neq \emptyset \text{ and } Z\backslash X \neq \emptyset \\ Epist(i, t_n) & \text{otherwise.} \end{cases}$$

It is worth noting that the factors that trigger the process of epistemic change are of two kinds: ontological and epistemological. The ontological condition of the rule 1 is the fact that agent i says that he does not know that a certain ontic situation holds. The epistemological condition is his epistemic state ($Y \in Epist(i, t_n)$), in which the agent knows that this situation holds ($K_Y(X)$).

Some other possible rules and their generalisations are presented and discussed in [6].

4   Ontology to Epistemology Transition

In order to investigate epistemic interactions within a group of agents in certain circumstances one has to build a detailed model of agents and their possible behaviour. The model has to contain information about agents' states of belief at any moment, possible actions that can have an influence on those states of beliefs and the details of that influence (in other words epistemic attitudes). Such a model is quite complex even for a small number of agents and possible actions. Usually, when systems like Perseus are used, models are described explicitly and *manually* – a user defines, step by step, the states of belief of all agents and their transitions after every possible action. That is a very laborous process and that fact strongly limits the possibility of application of model verifiers to the real life problems.

To avoid that problem we take advantage of the fact that the way rational agents change their beliefs strongly depends on their structure, especially on the kind of information thay have access to. We call that feature *epistemic capacities* of an agent. Thus, in the Hats Puzzle we can deduce that *Alice knows the colours of Bob's and Charlie's hats* because she can see the hats. From such facts one can build up a set of possible epistemic states of the agents. For example, Alice distinguishes between the situations in which Bob's hat has different colours and cannot distinguish the states that differ only in her own hat colour.

We automatise such a process of building the initial state of the system within our puzzle solver. Conseqently, we also build a model of the whole system and that model can be used as an input model for Perseus. We believe that the introduction of such a procedure is very promising in the prospective applications of Perseus and other similar systems.

At the moment in the puzzle solver we use the representation of epistemic capacities designed specifically for the Hats Puzzle in which the only element of such capacities is the relation of seeing. The possibility of generalisation of their description using RDF format is considered in [7].

5   Solving the Hats Puzzle within the General Model

To obtain the solution of the Hats Puzzle in our model, one needs the following input data:

- set $PossWorld$
- set of epistemic agents Agt,
- set of sets of epistemic states of any such agent at the initial moment t_1:
  $Epist(t_1) = \{Epist(i, t_1) : i \in Agt\}$,
- temporal sequence $Time = (t_n)$,
- function $dist : Time \rightarrow \wp(ElemSit)$.

The set $PossWorld$ of possible worlds and the description of the initial moment are generated automatically on the basis of the description of the possible features of the objects and epistemic capacities of the agents in the way describerd in the previous section. Function $dist$ is to distribute the agents' behaviour over the set of moments. In the hats puzzle we take into account only the activity of the public announcements described by the rule 1.

We assume that function $dist$ does not trigger more than one rule at a time. We also assume that epistemological states change only when a certain rule is triggered. After applying the last rule, say at moment t_k ($k \leq n$), we will reach one of the four possible outcomes: (1) in every epistemic state at t_k agent i knows that situation X holds (or does not hold), (2) in one epistemic state at t_k agent i knows that X holds (or does not hold) and in another epistemic state he or she does not know that, (3) in no epistemic state at t_k agent i knows that X holds (or does not hold) and (4) set $Epist(i, t_{n+1})$ is empty. Only the first case represents the situation in which we (or any other agent, for that matter) are in a position to solve the puzzle. On the other hand, the last situation implies that the puzzle was inconsistent.

That representation of the puzzle and its solution is implemented in a program that is able to solve the whole family of puzzles.

To introduce the conditions of a specific puzzle it is enough to specify the crucial elements of its description:

- list of agents
- list of features
- relation of 'seeing'

An example of such a file corresponding to the Hats Puzzle is shown below as a Prolog file.

```
% hats
colour(red, 3).    % There are three red hats
colour(black, 2).  % There are two black hats

% agents
agent('Alice').    % Alice is an agent
agent('Bob').      % Bob is an agent
agent('Charlie').  % Charlie is an agent

% epistemic capacities of the agents
sees('Alice','Bob').     % Alice sees Bob's hat
sees('Alice','Charlie'). % Alice sees Charlie's hat
sees('Bob','Charlie').   % Bob sees Charlie's hat
```

The first group of clauses states that there are three red hats and two black hats. The second is a list of agents. The third defines the relation of seeing, which is the only element of agents' epistemic capacities.

To obtain the solution for the puzzle one needs to:

1. generate a description of initial state;
2. describe the sequence of actions moving the whole system from one state to another;
3. analyse the final state of the system.

This can be done by the following Prolog query, in which the single element list of possible colours of Charlie's hat is given as the value of variable S[1].

```
all_agents_i_p_s(L),
change(not_knows,'Alice',L,M),
change(not_knows,'Bob',M,Q),
```

---

[1] The code one can be found here:
  http://l3g.pl/index.php?option=com_content&view=article&id=62&Itemid=1

```
member(('Charlie',W1),Q),
append(W1,W2),
possible_colours('Charlie',W2,S).
```

The first line is responsible for generating of the initial state. The two following lines represent epistemic actions – Alice says that she does not now the colour of her hat, and Bob says the same about himself. The remaining three lines allow the program to analyse the final state of the system – in the first line the Charlie's epistemic state is taken from the list of all agents' epistemic states, in the second line the list of possible worlds (with respect to Charlies epistemic state) is calculated and in the third one possible colours of Charlie's hat are gathered as a value of variable S.

The architecture of the puzzle solver based on the general model of epistemic interactions is depicted in the figure 2.

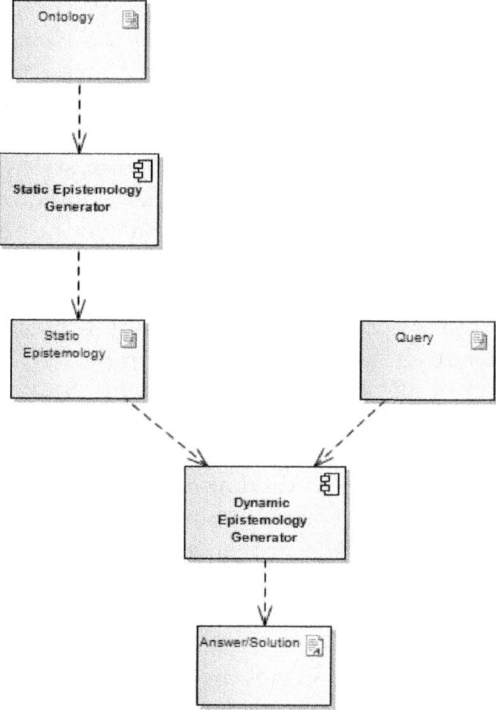

Fig. 2. The architecture of puzzle solver

6   Generating a Global Semantic Model

A characteristic feature of the presented general model of epistemic states and interaction, which makes it different from other models, including the one that is used by Perseus, is that it does not distinguish any possible states of the world (situations) as real. Thus the observer having access to everything that is encoded within the model has information about the world only through the agents' epistemic constitutions and behaviour. That approach corresponds to the setting of the hats puzzle. However, the model can be extended to include the information about the real situation. As a result we obtain the specification of a graph which can be used by the Perseus system which is generated automatically on the basis of the description of puzzle's details.

The underlying structure of both models is analogical – a set of possible worlds corresponds to a set of states, an elementary situation (element of possible world) points out which proposition variables are true in a state, and actions that trigger epistemic changes correspond to program variables. In the general model, for each agent, the set of possible worlds is divided into partitions using agent's indiscernibility relation at a certain moment in time (or equivalently after a certain combination of agent's actions). Those partitions are represented in the Perseus model by a doxastic function RB. However, the indiscernibility relation changes in time. In the Perseus model the change is represented by a combination of actions defined by a schema of a program. Thus we need a separate set of worlds to represent doxastic relations that hold after each of the possible programs (each combination of actions performed by agents).

In Perseus, there is also another relation between states – an interpretation I of program variables. Since a program variable is interpreted as a persuasive action it has influence only on agents' beliefs but not on the real world. Thus, the relation defined by interpretation I holds between *similar* states (states in which the set of true propositions is the same) in different time moments, if there is an action that triggers epistemic change between those moments.

Formally, we have to define the structure $\mathcal{M} = (S, RB, I, v)$ used by Perseus on the basis of a set of all possible epistemic states $Epist$ and rules describing epistemic changes after firing the epistemic trigger. Since we want to include in the model all the possible scenarios, we have to drop the time layer of the model and consider elements of $Epist$ as valid after performing a sequence of triggers. For this reason we will use for them symbols $Epist(x)$, $x \in \mathbb{N}$. Let $Epist(1)$ be an initial epistemic state. Let further $Epist^* \subseteq Epist$ be the smallest set containing $Epist(1)$ closed under the operation of applying an epistemic rule. Intuitively, $Epist^*$ is a set of epistemic states reachable from an initial state by agents actions.

Not all ontologically possible worlds are epistemically possible in every epistemic state, because epistemic rules exclude some of them. $\bigcup\bigcup Epist(x)$ is the set of possible worlds occurring in epistemic state $Epist(x)$. Let $S_x = \{\langle w, x \rangle : w \in \bigcup\bigcup Epist(x)\}$. Now, we can define $\mathcal{M} = (S, RB, I, v)$ in the following way:

$$S = \bigcup \{S_x : Epist(x) \in Epist^*\} \tag{3}$$

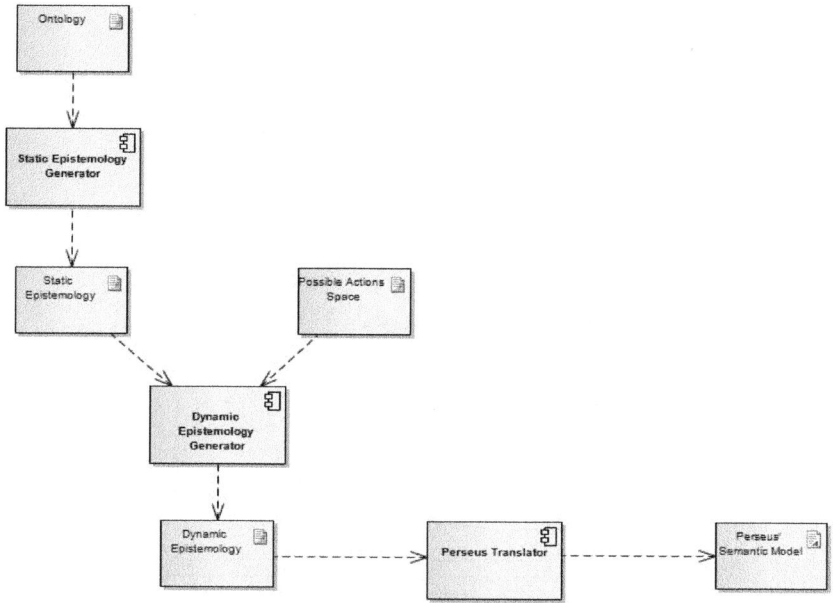

Fig. 3. The architecture of Perseus' semantic model generator

$$RB(i) = \qquad\qquad (4)$$
$$= \{\langle\langle s, x\rangle, \langle s', x'\rangle\rangle : x = x' \text{ and there exists } e \in Epist(i,x), \text{ such that } s, s' \in e\}$$

$$I(P)(i) = \{\langle\langle s, x\rangle, \langle s', x'\rangle\rangle : \qquad\qquad (5)$$
$$s = s' \text{ and action } P \text{ performed by agent } i \text{ leads from } Epist(k) \text{ to } Epist(k')\}$$

v is a valuation such that in state $\langle s, x\rangle$ a propositional variable P is assigned to value **1** iff a respective elementary situation $es \in s$ and to **0** otherwise.

On Figure 4 we present a graph automatically generated by the Perseus tool for Hats Problem.

7   Solution for the Hats Puzzle in Perseus

First of all let us observe that the assumptions of the puzzle are satisfied if for some $n_1, n_2 \in \mathbb{N}$ the following $\mathcal{AG}_n$ formula holds:

$$\Diamond(a : Alice)\Diamond(a : Bob)(M!^{n_1,n_1}_{Charlie}has\_Charlie\_r \vee M!^{n_2,n_2}_{Charlie}has\_Charlie\_b) \qquad\qquad (6)$$

where a is a verbal action in which an agent announces that he does not know what the colour of his hat is and $has\_Charlie\_r$, $has\_Charlie\_b$ are propositions true in every state in which Charlie has a red or black hat, respectively.

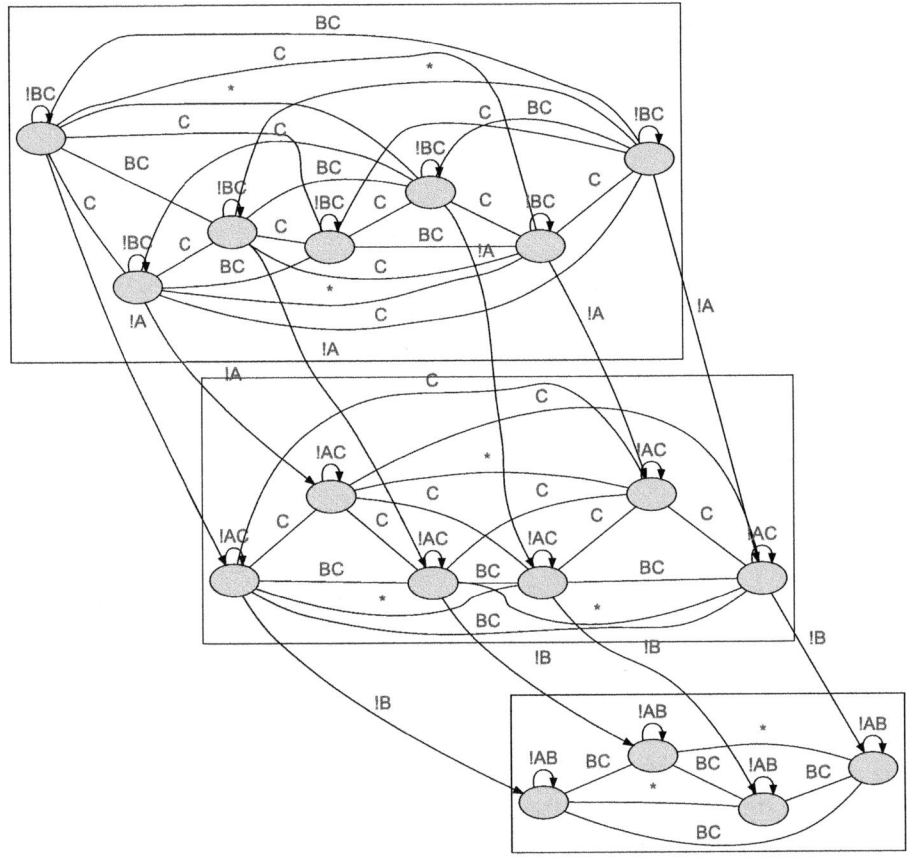

Fig. 4. The graph for epistemic relations of agents automatically generated by Perseus. The fragments of the graph representing different epistemic states are grouped in frames. Program variables are represented by lines labeled by '!' and initials of agents, doxastic function – just by agents' initials ('*' stands for all agents).

The formula intuitively says that "After Alice's announcement that she does not know the colour of her hat and Bob's announcement that he does not know the colour of his hat, Charlie believes with degree $\frac{n_1}{n_1}$ that he has a red hat or believes with degree $\frac{n_2}{n_2}$ that he has a black hat". It means that he is sure about that.

To solve the puzzle Perseus should search the model and point at a state (a set of states) in which formula 6 is satisfied. Then it should check which proposition $has\_Charlie\_r$ or $has\_Charlie\_b$ is true in this state (these states). Therefore, Perseus selects a state s and then using a parametric verification searches for values of unknowns $?_1, ?_2$ for which the expression

$$\Diamond(a : Alice)\Diamond(a : Bob)(M!_{Charlie}^{?_1,?_2}has\_Charlie\_r \vee M!_{Charlie}^{?_3,?_4}has\_Charlie\_b)$$

is true at s. If $?_1 =?_2 = n_1$ or $?_3 =?_4 = n_2$ then the assumptions of the puzzle are satisfied at s and Perseus tests whether the proposition $has\_Charlie\_r$ is satisfied at s. In consequence, Charlie has a red hat if for every state formula 6 implies proposition $has\_Charlie\_r$. Similarly, if for every state 6 implies $has\_Charlie\_b$ then Charlie has a black hat.

Apart from the ability to solve the puzzle, Perseus is equipped with tools which can help to analyse the scenario in a more detailed way. First of all, it answers the question which actions Alice and Bob should perform to influence Charlie's beliefs and cause that he will know the colour of his hat. In this case Perseus executes a parametric verification with the input expression

$$\Diamond(? : Alice)\Diamond(? : Bob)(M!_{Charlie}^{1,1}has\_Charlie\_r \vee M!_{Charlie}^{1,1}has\_Charlie\_b).$$

The other question concerns the agents who can influence Charlie's beliefs, i.e. who is the most successful performer of the announcement action

$$\Diamond(a :?)\Diamond(a :?)(M!_{Charlie}^{1,1}has\_Charlie\_r \vee M!_{Charlie}^{1,1}has\_Charlie\_b).$$

Finally, we could be interested in keeping track of the change of degrees of Charlie's beliefs. Then, the input question is

$$\Diamond(a : Alice)(M!_{Charlie}^{?,?}has\_Charlie\_r) \text{ or } \Diamond(a : Alice)(M!_{Charlie}^{?,?}has\_Charlie\_b).$$

8   Changing the Puzzle

The way of solving the puzzle is fairly general. Applying exactly the same algorithm we can change the number of agents, the number of colours and number of hats of different colours. Thus, we can approach any problem in which only one feature of the objects in concern is considered. As an example of an alternative application of our procedure let us consider the well known Muddy Children Problem.

In general settings the Muddy Children Puzzle can be defined as follows:

There are n children playing together. During their play some of the children, say k of them, get mud on their foreheads. Each can see the mud on others but not on his own forehead. Along comes a father, who says: 'At least one of you has mud on your head'. He then asks the following question, over and over: 'Can any of you prove that you have mud on your head?' Assuming that all the children are perceptive, intelligent, truthful, and that they answer simultaneously, what will happen?

For example, let us consider the case with n=3. We need to encode the probem within the Hats Puzzle language. We will do it in the following way.

- Muddy child - red hat.
- Clean child - black hat.
- At leats one of the children is muddy - there are three black hats and four red.

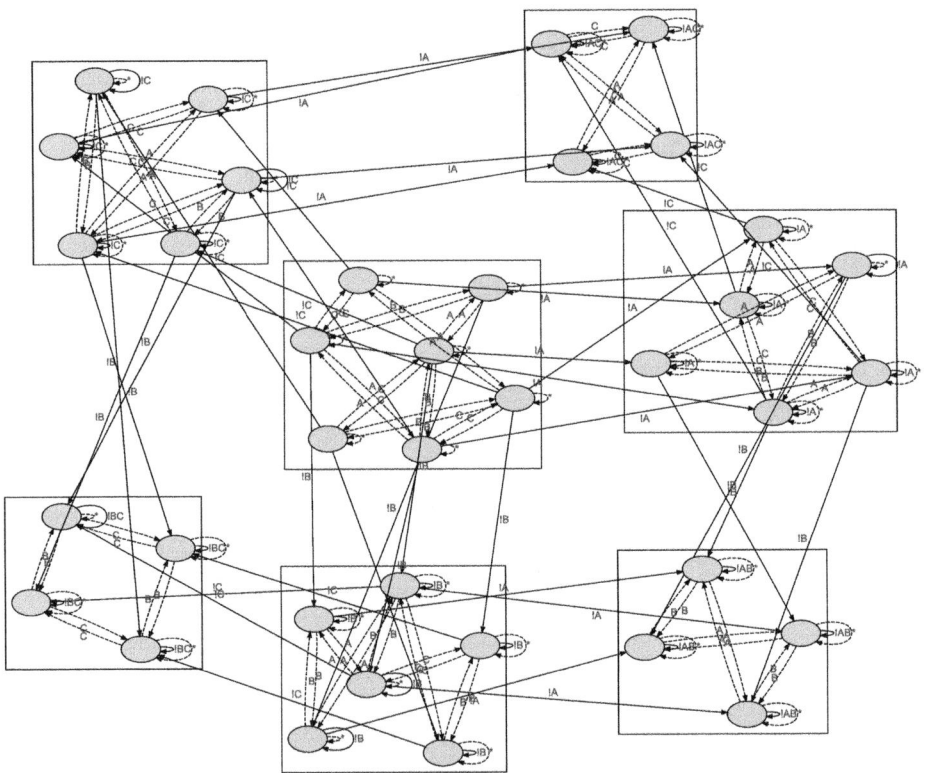

Fig. 5. The whole model constructed for Muddy Children Problem automatically generated by Perseus

Such encoding enables us to express the Muddy Children Problem in the form of the following Prolog file which can be used as an input to our program.

```
% hats
colour(red, 3).
colour(black, 2).

% agents
agent('Child_1').
agent('Child_2').
agent('Child_3').

% epistemic capacities of the agents
sees('Child_1','Child_2').
sees('Child_1','Child_3').
sees('Child_2','Child_1').
sees('Child_2','Child_3').
sees('Child_3','Child_1').
sees('Child_3','Child_2').
```

Using that file makes our program to generate a Perseus' graph for the Muddy Children Problem. The graph can be further used for many folded analyses of the problem as we shown for the case of the Hats Puzzle.

The model for Muddy Children Problem generated by the Perseus tool is shown in Figures 5 and 6.

9   Relation to Other Works

The application of the Perseus system to epistemic interactions places the present work among the considerations about tools for automated deduction for epistemic logic using systems like DEMO [13] or Aximo [14]. In general, those systems have similar expresive power and performance when applied to puzzles like the one considered in the paper. Since Perseus has features that enable it to express uncertain beliefs, it seems that using it may lead to more interesting results.

Verification of epistemic and temporal formulas is possible by means of model checkers like MCMAS [15] or Verics [16]. In comparison with them, Perseus is distinguished by two issues. First of all, it performs pure model checking and, what is more, parametric verification. It means that, given a model of a system, it can test automatically whether this model meets a given specification or given an input expressions with unknowns it can determine for which values of these unknowns the obtained logical formula is true in this model. Furthermore, Perseus is not limited to verification of formulas with epistemic and dynamic operators. It works also with graded doxastic modalities and, in the newest, enriched version, with probabilistic modalities [17].

In the field of verification of distributed systems, one of the crucial problems refers to the question how to build a model of a given system. The main challenge is to do it in an automatic way. The current paper provides one of the solutions which can be applied to the Perseus system. The Authors are not aware of any

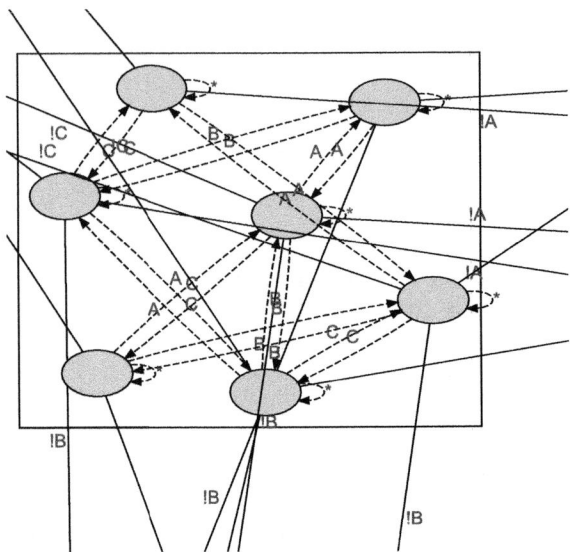

Fig. 6. The fragment of the graph from Figure 5 representing the initial state

other work aiming at automated generation of models that can be used as an input to the systems of automated deduction for epistemic logic.

10   Conclusion

The main contribution of the paper is using the existing software (the Perseus system) designed to represent the persuasion processes to model agent's knowledge acquisition. In order to do that we have designed and implemented an algorithm automatically generating a description of a graph that can be uploaded by the Perseus system, from the description of a situation in which knowledge acquisition takes place. It enables us to present the possible knowledge acquisition processes on diagrams generated by the Perseus system and perform a number of calculations that help us to understand the processes. Among other computations, the Perseus system is able to solve the hats puzzle, which was the initial task.

References

1. Meyer, J.-J.C., van der Hoek, W.: Epistemic logic for AI and computer science. Cambridge University Press, Cambridge (1995)
2. van Ditmarsch, H., van der Hoek, W., Kooi, B.: Dynamic Epistemic Logic. Synthese Library Series, vol. 337. Springer, Heidelberg (2007)
3. Fagin, R., Halpern, J.Y., Moses, Y., Vardi, M.Y.: Reasoning About Knowledge. MIT Press, Cambridge (2003)

4. Baltag, A., Moss, L.: Logics for epistemic programs. Knowledge, Rationality & Action (Synthese) 139, 165–224 (2004)
5. Garbacz, P., Kulicki, P., Lechniak, M., Trypuz, R.: Beyond public announcement logic: An alternative approach to some AI puzzles. In: Mertsching, B., Hund, M., Aziz, Z. (eds.) KI 2009. LNCS, vol. 5803, pp. 379–386. Springer, Heidelberg (2009)
6. Garbacz, P., Kulicki, P., Lechniak, M., Trypuz, R.: A formal model for epistemic interactions. In: Nguyen, N.T., Katarzyniak, R., Janiak, A. (eds.) New Challenges in Computational Collective Intelligence. SCI, pp. 205–216. Springer, Heidelberg (2009)
7. Kulicki, P., Garbacz, P., Trypuz, R., Lechniak, M.: Epistemic capacities, incompatible information and incomplete beliefs. In: Arrazola, X., Ponte, M. (eds.) LogKCA 2010. Proceedings of the Second ILCLI International Workshop on Logic and Philosophy of Knowledge, Communication and Action, pp. 255–273. University of the Basque Country Press (2010)
8. Budzyńska, K., Kacprzak, M.: A logic for reasoning about persuasion. Fundamenta Informaticae 85, 51–65 (2008)
9. Budzyńska, K., Kacprzak, M., Rembelski, P.: Perseus. software for analyzing persuasion process. Fundamenta Informaticae 93, 65–79 (2009)
10. Kacprzak, M., Kulicki, P., Trypuz, R., Budzynska, K., Garbacz, P., Lechniak, M., Rembelski, P.: Using perseus system for modelling epistemic interactions. In: Jędrzejowicz, P., Nguyen, N.T., Howlet, R.J., Jain, L.C. (eds.) KES-AMSTA 2010. LNCS (LNAI), vol. 6070, pp. 315–324. Springer, Heidelberg (2010)
11. Petty, R.E., Cacioppo, J.T.: Attitudes and Persuasion: Classic and Contemporary Approaches. Westview Press (1996)
12. Russell, B.: On Denoting. Mind 14, 479–493 (1905)
13. Eijck, J.V., Orzan, S.: Modelling the epistemics of communication with functional programming. In: 6th Symposium on Trends in Functional Programming, TFP 2005, pp. 44–59 (2005)
14. Richards, S., Sadrzadeh, M.: Aximo: Automated axiomatic reasoning for information update. Electronic Notes in Theoretical Computer Science, ENTCS (2009)
15. Lomuscio, A., Qu, H., Raimondi, F.: MCMAS: A model checker for the verification of multi-agent systems. In: Bouajjani, A., Maler, O. (eds.) CAV 2009. LNCS, vol. 5643, pp. 682–688. Springer, Heidelberg (2009)
16. Kacprzak, M., Nabiałek, W., Niewiadomski, A., Penczek, W., Półrola, A., Szreter, M., Woźna, B., Zbrzezny, A.: Verics 2008 - a model checker for time petri nets and high-level languages. In: Proc. of the International Workshop on Petri Nets and Software Engineering (PNSE 2009), pp. 119–132. University of Hamburg, Department of Informatics, Paris, France (2009)
17. Budzyńska, K., Kacprzak, M., Rembelski, P.: Update of probabilistic beliefs: Implementation and parametric verification. Fundamenta Informaticae 102(1), 35–48 (2010)

Reduction of Faulty Detected Shot Cuts and Cross Dissolve Effects in Video Segmentation Process of Different Categories of Digital Videos

Kazimierz Choroś

Institute of Informatics, Wrocław University of Technology,
Wybrzeże Wyspiańskiego 27, 50-370 Wrocław, Poland
`kazimierz.choros@pwr.wroc.pl`

Abstract. Video segmentation is an important computer vision research field being applied in many digital video analysis domains, such as: video compression, video indexing and retrieval, video scene detection, video content analysis, video object tracking in dynamic scenes, and many others. Video has temporal properties. The temporal segmentation process leads to the partition of a given video into a set of meaningful and individually manageable temporal segments. An effective segmentation technique is able to detect not only abrupt changes but also gradual scene changes, such as fade and dissolve transitions. The effectiveness of four methods was analyzed for five different categories of movie: TV talk-show, documentary movie, animal video, action & adventure, and pop music video. The tests have shown that the specific nature of videos has an important influence on the effectiveness of temporal segmentation methods. Furthermore, the knowledge on these specific features of the style of video editing has been used to reduce the number of faulty detected shot cuts and faulty detected cross dissolve effects.

Keywords: digital video indexing, temporal segmentation, scene changes, cuts, cross dissolve effects, movie categories.

1 Introduction

Multimedia indexing and retrieval methods should not apply only traditional techniques used for example by Internet search engines for retrieving textual parts of Web pages. We also expect efficient solutions for the retrieval of other kind of media like images, audio and video clips. The text is auto descriptive, it is composed of natural language words which can be treated as index terms used in retrieval. The process of text indexing is usually limited to the identification of words or expressions in the text.

Let's notice that the text has structural features. These are: language of the text, its length, number of standard pages or paragraphs, number of words or characters, number of columns, the size of characters, and many other statistical and editorial properties.

N.T. Nguyen (Ed.): Transactions on CCI V, LNCS 6910, pp. 124–139, 2011.

In many cases the textual information retrieval systems also retrieve other multimedia objects. They are processed similarly to texts, i.e. the multimedia are indexed by textual indexes derived from the texts accompanying these multimedia objects. A multimedia retrieval system should analyze the content in all media forms, so, not only textual parts. Furthermore, we should be able to express in our requests different aspects of the media we need. This leads to the necessity of analyzing and of indexing the multimedia documents using specific features of each media. The other media are not of the same nature as text. Images as well as audio and video clips are much more expressive than traditional documents containing only text but they do not explicitly include index terms. The multimedia information stored in a document should be represented by a set of specific features, i.e. by textual, structural as well as by the content-descriptive metadata specific for each medium [11].

Visual information can be described by traditional bibliographic data such as title, abstract, subject, genre, but also by technical or structural data such as color, texture, shape for a static image, or a hierarchy of movie, segment, motion, pan, zoom, scene, and finally shot for a movie. These characteristics are derived on the bases of textual description or from relatively easy measured technical and structural parameters.

Users could certainly benefit from a retrieval in which one could refer to content semantics, i.e. to events, emotions or meaning associated with visual information. These data are called content-descriptive metadata. Content of a still image [19] is expressed by its perceptual properties, like color, texture, shape, and spatial relationships, but also by semantic primitives corresponding to abstractions, like objects, roles, and scenes, and finally by such imprecise features like impressions, emotions, and meaning associated with the perceptual features combined together.

The indexing process of digital video clips can be performed at several levels:

- text annotation – traditional approach leading to the identification of index terms describing the content of the video clip – words in natural languages can be also detected directly in the image or video [12];
- analysis of technical features [21];
- automatic analysis of video content [2, 10, 16, 17].

A temporal segmentation is a process leading to the identification of meaningful video units, like shots, episodes or scenes [8]. Generally, it is the first step of decomposition of a video clip aiming to the partition of a given video into a set of meaningful and individually manageable temporal segments, which then can serve as basic units for content analysis and indexing as well as video summarization [18].

2 Temporal Segmentation Process

A video clip is also structured - like a text - into a strict hierarchy [10]. A clip is divided into some scenes, and a scene is composed of one or more camera shots. A scene usually corresponds to some logical event in a video such as a sequence of shots making up a dialogue scene, or an action scene in a movie. A shot is usually defined as a continuous video acquisition with the same camera, so, it is as a sequence of interrelated consecutive frames recorded contiguously and representing a continuous action in time or space.

A shot change occurs when a video acquisition is done with another camera. The cut is the simplest and the most frequent way to perform a change between two shots. In this case, the last frame of the first video sequence is directly followed by the first frame of the second video sequence. Cuts are probably the easiest shot changes to be detected. But software used for digital movie editing is more and more complex and other shot changes are now available. They include effects or transitions like a wipe, a fade, or a dissolve [19]. A wipe effect is obtained by progressively replacing the old image by the new one, using a spatial basis. A dissolve is a transition where all the images inserted between the two video sequences contain pixels whose values are computed as linear combination of the final frame of the first video sequence and the initial frame of the second video sequence. Cross dissolve describes the cross fading of two scenes. Over a certain period of time (usually several frames or several seconds) the images of two scenes overlay, and then the current scene dissolves into a new one. Fades are special cases of dissolve effects, where a most frequently black frame replaces the last frame of the first shot (fade in) or the first frame of the second shot (fade out). There are also many other kinds of effects combining for example wipe and zoom, etc.

A temporal segmentation of video clips is a process of partitioning a video frame sequence into shots and scenes. It is the first and indispensable step towards video-content analysis and content-based video browsing and retrieval.

There are many methods of temporal segmentation and they are still being refined [1, 3, 4, 5, 7, 14, 19, 20, 22]. The simplest methods are those analyzing individual pixels of the consecutive frames, the most complex are based on the histogram analysis and the detection of the motion during the video sequence. Several categories can be distinguished [15]:

- pixel pair differences,
- histogram differences of frames,
- block sampling of video frames,
- feature-based methods,
- motion-based methods, and
- combination of approaches.

The fundamental method is a shot change detection method based on pixel pair difference. It is known as the template matching. For every two successive frames, the values of intensity differences are computed for pixel pairs having the same spatial position in these two frames. Then, the cumulated sum of intensity differences is compared with a fixed threshold in order to determine if a shot change has been detected. Several other statistical measures have been proposed, among others the normalized difference energy and the normalized sum of absolute differences.

Two images can be also compared using global features instead of local features (pixels). Histogram is the best global image feature widely used in image processing. The main advantage of histogram-based methods is their global aspect. There are several methods which compute differences between histograms or weighted differences between histograms. The other methods define an intersection operator between histograms, different distances or different similarity measures.

The main advantage of the third group of segmentation methods that use the block sampling of video frames is the decrease of the computation time. The algorithms proposed for pixel or histogram analysis methods are applied for block representation of images. The other advantage of block-based methods is their relatively weak sensitivity to noise and camera or object motion.

The next group of temporal segmentation methods takes into consideration sophisticated features of images, such as [15]:

- moment invariants combined with histogram intersection,
- contour lines extracted from the image,
- some feature points extracted using Hough transform,
- planar points – points contained in a flat neighbourhood of the hyper surface,
- comparing of color histograms of regions of two successive frames,
- modeling of the video transition effects,
- use of some decision process as Bayesian methods,
- features computed from classical statistical approaches, and
- use of hidden Markov models.

Among the motion-based methods are the methods based on global (or camera) motion, motion vectors, optical flow, and correlation in the frequency domain.

The last group of methods relays upon the shot change detection by combining two or several algorithms.

3 Features of Different Video Categories

The question arises whether the dynamic nature and editing style of video clips has an influence on the effectiveness of temporal segmentation methods. Generally, the more dynamic video editing, the easier cut detection. In a dynamic clip there are usually no cross dissolve effects.

Most frequently categories of movies are defined on the basis of theme of movies. But we can define other criteria to categorize movies. The dynamism, style, and richness of movie storyboard and editing are very significant: dialog (audio) speed or pace of the narration, camera motion, light changes, action dynamism, and special effects.

We have decided to measure the influence of the movie features on effectiveness of the temporal segmentation using five digital videos of different types: TV talk-show, documentary movie, animal video, action & adventure, and pop music video.

TV talk-show is generally special video shot realized in the TV studio, with a static scene, almost without camera movements and without object movements, without colour changes of the scene, without light effects and without special editing effects.

Documentary video is also static in nature, also without dynamic changes on the scene, but some fragments of such a video could be clearly different. In documentary videos many effects such as fades and dissolves are usually used.

Animal videos are totally different. Objects of the scene (mainly animals) are moving, but rather in a slaw manner, also camera is moving also in a slow manner, rather constant but very rich variety of colour used in every episode. The dissolve effects are rather long.

Adventure video is a video composed of dynamic, short clips. We observe in such movies dynamic camera movements, also dynamic object movements on the scene, rich colours, contrast quickly changing, changing light, and many effects.

In pop music videos the editing style is extremely dynamic, many images are rapidly juxtaposed together, many very rapid movements of cameras, lights, as well as objects of the scene. The clips of the video are very short, even less then 1 second, cuts are very frequent, dissolve effects are relatively rare, contrary to light effects which are often used.

The following five representatives of the discussed above types of videos were used in experiments with temporal segmentation methods:

- TV talk-show – resolution: 576x432, duration: 5:05, frame rate: 25 fps, number of cuts: 61, number of cross dissolves: 0;
- documentary video – resolution: 512x320, duration: 5:12, frame rate: 25 fps, number of cuts: 45, number of cross dissolves: 8;
- animal video – resolution: 640x352, duration: 5:01, frame rate: 25 fps, number of cuts: 66, number of cross dissolves: 2;
- adventure video – resolution: 640x272, duration: 5:06, frame rate: 25 fps, number of cuts: 98, number of cross dissolves: 0;
- POP music video – resolution: 436x4370, duration: 1:56, frame rate: 25 fps, number of cuts: 93, number of cross dissolves: 13.

4   Tests and Results

Four main well-known methods of a temporal segmentation have been implemented [13]. These methods are:

- pixel pair differences,
- likelihood ratio method based on block sampling of video frames,
- histogram differences of frames,
- twin threshold comparison.

These methods process non-compressed video files. Experimental results will be presented to demonstrate the performance of various algorithms. The algorithms have some parameters. In the tests several sets of specific parameters have been used to demonstrate their influence on the effectiveness of the temporal segmentation methods.

The Tables 1 to 4 present the results obtained in the tests. These results were early reported in [6]. Notations used in the tables:

PT   - processing time (minutes:seconds),
C   - number of recognized cuts,
CC   - number of cuts correctly recognized,
OC   - number of omitted cuts (not-recognized),
FC   - faulty cuts,
D   - number of recognized cross dissolve effects,
CD   - number of cross dissolves correctly recognized,
OD   - number of omitted cross dissolves (not-recognized),
FD   - faulty cross dissolves,
R   - recall,
P   - precision.

Table 1. Experimental results of temporal segmentation for pixel pair differences. Two pixels are different if the difference of their values is greater than t. There is a cut between two frames if T % of pixels of two consecutive frames is different.

Parameters			Cuts				Cross Dissolves				Effectiveness of effect detection	
TV Talk-Show												
t	T	PT	C	CC	OC	FC	D	CD	OD	FD	R	P
20	20	07:40	278	61	0	217	0	0	0	0	**1.00**	**0.22**
30	50	07:45	61	61	0	0	0	0	0	0	**1.00**	**1.00**
40	30	07:48	61	61	0	0	0	0	0	0	**1.00**	**1.00**
100	20	07:34	17	17	44	0	0	0	0	0	**0.28**	**1.00**
Documentary Video												
t	T	PT	C	CC	OC	FC	D	CD	OD	FD	R	P
20	20	05:21	524	45	0	479	1	1	7	0	**0.87**	**0.09**
30	50	05:24	43	43	2	0	0	0	8	0	**0.81**	**1.00**
40	30	05:20	45	45	0	0	0	0	8	0	**0.85**	**1.00**
100	20	05:19	36	36	9	0	0	0	8	0	**0.68**	**1.00**
Animal Video												
t	T	PT	C	CC	OC	FC	D	CD	OD	FD	R	P
20	20	06:45	925	60	6	865	0	0	2	0	**0.88**	**0.06**
30	50	06:48	53	52	14	1	0	0	2	0	**0.76**	**0.98**
40	30	06:48	74	54	12	20	0	0	2	0	**0.79**	**0.73**
100	20	06:50	22	22	44	0	0	0	2	0	**0.32**	**1.00**
Adventure Video												
t	T	PT	C	CC	OC	FC	D	CD	OD	FD	R	P
20	20	05:37	2596	98	0	2498	0	0	0	0	**1.00**	**0.04**
30	50	05:37	132	91	7	41	0	0	0	0	**0.93**	**0.69**
40	30	05:36	274	97	1	177	0	0	0	0	**0.99**	**0.35**
100	20	05:37	65	52	46	13	0	0	0	0	**0.53**	**0.80**
POP Music Video												
t	T	PT	C	CC	OC	FC	D	CD	OD	FD	R	P
20	20	03:07	585	95	0	490	8	8	5	0	**0.95**	**0.17**
30	50	03:09	72	70	25	2	2	2	11	0	**0.67**	**0.97**
40	30	03:10	105	95	0	10	2	2	11	0	**0.90**	**0.91**
100	20	03:03	57	57	38	0	0	0	13	0	**0.53**	**1.00**

Table 2. Experimental results of temporal segmentation for the likelihood ratio method based on block sampling of video frames. Two blocks are different if the difference of their average values is greater than t. There is a cut between two frames if T % of blocks of two consecutive frames is different.

Parameters				Cuts				Cross Dissolves				Effectiveness of effect detection	
TV Talk-Show													
blocks	t	T	PT	C	CC	OC	FC	D	CD	OD	FD	R	P
4x3	2	30	14:48	51	50	11	1	0	0	0	0	**0.82**	**0.98**
4x3	3	20	14:46	44	43	18	1	0	0	0	0	**0.70**	**0.98**
8x6	2	40	14:36	68	61	0	7	0	0	0	0	**1.00**	**0.90**
16x9	1	80	14:48	296	61	0	235	0	0	0	0	**1.00**	**0.21**
Documentary Video													
blocks	t	T	PT	C	CC	OC	FC	D	CD	OD	FD	R	P
4x3	2	30	09:39	41	41	4	0	0	0	8	0	**0.77**	**1.00**
4x3	3	20	09:32	40	40	5	0	0	0	8	0	**0.75**	**1.00**
8x6	2	40	09:45	45	45	0	0	0	0	8	0	**0.85**	**1.00**
16x9	1	80	09:46	638	45	0	593	7	7	1	0	**0.98**	**0.08**
Animal Video													
blocks	t	T	PT	C	CC	OC	FC	D	CD	OD	FD	R	P
4x3	2	30	12:15	67	60	6	7	0	0	2	0	**0.88**	**0.90**
4x3	3	20	12:23	73	58	8	15	0	0	2	0	**0.85**	**0.79**
8x6	2	40	12:08	82	65	1	17	0	0	2	0	**0.96**	**0.79**
16x9	1	80	12:16	1587	66	0	1521	2	2	0	0	**1.00**	**0.04**
Adventure Video													
blocks	t	T	PT	C	CC	OC	FC	D	CD	OD	FD	R	P
4x3	2	30	09:57	118	86	12	32	0	0	0	0	**0.88**	**0.73**
4x3	3	20	09:59	100	76	22	24	0	0	0	0	**0.78**	**0.76**
8x6	2	40	09:54	142	93	3	47	0	0	0	0	**0.95**	**0.65**
16x9	1	80	09:55	2839	98	0	2741	0	0	0	0	**1.00**	**0.03**
POP Music Video													
blocks	t	T	PT	C	CC	OC	FC	D	CD	OD	FD	R	P
4x3	2	30	06:04	72	60	35	12	7	4	9	3	**0.59**	**0.81**
4x3	3	20	06:06	65	52	43	13	5	5	8	0	**0.53**	**0.81**
8x6	2	40	06:03	102	87	8	15	5	5	8	0	**0.85**	**0.86**
16x9	1	80	06:04	0	0	95	0	0	0	13	0	**0.00**	**0.00**

Table 3. Experimental results of temporal segmentation for histogram differences of frames. There is a cut between two frames if T % of values of the histograms of two consecutive frames is different.

Parameter		Cuts				Cross Dissolves				Effectiveness of effect detection	
TV Talk-Show											
T	PT	C	CC	OC	FC	D	CD	OD	FD	R	P
20	05:36	61	61	0	0	0	0	0	0	**1.00**	**1.00**
40	05:40	39	39	22	0	0	0	0	0	**0.64**	**1.00**
60	06:19	0	0	61	0	0	0	0	0	**0.00**	**0.00**
80	06:18	0	0	61	0	0	0	0	0	**0.00**	**0.00**
Documentary Video											
T	PT	C	CC	OC	FC	D	CD	OD	FD	R	P
20	04:07	60	44	1	16	3	3	5	0	**0.89**	**0.75**
40	04:08	34	34	11	0	0	0	8	0	**0.64**	**1.00**
60	04:07	16	16	29	0	0	0	8	0	**0.30**	**1.00**
80	04:09	3	3	42	0	0	0	8	0	**0.06**	**1.00**
Animal Video											
T	PT	C	CC	OC	FC	D	CD	OD	FD	R	P
20	04:52	98	64	2	34	1	1	1	0	**0.96**	**0.66**
40	04:49	36	36	30	0	0	0	2	0	**0.53**	**1.00**
60	04:50	21	21	45	0	0	0	2	0	**0.31**	**1.00**
80	04:50	5	5	61	0	0	0	2	0	**0.07**	**1.00**
Adventure Video											
T	PT	C	CC	OC	FC	D	CD	OD	FD	R	P
20	04:16	135	90	8	45	0	0	0	0	**0.92**	**0.67**
40	04:15	61	48	50	13	0	0	0	0	**0.49**	**0.79**
60	04:15	22	19	79	3	0	0	0	0	**0.19**	**0.86**
80	04:17	5	5	93	0	0	0	0	0	**0.05**	**1.00**
POP Music Video											
T	PT	C	CC	OC	FC	D	CD	OD	FD	R	P
20	02:18	95	66	29	29	4	4	9	0	**0.65**	**0.74**
40	02:21	6	5	90	1	0	0	13	0	**0.05**	**0.83**
60	02:21	1	1	94	0	0	0	13	0	**0.01**	**1.00**
80	02:20	0	0	95	0	0	0	13	0	**0.00**	**0.00**

Table 4. Experimental results of temporal segmentation for the twin threshold comparison method. In the twin comparison threshold method the twin thresholds Tb is used for cut detection and Ts is used for special effect detection. l, k – additional parameters.

Parameter					Cuts				Cross Dissolves				Effectiveness of effect detection	

TV Talk-Show

l	k	T_s	T_b	PT	C	CC	OC	FC	D	CD	OD	FD	R	P
1	2	2	9	12:55	85	61	0	24	78	0	0	78	**1.00**	**0.37**
2	4	3	17	13:02	61	61	0	0	32	0	0	32	**1.00**	**0.66**
3	6	5	24	12:49	59	59	2	0	14	0	0	14	**0.97**	**0.81**
4	8	6	32	12:38	55	55	6	0	7	0	0	7	**0.90**	**0.89**

Documentary Video

l	k	T_s	T_b	PT	C	CC	OC	FC	D	CD	OD	FD	R	P
1	2	2	11	08:48	128	45	0	83	145	8	0	137	**1.00**	**0.19**
2	4	5	20	08:47	56	44	1	12	47	8	0	39	**0.98**	**0.50**
3	6	7	29	08:50	42	39	6	3	22	6	2	16	**0.85**	**0.70**
4	8	9	38	08:52	34	33	12	1	10	5	3	5	**0.72**	**0.86**

Animal Video

l	k	T_s	T_b	PT	C	CC	OC	FC	D	CD	OD	FD	R	P
1	2	3	14	10:50	169	66	0	103	104	2	0	102	**1.00**	**0.25**
2	4	5	25	11:00	67	58	8	9	51	1	1	50	**0.87**	**0.50**
3	6	8	36	11:17	42	41	25	1	23	1	1	22	**0.62**	**0.65**
4	8	11	47	11:29	30	30	36	0	11	1	1	10	**0.46**	**0.76**

Adventure Video

l	k	T_s	T_b	PT	C	CC	OC	FC	D	CD	OD	FD	R	P
1	2	4	16	09:33	154	95	3	59	167	0	0	167	**0.97**	**0.30**
2	4	7	28	09:35	99	76	22	23	38	0	0	38	**0.78**	**0.55**
3	6	11	40	09:37	59	47	51	12	7	0	0	7	**0.48**	**0.71**
4	8	15	52	09:38	36	30	68	6	4	0	0	4	**0.31**	**0.75**

POP Music Video

l	k	T_s	T_b	PT	C	CC	OC	FC	D	CD	OD	FD	R	P
1	2	4	15	05:19	140	83	12	57	64	12	1	52	**0.88**	**0.47**
2	4	8	26	05:15	37	29	66	8	24	9	4	15	**0.35**	**0.62**
3	6	12	36	05:14	7	5	90	2	6	6	7	0	**0.10**	**0.85**
4	8	17	47	05:16	3	3	92	0	1	0	13	1	**0.03**	**0.75**

5   Best Results of Recall and Precision

Let us examine now the values of the best results of recall and precision achieved for the tested categories of video, i.e. the values achieved using one of the methods of temporal segmentation, no matter which one, implemented for the experiments. It may signal what is the highest level of temporal segmentation efficiency possible to attained by known methods for different categories of video. Nevertheless, it is obvious that a method applied for one category of videos can be less effective for another category.

5.1   Best Results of Recall

The highest values of recall have been obtained using the twin threshold comparison method, but for this method with the best parameters of processing and in consequence the best results of recall we observe relatively very low results of precision. The simple histogram difference method produced good results of recall as well as of precision.

Table 5. The best results of recall of temporal segmentation methods received for every category of video

Results with the best RECALL	Pixel pair differences		Likelihood ratio method		Histogram differences		Twin threshold comparison	
	R	P	R	P	R	P	R	P
TV Talk-Show	1.00	1.00	1.00	0. 90	1.00	1.00	1.00	0.66
Documentary Video	0.87	0.09	0.98	0.08	0.89	0.75	1.00	0.19
Animal Video	0.88	0.06	1.00	0.04	0.96	0.66	1.00	0.25
Adventure Video	1.00	0.04	1.00	0.03	0.92	0.67	0.97	0.30
POP Music Video	0.95	0.17	0.85	0.86	0.65	0.74	0.88	0.47

5.2   Best Results of Precision

In the case of precision the highest values of recall have been obtained using the histogram difference method. Notice, however, that the more dynamic editing style of video, the lower the value of recall. For the adventure video and music video the value of recall is not acceptable (only 0.05 and 0.01).

Table 6. The best results of precision of temporal segmentation methods received for every category of video

Results with the best PRECISION	Pixel pair differences		Likelihood ratio method		Histogram differences		Twin threshold comparison	
	R	P	R	P	R	P	R	P
TV Talk-Show	1.00	1.00	0.82	0.98	1.00	1.00	0.90	0.89
Documentary Video	0.85	1.00	0.85	1.00	0.64	1.00	0.72	0.86
Animal Video	0.32	1.00	0.88	0.90	0.53	1.00	0.46	0.76
Adventure Video	0.53	0.80	0.78	0.76	0.05	1.00	0.31	0.75
POP Music Video	0.67	1.00	0.85	0.90	0.01	1.00	0.10	0.85

Generally, when we like to receive the best values of the recall ratio, the twin threshold comparison method is recommended. The histogram difference method leads to the best values of the precision ration.

6 Precision Improvements

The effectiveness of the shot detection methods may be improved when the specificity of a given movie category is taken into account. It was observed that the lengths of shots vary in different movie categories. The more dynamic the movie and the wider the framing, the shorter the shots are, the more static the content and narrower the framing, the longer the shots are. The main assumption for further software improvements is that shots are not shorter than one second in dynamic adventure movie and not shorter than two seconds in other categories of movies.

6.1 Faulty Shot Cuts Reduction in Adventure Movie

The recall of the segmentation process of an adventure movie using pixel pair differences technique was sufficiently high (0.93), but its precision, for example with parameters 30 and 50 (Tab. 1), was rather not satisfactory (0.69). It was due to the fact that in the adventure movie the movie action is very dynamic. As it was already mentioned in such movies we observe dynamic camera movements, also dynamic object movements on the scene, rich colors, contrast quickly changing, changing light, and many effects. This specificity promotes the detection of faulty shot cuts or cross dissolve effects.

Shots in an adventure movie are very short but practically not shorter than one second. So, the first procedure implemented to improve the precision was the filtering of shots detected during the segmentation process. All shots shorter than one second have been not accepted. It leads to the significant increase of precision (from 0.69 to 0.95) with rather negligible decrease of recall (from 0.93 to 0.89).

Table 7. Comparison of the effectiveness of shot cuts detection without and with additional filtering for minimal length of shots equal to one second in temporal segmentation process based on pixel pair differences technique

Cuts				Effectiveness	
C	CC	OC	FC	R	P
Without filtering					
132	91	7	41	0.93	0.69
With additional filtering					
92	87	11	5	0.89	0.95

6.2 Faulty Shot Cuts and Cross Dissolves Reduction in Documentary Video

The recall of the segmentation process of a documentary video using twin threshold comparison technique was very high (0.98), but its precision, for example with parameters 5 and 20 (Tab. 4), was relatively low (0.50).

Shots in a documentary video are not so short as in the case of adventure movies. Therefore, in the procedure implemented to improve the precision only shots longer than two second have been accepted. It also leads to the significant increase of precision (from 0.50 to 0.94) with rather slight decrease of recall (from 0.98 to 0.96).

Table 8. Comparison of the effectiveness of shot cuts and cross dissolve detection without and with additional filtering for minimal length of shots and dissolve equal to two second in temporal segmentation process based on twin threshold comparison technique

Cuts				Cut detection effectiveness		Cross dissolve effects				Cross dissolve detection effectiveness	
C	CC	OC	FC	R	P	D	CD	OD	FD	R	P
Without filtering											
56	44	1	12	0.98	0.79	47	8	0	39	1.00	0.17
With additional filtering											
45	43	2	2	0.96	0.96	9	8	0	1	1.00	0.89

The increase of precision of cut detection is significant (from 0.79 to 0.96), but what is much more surprising the increase of precision of cross dissolve detection is extremely high (from 0.17 to 0.89).

6.3   Faulty Shot Cuts in Animal Video

The recall of the segmentation process of an animal video using likelihood ratio method was sufficiently high (0.96), its precision, for example with blocks 8x6 and parameters 2, 40 (Tab. 2), was quiet good (0.79).

The likelihood ratio method enables us to detect only shot cuts. Nevertheless, cross dissolves are rare in an animal video. To speed the computing time the binary algorithm has been implemented to find an adequate frame. In the binary algorithm the step of 16 frame was applied. Such a procedure led not only to the increase of the precision (from 0.79 to 0.97) without changing the recall but also to the significant diminution of computing time (eight times).

Table 9. Comparison of the effectiveness of shot cuts detection without and with additional filtering in temporal segmentation process based on likelihood ratio method

Cuts				Cross dissolve effects				Effectiveness of cut and cross dissolve detection		Processing time
C	CC	OC	FC	D	CD	OD	FD	R	P	PT
Without filtering										
82	65	1	17	0	0	2	0	0.96	0.79	12:08
With additional filtering										
67	65	1	2	0	0	2	0	0.96	0.97	1:33

6.4   Faulty Shot Cuts in Documentary Video

The same change in cut detection procedure has been implemented to documentary video category tested by histogram difference method.

The histogram difference method enables us to detect only shot cuts. Nevertheless, cross dissolves are rare in an animal video. To speed the computing time the binary algorithm has been implemented to find an adequate frame. In the binary algorithm the step of 16 frame was applied. Such a procedure led not only to the increase of the precision (from 0.75 to 0.92) without changing the recall but also to the significant diminution of computing time (even ten times).

Table 10. Comparison of the effectiveness of shot cuts detection without and with additional filtering in temporal segmentation process based on histogram difference method

Cuts				Cross dissolve effects				Effectiveness of cut and cross dissolve detection		Processing time
C	**CC**	**OC**	**FC**	**D**	**CD**	**OD**	**FD**	**R**	**P**	**PT**
Without filtering										
60	44	1	16	3	3	5	0	0.89	0.75	4:07
With additional filtering										
48	44	1	4	3	3	5	0	0.89	0.92	0:25

7 Conclusions

The temporal segmentation process leads to the partition of a given video into a set of meaningful and individually manageable segments, which then can serve as basic units for indexing. Video has temporal properties such as camera motion, object movements on the scene, sequential composition, and interframe relationships. An effective segmentation technique is able to detect not only abrupt changes but also gradual scene changes, such as fade and dissolve transitions.

The nature of movies, mainly the style of video editing has an influence on the effectiveness of temporal segmentation methods. In the experiments and tests performed the effectiveness of four methods was analyzed for five different categories of movie: TV talk-show, documentary movie, animal video, action & adventure, and pop music video. The cuts have been recognized as well as cross dissolve effects.

The tests have shown that the specific nature of the style of video editing for different video categories has an important influence on the effectiveness of temporal segmentation methods, fundamental methods of video indexing. Taking into account these specific features for different movie categories we can significantly reduce the number of faulty detected cuts and faulty detected cross dissolves effects.

The tests have been performed using the Automatic Video Indexer software. The Automatic Video Indexer AVI [10] is a research project investigating tools and techniques of automatic video indexing, mainly based on automatic content analysis for retrieval systems. The main goal of the project is to develop efficient techniques of content-based video indexing and retrieval, such as temporal segmentation of videos, key-frames selection, shot analysis and clustering, shot retrieving, repetitive editing pattern identification [9].

Two main modules have been already implemented in the Automatic Video Indexer: the Automatic Shot Detector ASD responsible for temporal segmentation as well as for shot categorization and the Automatic Scene Analyzer ASA responsible for shot clustering, scene detection, and content analysis of scenes. The next parts of the AVI software will classify scenes and will detect important events and people in videos. The automatic extraction of the most interesting highlights in videos will facilitate browsing and retrieval of video.

Content-based indexing and retrieval of videos is all the time a research topic of increasing importance, sometimes difficult but surely fascinating. It is a scientific problem as well as practical task leading to the development and to the application of efficient methods of organization, indexing, browsing, and retrieval of videos in archives using high-level semantic features.

References

1. Barbu, T.: Novel automatic video cut detection technique using Gabor filtering. Computers and Electrical Engineering 35, 712–721 (2009)
2. Bertini, M., Del Bimbo, A., Pala, P.: Content-based indexing and retrieval of TV news. Pattern Recognition Letters 22, 503–516 (2001)
3. Chasanis, V., Likas, A., Galatsanos, N.: Simultaneous detection of abrupt cuts and dissolves in videos using support vector machines. Pattern Recognition Letters 30, 55–65 (2009)
4. Chena, L.-H., Laib, Y.-C., Liaoc, H.-Y.M.: Movie scene segmentation using background information. Pattern Recognition 41, 1056–1065 (2008)
5. Cheong, L.-F.: Scene-based shot change detection and comparative evaluation. Computer Vision and Image Understanding 79, 224–235 (2000)
6. Choroś, K., Gonet, M.: Effectiveness of video segmentation techniques for different categories of videos. In: Zgrzywa, A., et al. (eds.) New Trends in Multimedia and Network Information Systems, pp. 34–45. IOS Press, Amsterdam (2008)
7. Choroś, K.: Cross dissolve detection in a temporal segmentation process for digital video indexing and retrieval. In: Grzech, A., et al. (eds.) Information Systems Architecture and Technology: Information Systems and Computer Communication Networks, pp. 189–200. Oficyna Wydawnicza Politechniki Wrocławskiej, Wrocław (2008)
8. Choroś, K.: Video shot selection and content-based scene detection for automatic classification of TV sports news. In: Tkacz, E., Kapczynski, A. (eds.) Internet – Technical Development and Applications. AISC, vol. 64, pp. 73–80. Springer, Heidelberg (2009)
9. Choroś, K., Pawlaczyk, P.: Content-based scene detection and analysis method for automatic classification of TV sports news. In: Szczuka, M., Kryszkiewicz, M., Ramanna, S., Jensen, R., Hu, Q. (eds.) RSCTC 2010. LNCS (LNAI), vol. 6086, pp. 120–129. Springer, Heidelberg (2010)
10. Choroś, K.: Video structure analysis and content-based indexing in the Automatic Video Indexer AVI. In: Nguyen, N.T., Zgrzywa, A., Czyżewski, A. (eds.) Advances in Multimedia and Network Information System Technologies. AISC, vol. 80, pp. 79–90. Springer, Heidelberg (2010)
11. Del Bimbo, A.: Visual Information Retrieval. Morgan Kaufmann Publishers, San Francisco (1999)
12. Jung, K., Kim, K.I., Jain, K.A.: Text information extraction in images and video: a survey. Pattern Recognition 37, 977–997 (2004)
13. Koprinska, I., Carrato, S.: Temporal video segmentation: A survey. Signal Processing: Image Communication 16, 477–500 (2001)
14. Küçüktunç, O., Güdükbay, U., Ulusoy, Ö.: Fuzzy color histogram-based video segmentation. Computer Vision and Image Understanding 114, 125–134 (2010)

15. Lefèvre, S., Holler, K., Vincent, N.: A review of real-time segmentation of uncompressed video sequences for content-based search and retrieval. Real-Time Imaging 9, 73–98 (2003)
16. Lew, M.S., Sebe, N., Gardner, P.C.: Principles of visual information retrieval. Springer, London (2001)
17. Lew, M.S., et al.: Content-based multimedia information retrieval: state of the art and challenges. ACM Transactions on Multimedia Computing, Communications, and Applications 2, 1–19 (2006)
18. Money, A.G., Agius, H.: Video summarisation: A conceptual framework and survey of the state of the art. J. of Visual Communication and Image Representation 19, 121–143 (2008)
19. Porter, S., Mirmehdi, M., Thomas, B.: Temporal video segmentation and classification of edit effects. Image and Vision Computing 21, 1097–1106 (2003)
20. Smeaton, A.F., Browne, P.: A usage study of retrieval modalities for video shot retrieval. Information Processing and Management 42, 1330–1344 (2006)
21. Smeaton, A.F.: Techniques used and open challenges to the analysis, indexing and retrieval of digital video. Information Systems 32, 545–559 (2007)
22. Yu, J., Srinath, M.D.: An efficient method for scene cut detection. Pattern Recognition Letters 22, 1379–1391 (2001)

Using Knowledge Integration Techniques for User Profile Adaptation Method in Document Retrieval Systems

Bernadetta Mianowska and Ngoc Thanh Nguyen

Wroclaw University of Technology,
Wyb. Wyspianskiego 27, 50-370 Wroclaw, Poland
Bernadetta.Mianowska@pwr.wroc.pl
Ngoc-Thanh.Nguyen@pwr.edu.pl

Abstract. Knowledge integration is a very important and useful technique to combine information from different sources and different formats. In the Information Retrieval field, integration of knowledge can be understood in many ways. In this paper a method of user personalization in information retrieval using integration technique is presented. As user delivers new knowledge about himself, this knowledge should be integrated with previous knowledge contained in the user profile. Our proposed method is analyzed in terms of integration postulates. A list of desirable properties of this method and its proofs are presented. Simulated experimental evaluation has shown that proposed method is effective and the updated profile is proper since it is closer and closer to the user preferences.

Keywords: knowledge integration postulates, user profile adaptation.

1 Introduction

Knowledge integration is used very often for user personalization in information retrieval systems. Information about user interests, habits, preferences, etc. can change with in time. In many systems user profiles are built to formalize this knowledge about the user. A problem arises when users' interests are changing and the system needs to have up-to-date information. New knowledge should be joined with the previous knowledge. In this context, a user profile adaptation method can be treated as a kind of integration of knowledge about the user. Integrated knowledge about the user should satisfy a set of requirements to keep the consistency of knowledge state. In particular, the following intuitive postulates derived from standard integration postulates should be met: when user starts to be interested in some concepts, the importance of these concepts should increase in user profile, when user is not interested in some terms, these terms should be forgotten with time [11].

Nowadays, the problem of knowledge integration is getting more important because there exist many knowledge sources that cannot be unified in a simple way.

In information retrieval domain this problem is even more visible regarding the following aspects: information obtained from different search engines has different formats - then the integration process is connected with merging the structures, and it

N.T. Nguyen (Ed.): Transactions on CCI V, LNCS 6910, pp. 140–156, 2011.

often happens that they have different semantics, thus some inconsistency between them can appear.

Knowledge integration can be understood in many ways. On the most general level, knowledge integration is defined in [22] as "the task of creating a new piece of knowledge on the basis of other different pieces of knowledge". This task is connected with data inconsistency problem – in these terms integration processes can be treated in two ways: integration of different knowledge bases and integration of different knowledge representations but on different levels of representation. A more popular approach is to add new knowledge to the previous knowledge in such way that the updated knowledge base is still consistent.

The aim of this paper is to check if desirable properties of the proposed method of integrating the previous knowledge included in user profile with the new knowledge delivered to the system by user activity observations are satisfied. Several intuitive properties are proposed and their proofs are presented. To find out whether a developed system of user profiling is effective in term of distance measure between user preferences and adapted user profile, experimental evaluation has been done.

The paper is organized as follows: in Section 2 we present the related works connected with knowledge integration in different approaches. Section 3 describes the way of integrating new knowledge about the user with the previous knowledge. In Section 4 we analyze several properties of the method in term of integration knowledge postulates. Experimental evaluation and results are contained in Section 5. In the last Section conclusions and future works are presented.

2 Related Works

Integration processes are required in any system where there is more than one source of information. Knowledge integration is used in many domains such as multiagent systems. In this process agents have different observations and in order to communicate and cooperate they need to establish the same consistent knowledge state [22]. Authors of [28] propose also integration in law domain to support decision making processes.

Aamodt and Nygard [1] present the integration problem in the context of data, information and knowledge level in computer-based decision support system. They define these concepts in the context of decision making as follows:

- Data are syntactic entities - patterns with no meaning; they are input to an interpretation process, i.e. to the initial step of decision making;
- Information is interpreted data - data with meaning; it is the output from data interpretation as well as the input to, and output from, the knowledge-based process of decision making;
- Knowledge is learned information - information incorporated in an agent's reasoning resources, and made ready for active use within a decision process; it is the output of a learning process.

They also indicate the role of knowledge: to play the active part in the processes of transforming data into information, deriving other information and acquiring new knowledge - i.e. to learn. The paper presents a few case-based approaches to integration data, information and knowledge.

Brewka and Eiter [5] present the application of integration on information level to knowledge mediation. They claim that mediation of data and knowledge, which provides services on an abstract level, go far beyond technical aspects of integration and should take into account different aspects such as situation awareness, social context and goals of a user.

Knowledge management also applied integration techniques to obtain more information [2, 7, 12]. Huge heterogeneity of knowledge sources coming from the system and from people is the main problem in this area. A similar approach is presented in [23] where explicit and tacit knowledge is joined. Tacit knowledge includes the beliefs, perspectives and mental models so ingrained in a person's mind that they are taken for granted. On the other hand, explicit knowledge is "knowledge that can be expressed formally using a system of language, symbols, rules, objects, or equations, and can thus be communicated to others; it consists of quantifiable data, written procedures, universal principles, mathematical models, etc". Integration in this terms can be treated as formalization of tacit knowledge.

Merugu and Ghosh [15] consider integration of knowledge coming from many heterogeneous data sources in the term of probabilistic model. They provide a mathematical formulation of the model integration problem using the maximum likelihood and maximum entropy principles and describe iterative algorithms that are necessary to converge to the optimal solution. The empirical results for various learning tasks such as clustering and classification of different kinds of datasets consisting of continuous vector, categorical and directional attributes show that high quality global models can be obtained without much loss of privacy. Privacy in this context is connected with his own data source distributions. Integration process is divided into two subproblems: learning probabilistic models from the local data while adhering to information-theoretic privacy constraints and integrating the local models effectively to obtain an appropriate "global" model. This separation of privacy and integration issues also allows the individual parties to use their own means of sanitizing the local models during the local learning process.

In many cases knowledge integration can be considered on the structural and semantic levels. This problem is more precisely defined using particular structure of knowledge but there still remains problem on the semantic level. The most popular integration on the structure level are trees, for example XML and DTD integrations [4, 13].

A similar approach of knowledge integration is presented in the terms of classification problem and taxonomy integration [29]. The Rocchio algorithm [25] and the Naïve Bayes algorithm [20] have been applied to the ontology mapping problem. Ontology-based knowledge integration is also presented by Chen [6]. Ontology integration includes two phases: ontology mapping and ontology merging. In the ontology integration, ontology mapping is used initially to identify similar knowledge concepts between local ontology and global ontology, and then to become a newly integrated global ontology through ontology merging.

Another interpretation of knowledge integration is presented in [3] where knowledge integration is applied to customer recommendation. An integrative model for better predictions and classifications is proposed. It efficiently combines the currently-in-use statistical and artificial intelligence models, e.g. by integrating the models such as association rule, frequency matrix and tree-based models. The results of the experiments show that the performance of integrated model is superior the other one.

In information retrieval domain, knowledge integration is also very useful technique [8]. Suzuki et al. [26] propose integration of results' list obtained from different search engines. The position of result in every list is taken into account in modified Shannon measure. As a result they prepare final list of results to present to the user. Ding [10] presents a method of metadata integration in digital libraries environment in which different library have different formats of metadata. Heterogeneity of source descriptions is the main difficulty to realize integration process.

Riano et al. [24] propose the model of knowledge management coming from the Internet. They also claim that the main problem of integration in such heterogeneous environment is that knowledge is not always easily expressed in terms of a formal representation language (tacit knowledge).

Our researches are connected with personalization in information retrieval systems. Our previous works present the personalization of information searching domain in the context of agent-based Personal Assistant [16, 17]. A model of user profile and an adaptation method have been proposed in [19]. Due to the fact that experimental validation of our algorithms will take a long time, we decided to prepare the simulation environment, in particular to simulate user behaviour in information retrieval tasks. The algorithm for judging if the obtained document is relevant to the user query and his information needs was proposed in [18]. Based on the information about user interests and his activities in the system we try to keep his profile up-to-date. As a result in some fixed period of time the profile is updated. The main aim of profile adaptation method is to decrease the distance between user profile and his preferences in subsequent adaptation steps. Preliminary experimental evaluations have shown that proposed methods are effective in this case.

The next part of researches refers to formal analysis of developed method, especially the important task is to show that when we have a new information about the user (from his activity observation) we can integrate it with the knowledge obtained previously and the result of the integration process is better (built profile is closer to real user interests).

In this paper knowledge integration is understood as a task of combining new knowledge about user activities with the previous one, saved in his profile. In user personalization domain knowledge integration is important during gathering information about user interests, habits, etc. Information about user can be divided into two parts: the first one connected with his preferences (usually obtained in indirect way from the user) and the second – usage data – information about user activities (in this case, list of documents that were useful for the user). Combining these pieces of information in user profile is important task to keep up-to-date knowledge about the user. This new knowledge can be treated as tacit knowledge defined in [23] that should be formalized and added to the existing knowledge state in user profile.

3 Knowledge Integration in User Profile Building

In this section we present the knowledge integration process in the case of building user profile in information retrieval domain. The document representation, user profile structure and a method of knowledge integration are presented. When a user is active in the system, his profile is built and updated according to the proposed method of integrating new knowledge about the user with previous knowledge contained in user profile.

3.1 Document Representation

We assume the following representation of document: each document is described by its title and a set of complex terms (here called 'appellations'):

$$d = (tit, \{a_1, a_2, ..., a_L\}) \tag{1}$$

where *tit* is the title of the book and L is the number of appellations for considered document and each appellation is constructed as follows:

$$a_l = (a_m^l, a_{wg}^l, a_{wh}^l, a_s^l) \text{ for } l \in \{1, ..., L\} \tag{2}$$

and $a_m^l, a_{wg}^l, a_{wh}^l, a_s^l$ are respectively: the main term (with different wording but with the same meaning), sets of broader terms, narrower terms and correlated terms ("see also"). Correlated terms are often used to mark that these terms can be loosely connected with the main term but this relationship is not as strong as synonym. Selected documents may have some of these terms undefined.

The most important terms are those in the set of main terms – they are the most fitted keywords that describe the document. The rest of terms (broader, narrower and correlated) are also useful – they help to place the right meaning of the main term, especially when the main term is ambiguous.

An exemplary document is presented as follows:

Title: *Algorithms and data structures: selected issues*
Authors: *Zbigniew J. Czech, Sebastian Deorowicz, Piotr Fabian*
Description: *Algorithms – handbook*
                 Data Structures – handbook
                 Discrete Mathematics

Algorithms, *Data Structure* and *Discrete Mathematics* are basic complex terms (some additional specification is added like "*handbook*" to specify that this is a handbook about algorithms and data structures). The appellation "*Data Structure*" has the following form:

$a_m = \{Data\ transforming,\ Data\ organization\}$;
$a_{wg} = \{Computer\ science,\ Databases,\ Files\}$;
$a_{wh} = \{Abstract\ data\ types,\ Data\}$;
$a_s = \{Data\ transformation\}$.

3.2 User Profile

According to Danilowicz [9] a profile of a user is understood as the representation of his (her) information needs, which are assumed to be relatively stable in some period of time. In traditional information retrieval systems, a user expresses his (her) temporary information needs only by means of queries, which often are insufficient to establish the relevance degree of documents in a database. Experiments have proved that different users may expect different answers for the same query, and the same user for the same query may expect different answers in different periods of time. This means that the information preferences (or profile) of a user should be changeable in retrieval processes [21]. It implies that the abilities of creation and modification of user profiles should be the most important feature of an information agent.

As presented in our previous work [19] the user profile can be presented as a tree structure – acyclic and coherent graph $G = (V, E)$, where V is a set of nodes containing the vector of weighted terms describing concepts with their synonyms and a time stamps when the user was interested in those concepts for the last time. The E is a set of edges representing "is a" relation between two nodes taken from WordNet ontology [27]. If two nodes v_1 and v_2 are connected by edges $e(v_1,v_2)$, it means that concept from node v_2 is a kind of concept in node v_1. Terms contained in the same concepts are synonyms. Figure 1 presents an example of user profile structure.

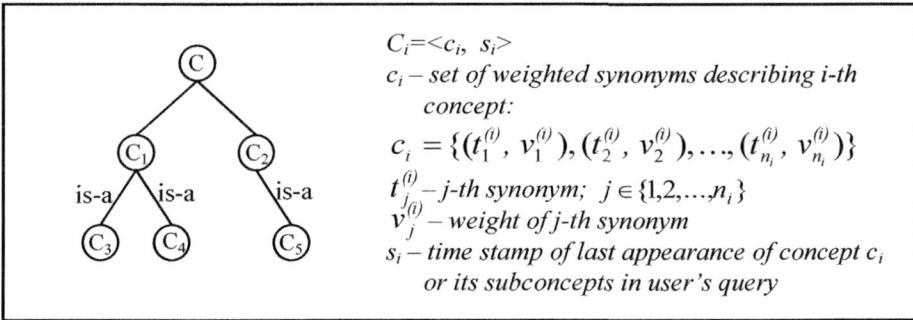

Fig. 1. Structure of user profile

The root of this tree is not a concept in WordNet meaning but only an artificial node. The nodes of the first level (roots' children) are the main areas of user interests or concepts connected with them. The profile of the user with many different interests will be broad (many children of the root) and the deeper the user profile is, the more specialized information about the user the system will have.

The terms in the user profile are obtained from users' queries. Term in this context means a word or a few words used by the user to express his information needs. The intuition in this situation is that if the user is asking about some information, he is interested in it and even if there are other terms connected with users' ones, it is not obvious that the user is interested also in those additional terms.

The procedure of building the profile structure assumes that when a new term occurs in user queries, it is added to the user profile to the proper place e.g. when a new term is a hypernym term of a term in user profile, this new term is added as a descendant of existing term in user profile. The timestamps of appropriate concepts are also added or actualized.

3.3 User Profile Adaptation

The main objective of building the user profile is to integrate all facts and figures of the user, including the newly gathered information (knowledge) and the knowledge accumulated in the previous version of the profile.

The integration process can be considered on two different levels: structural when new term is added or deleted (this situation is described above) and on the level of terms and theirs weights. When the user enters a few queries and selects the relevant documents from the obtained results, his profile should be adapted according to the new knowledge about his interests. If user queries contain terms that were previously in his profile, its weight should be updated and if a new term, that was not used before, occurs in user query, then the term should be added to the user profile at the appropriate place and its weight is calculated using the proposed procedure.

User information retrieval process (e.g. entering the queries, obtaining the results and selecting the needed documents) is divided into sessions. A session is set of user activities from login to logout of the system. In every session user submits a few queries and to each query he obtains a list of documents. In practical information retrieval system user chooses the documents that are relevant to his information needs. Each document is described by the title and a set of appellations. In our system, after each session for each term, the mean value of its weights is calculated.

- Documents set from a single session with appropriate query:

$$D(s) = \{(q_i^{(s)}, d_{i_j}^{(s)})\} \tag{3}$$

where s is session's number, i is query's number and i_j is a number of documents relevant to query $q_i^{(s)}$;

- Weight of t_j-th term after s-th session:

$$w_d^{(s)}(t_j) = \frac{1}{n_s} \sum_{i=1}^{n_s} w_{d_i}^{(s)}(t_j) \tag{4}$$

where $w_d^{(s)}(t_j)$ is average value of weights in documents set and $w_{d_i}^{(s)}(t_j)$ is weight of term in single document in current session.

The main objective of calculated above values is to get know if the user is interested in a particular term and if (and in what way) his interests are changing. The most popular measure of interest change is calculating the difference between previous and current values of interest level (weights calculated using formula (4)). In a normalized interval a big value of this difference can mean that user dramatically changes his preferences while it is not obvious that small changes mean the small changes of interests, e.g. the difference equal to 0.1 in the case when current weight is 0.7 ($w_d^{(s)}(t_j) = 0.7$) and previous weight $w_d^{(s)}(t_j)$ was equal to 0.6 has different meaning then in the case when the current weight is 0.2 and previous one was 0.1. Due to this fact we propose a measure of relative change of user interests between the sessions.

- Relative change of user interests in term t_j after the session s:

$$\Delta w_{t_j}(s) = \begin{cases} \dfrac{w_{d_i}^{(s)}(t_j) - w_{d_i}^{(s-1)}(t_j)}{w_{d_i}^{(s-1)}(t_j)}, & \text{if } w_{d_i}^{(s-1)}(t_j) > 0 \\ w_{d_i}^{(s)}(t_j), & \text{otherwise} \end{cases} \tag{5}$$

where $w_{d_i}^{(s)}(t_j)$ is a weight of term t_j after current session and $w_{d_i}^{(s-1)}(t_j)$ is a weight of term t_j after previous session.

Using the measure proposed in formula (6), the system can differentiate two cases described above: when the previous weight was 0.6 and current equals to 0.7 system know that user is still interested in this term while in the second case (previous weight = 0.1 and current weight = 0.2) the relative change is high (equals to 1) what can mean that level of user interests in this term is significantly greater. The disadvantage of this measure is that its values are not normalized.

The knowledge obtained using proposed method is a base to keep the user profile up-to-date. The relative changes of user interests in each term from user queries have influence on the adaptation in knowledge integration process.

The new weight of term t_j in user profile in the session $s+1$ is calculated as follows:

$$w_{t_j}(s+1) = \alpha \cdot w_{t_j}(s) + (1-\alpha) \cdot \left(\frac{A}{1 + \exp(-B \cdot \Delta w_{t_j}(s) + C)} \right) \tag{6}$$

where $w_{t_j}(s+1)$ is weight of term t_l in user profile in session $s+1$; A, B, C and $\alpha \in [0, 1]$ are parameters that should be attuned in experimental evaluation.

In the next section the intuitive postulates of knowledge integration are analyzed and proofs of the required properties are presented.

3.4 Example

Let consider the following example of user query (simplifying to conjunction of the keywords) "*theory* AND *knowledge* AND *learning*". The results obtained in the data-base of Main Library of Wroclaw University of Technology are gathered in Table 1.

Based on the series of user queries and results that user has treated as relevant, the procedure of building the profile and updating it is applied. An example of weights values for term "*theory*" has been considered. This term was absent in user queries in the first and second blocks of sessions and in the third block term "*theory*" has appeared and till the end of presented blocks interval, user was interested in this term.

Table 1. A sample of user query and results

User query	Description of documents obtained for query

theory
 AND
 knowledge
 AND
 learning
	Title: Futures thinking, learning, and leading: applying multiple intelligences
	 to success and innovation
	 Authors: Irving H. Buchen.
	 Description: *Cultural pluralism in the work*
	                 Knowledge Management
	                 Organization of self-learning

	Title: The theory of organizational changes in the companies of the
	 information age (some aspects and tools)
	 Author: Kazimierz Krupa.
	 Description: *Organizational innovations – management*
	                 Organization of self-learning
	                 Knowledge management - Information systems

The values of term weights in user profile obtained in the process of integration new knowledge about user activity and previous knowledge saved in user profile in the subsequent steps of updating are collected in Fig. 2.

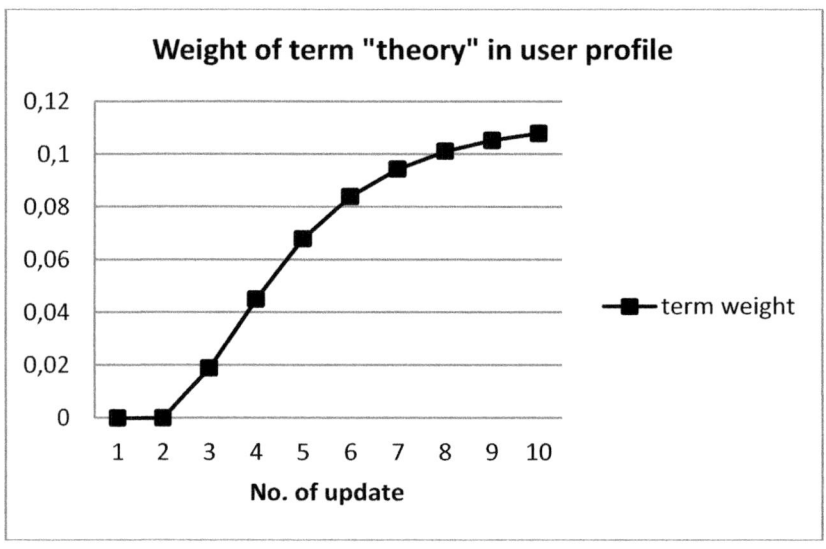

Fig. 2. Weights of single term in user profile in 10 subsequent profile updates

When the term was not used by the user, its weight was equal to 0 and then user started to search for this term and till the 10th block of sessions he was interested in it. Through the blocks no. 3 – 6, weight of this term is increasing because the user was interested in this term, while after the 7th block, weight is not growing so fast. The reason of this situation is that user was not using this term in his queries frequently, but still he was interested in this term. If he would like to use the term *"theory"* in his further queries more frequently, the weight would increase and when the user would not use it any more the weight would decrease in further blocks of sessions.

4   Properties Analysis

For the proposed model of user profile, some intuitive properties of adaptive functions that satisfy knowledge integration postulates were found to be true. Below we present the formal descriptions and proofs of them (weights are connected with only one term so the argument will be omitted to clarify notation):

Property 1: *When a new term occurs in user queries, then the weight of this term in the user profile should increase. In other words, increase of user interests should implicate increase of appropriate weight in user profile, i.e.*

$$\text{If } w_{d_i}^{(s-1)} = 0 \text{ and } w_{d_i}^{(s)} \neq 0, \text{ then } w(s+1) > w(s).$$

Proof

Let assume that function f is an updating component of function (eq. (6)) connected with the relative change of user interests (called updating function):

$$f(\Delta w_{t_l}(s)) = \frac{A}{1 + \exp(-B \cdot \Delta w_{t_l}(s) + C)} \tag{7}$$

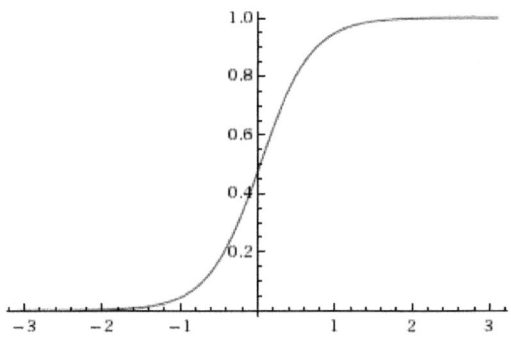

Fig. 3. The plot of updating function component f connected with relative change of user interests (eq. 8), parameters' values: $A=1$; $B=3$ and $C=-0,3$

This updating function contains some parameters that have influence to the update process. During previous experiments those parameters were attuned with the following values: $A=1$; $B=3$ and $C=-0,3$. The plot of this function is presented in Figure 3. For the purpose of properties analysis those values of parameters will be assumed.

If a term has not occurred in previous session, its weight equals zero:

$$w_{d_i}^{(s-1)} = 0$$

and in current session this term occurs so its weight is greater than zero:

$$w_{d_i}^{(s)} > 0$$

then relative change is also greater than zero:

$$\Delta w_{t_j}(s) = w_{d_i}^{(s)} > 0.$$

The value of t_j-th term in user profile in next session will be calculated using formula (7). The result – weight of considered term will be greater than zero:

$$w_{t_j}(s+1) = (1-\alpha) \cdot \left(\frac{A}{1+\exp(-B \cdot w_{d_i}^{(s)} + C)} \right) > 0$$

This means that weight of the term increases in user profile when this term occurs in user interests (and user queries). ∎

Property 2: *When user is very interested in a term during more blocks of sessions, the weight of this term should not change too much. In other words, a small change of user interests in one term between two blocks should implicate a small change of weight of this term in user profile, i.e.*

If $w_{d_i}^{(s-1)} >> 0$ ($w_{d_i}^{(s-1)} \cong f(0)$) *and* $w_{d_i}^{(s)} \cong w_{d_i}^{(s-1)}$, *then* $w(s+1) \cong w(s)$.

Proof

If user has been interested in term in previous blocks of sessions, the weight of this term was significantly greater than zero (its value was comparable with the value of updating component function f at the point zero):

$$w_{d_i}^{(s-1)} >> 0 \text{ and } w_{d_i}^{(s-1)} \cong f(0)$$

and in current block he is still interested in this term, i.e. an interests degree of this term is approximately the same as in previous blocks:

$$w_{d_i}^{(s)} \cong w_{d_i}^{(s-1)}$$

then relative change of weight is close to zero:

$$\Delta w_{t_j}(s) \cong 0.$$

We should check if the difference between weight values in user profile in two sequent sessions is also close to 0. We check if the following formula is met:

$$w(s+1) - w(s) \cong 0 \tag{8}$$

Using formula (6), we should check if:

$$(\alpha-1) \cdot w_{t_j}(s) + (1-\alpha) \cdot \left(\frac{A}{1+\exp(-B \cdot \Delta w_{t_j}(s) + C)} \right) = 0 \tag{9}$$

After some simple transformations of eq. (9), we have:

$$(1-\alpha)\cdot w_{t_j}(s) = (1-\alpha)\cdot\left(\frac{A}{1+\exp(-B\cdot\Delta w_{t_j}(s)+C)}\right) \tag{10}$$

and calculating the weight of the term t_j we obtain the value that is approximately the same as value of updating component function f in the point zero:

$$w_{t_j}(s) = \left(\frac{A}{1+\exp(-B\cdot\Delta w_{t_j}(s)+C)}\right) \cong f(0) \tag{11}$$

We have obtained that term's weight is approximately equal to the value of updating component function f at point 0 (see eq. (7)). Therefore, the equation $w(s+1)\cong w(s)$ is satisfied. ■

Property 3: *When user is not interested in a term for a few blocks of sessions, weight of this term should slightly decrease with time (in subsequent moments of adaptation processes). In other words significant decrease of user interests connected with selected term should implicate decrease of weight value in user profile, i.e.*

$$\textit{If } w_{d_i}^{(s-1)} \neq 0 \textit{ and } w_{d_i}^{(s)} = 0, \textit{ then } w(s+1) < w(s).$$

Proof

If user has been interested in term and weight of this term was greater than zero:

$$w_{d_i}^{(s-1)} > 0$$

and in current session this term is not occurring in user queries (he is no more interested in this term at this moment)

$$w_{d_i}^{(s)} = 0,$$

then value of relative change calculated using formula (6) equals -1, i.e:

$$\Delta w_{t_j}(s) = \frac{0 - w_{d_i}^{(s-1)}(t_j)}{w_{d_i}^{(s-1)}(t_j)} = -1.$$

The value of k_l-*th* term in user profile in next session equals (according to eq. (6)):

$$w_{t_j}(s+1) = \alpha\cdot w_{t_j}(s) + (1-\alpha)\cdot\left(\frac{A}{1+\exp(B+C)}\right)$$

The new value of weight in user profile $w_{t_j}(s+1)$ is smaller than the previous one $w_{t_j}(s)$ because the value of update function component $f(-1)$ is close to 0 (compare Fig. 3.) and $\alpha\ll1$, so required inequality $w(s+1) < w(s)$ is satisfied. ■

Presented intuitive properties are expected and satisfy postulates of knowledge integration process.

5 Experimental Evaluation

To evaluate proposed method a series of experiment have been performed. The adaptation method is effective if the distance between current user preferences and built and updated profile is decreasing when the user uses the system (with the growing number of updated steps).

5.1 Data Set

Similarly as in our previous work [8] we use a set of documents obtained from The Main Library and Scientific Center in Wroclaw University of Technology [14]. The formal document representation was described in Subsection 3.1.

These database of documents contains over 160 000 books descriptions and the cardinality of appellations' set is close to 90 000. Description of each document (appellation) has at least one main term and usually a few broader, narrower or correlated terms.

5.2 User Behaviour Simulation

Performing the experimental evaluations in practical system would be a time-consuming process so we decide to prepare simulation environment. We propose a simulation of user behaviour in information retrieval situation instead of using real usage data. Such solution is better than using real user because we save time needed to perform such experiment. We assume that user has 10 weighted terms in his preferences and they change randomly from session to session. Session is defined as 5 user queries entered to the search engine. After each block of 10 sessions, one term with the lowest weight is replaced by a new one with randomly selected weight (weights are normalized).

Here we present the plan of experiment similar to the experiments performed and described in [19]:

1. Determine a domain and set of terms T that will be used in experiment. Determine user preferences *Pref*.
2. Generate a query q – select randomly 3 terms from user preferences set $\{t_1, t_2, ..., t_{10}\}$, set these terms in proper order according to decreasing weights and send query to search engine.
3. Get documents descriptions $d = (tit, \{a_1, a_2, ..., a_L\})$ from the returned list of results.
4. Calculate probabilities $P(d_i = rel \mid q)$ that retrieved document is relevant to user query using formula (12) for each document.
5. Mark documents that meet the condition $P(d_i = rel \mid q) \geq \rho; \rho \in (0;1)$ as 'relevant'; $D = \{d_1^{(s)}, d_2^{(s)}, ..., d_{n_s}^{(s)}\}$.

6. After 3 blocks of 10 sessions update the profile using adaptation method presented in equation (6).

7. Calculate the distance between user profile and user preferences using Euclidean distance between those two extended vectors.

Proposed adaptation method takes into account user queries and relevant documents from 3 blocks of sessions. In [18] we have proposed mechanism to judge the relevance of results obtained from search engine.

$$P(d_i = rel \mid q) = \frac{1}{j} \sum_j P(d_i = rel \mid q_j) = \frac{1}{j} \sum_j (\frac{1}{L} \sum_{l=1}^{L} v_j \cdot w(t_l)) \tag{12}$$

where:

- q_j is the j-th term from user query q

- $w(t_l)$ is a weight of term in l-th appellation of considered document; $l \in \{1, L\}$. The value of particular term depends on the importance of this term in appellation – these values are presented below:

$$w(t_l) = \begin{cases} 1 & \text{if } t_l \subset \{a_m^l, tit^l\} \\ 0.75 & \text{if } t_l \subset \{a_{wg}^l, a_{wh}^l\} \text{ AND } t_l \not\subset \{a_m^l, tit^l\} \\ 0.5 & \text{if } t_l \subset a_s^l \text{ AND } t_l \not\subset \{a_m^l, a_{wg}^l, a_{wh}^l, tit^l\} \\ 0 & \text{otherwise} \end{cases} \tag{13}$$

where $a_m^l, a_{wg}^l, a_{wh}^l, a_s^l$ are respectively: the main term (with different wording but with the same meaning), sets of broader terms, narrower terms and correlated terms ("see also").

The interpretation of presented formula (12) is the probability that considered document is relevant to the user query is a sum of probabilities that this document is relevant to each of query terms. Probability that document is relevant to a term can be calculated as a mean value of user interests v_j connected with this term multiplied by probability that the term occurs in the document description.

Documents with value of query-document relevance greater than assumed threshold are taken into account in adaptation process. In the first step of adaptation new profile for the user is created and in each update process, new knowledge is combined with previous profile.

5.3 Experimental Results

The goal of experiment was to show that user profile built and updated using proposed methods is getting closer to user preferences in subsequent steps. The obtained results were gathered in the following diagrams.

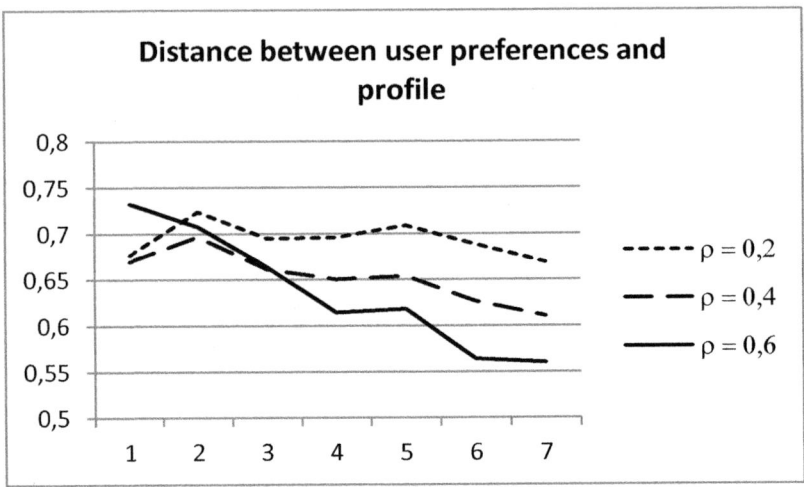

Fig. 4. Euclidean distance between user preferences and user profile updated 7 times

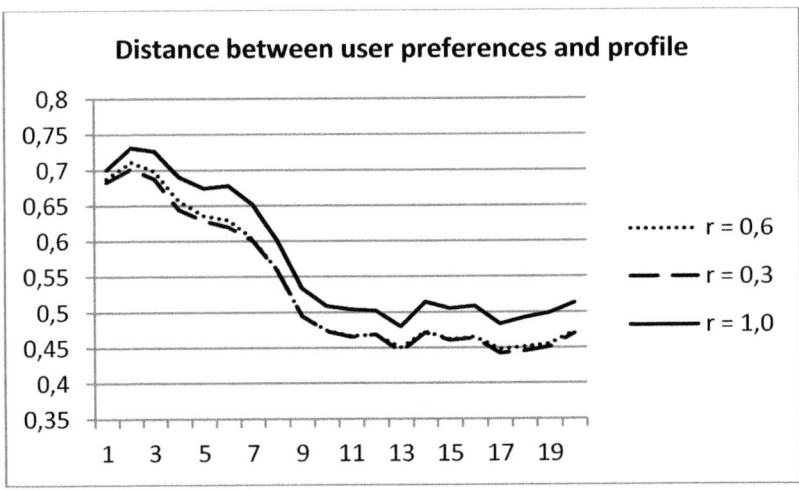

Fig. 5. Euclidean distance between user preferences and user profile updated 20 times

To check the quality of proposed method, updated user profile and user preferences are compared using extended Euclidean measure to appropriate weights. The results are presented in Fig. 4 and Fig. 5. for different values of relevance threshold ρ and different series of experiment. The distances between user preferences and updated profile become smaller with growing number of updates. At the beginning this distance can grow up because new terms are occurring in user profile but after a few block of session method of user profile adaptation seems to be effective (in mean of this measure user profile is getting closer to user preferences with a subsequent update processes). Comparing the results obtained for different relevance threshold values we can see that the greater value of threshold implies smaller distance between user profile and preferences so that the user profile is closer to user preferences. Some problems can occur when relevance threshold is greater (close to 1) because there can be no documents with such big relevance value. In the longer horizons, the difference between user preferences and user profile is decreasing and after some update steps, this distance is not decreasing so fast. It can mean that user profile is fitted to the current user preferences that were not changing dramatically in a few last blocks of sessions.

6 Conclusion Remarks and Future Works

In this paper we have presented a method of knowledge integration gathered in user profile with new knowledge obtained from user activity observations. The postulates of integration process have been presented and expected properties of presented adaptation method were proved for a single term of user interests. Performed experiments show that in an overall approach using presented method of adapting user profile can estimate user preferences.

In future works adaptation method should be formally analyzed in terms of convergence of built and updated user profile to user preferences.

Acknowledgments. This research was partially supported by European Union within European Social Fund under the fellowship and by Polish Ministry of Science and Higher Education under grant no. N N519 407437 (2009-2012).

References

1. Aamodt, A., Nygard, M.: Different roles and mutual dependencies of data, information, and knowledge - An AI perspective on their integration. Data & Knowledge Engineering 16, 191–222 (1995)
2. Abecker, A., Decker, S.: Organizational Memory: Knowledge Acquisition, Integration, and Retrieval Issues. In: Puppe, F. (ed.) XPS 1999. LNCS (LNAI), vol. 1570, pp. 113–124. Springer, Heidelberg (1999)
3. Bae, J.K., Kim, J.: Integration of heterogeneous models to predict consumer behavior. Expert Systems with Applications 37, 1821–1826 (2010)
4. Barthelemy, J.P.: The Median Procedure for n-Trees. Journal of Classification 3, 329–334 (1986)
5. Brewka, G., Eiter, T.: From Data Integration towards Knowledge Mediation. In: Erdem, E., Lin, F., Schaub, T. (eds.) LPNMR 2009. LNCS, vol. 5753, pp. 610–612. Springer, Heidelberg (2009)
6. Chen, Y.J.: Knowledge integration and sharing for collaborative molding product design and process development. Computers in Industry 61, 659–675 (2010)
7. Cohen, W.W.: Integration of Heterogeneous Databases Without Common Domains Using Queries Based on Textual Similarity. ACM SIGMOD Record Homepage 27(2) (1998)
8. Conesa, J., Storey, V.C., Sugumaran, V.: Improving web-query processing through semantic knowledge. Data & Knowledge Engineering 66, 18–34 (2008)
9. Daniłowicz, C.: Models of Information Retrieval Systems with Special Regard to Users' Preferences. Scientific Papers of the Main Library and Scientific Information Center of the Wrocław University of Technology, No.6 Monographs, No.3 Wrocław (1992)

10. Ding, H.: Towards the Metadata Integration Issues in Peer-to-Peer Based Digital Libraries. In: Jin, H., Pan, Y., Xiao, N., Sun, J. (eds.) GCC 2004. LNCS, vol. 3251, pp. 851–854. Springer, Heidelberg (2004)
11. Dingming, W., Dongyan, Z., Xue, Z.: An Adaptive User Profile Based on Memory Model. In: The Ninth International Conference on Web-Age Information Management. IEEE, Los Alamitos (2008)
12. Jlaiel, N., Ben Ahmed, M.: Ontology and Agent Based Model for Software Development Best Practices' Integration in a Knowledge Management System. In: Meersman, R., Tari, Z., Herrero, P. (eds.) OTM 2006 Workshops. LNCS, vol. 4278, pp. 1028–1037. Springer, Heidelberg (2006)
13. Lee, M.L., Yang, L.H., Hsu, W., Yang, X.: XClust: Clustering XML Schemas for Effective Integration. In: CIKM 2002, McLean, Virginia, USA, November 4-9 (2002)
14. Main Library and Scientific Information Centre in Wroclaw University of Technology, http://www.bg.pwr.wroc.pl/
15. Merugu, S., Ghosh, J.: A Distributed Learning Framework for Heterogeneous Data Sources. In: KDD 2005, Chicago, Illinois, USA, August 21-24 (2005)
16. Maleszka, M., Mianowska, B., Nguyen, N.T.: Agent Technology for Information Retrieval in Internet. In: Håkansson, A., Nguyen, N.T., Hartung, R.L., Howlett, R.J., Jain, L.C. (eds.) KES-AMSTA 2009. LNCS, vol. 5559, pp. 151–162. Springer, Heidelberg (2009)
17. Mianowska, B., Nguyen, N.T.: A Framework of an Agent-Based Personal Assistant for Internet Users. In: Jędrzejowicz, P., Nguyen, N.T., Howlet, R.J., Jain, L.C. (eds.) KES-AMSTA 2010. LNCS, vol. 6070, pp. 163–172. Springer, Heidelberg (2010)
18. Mianowska, B., Nguyen, N.T.: A Method of User Modeling and Relevance Simulation in Document Retrieval Systems. In: O'Shea, J., Nguyen, N.T., Crockett, K., Howlett, R.J., Jain, L.C. (eds.) KES-AMSTA 2011. LNCS (LNAI), vol. 6682, pp. 138–147. Springer, Heidelberg (2011)
19. Mianowska, B., Nguyen, N.T.: A Method for User Profile Adaptation in Document Retrieval. In: Nguyen, N.T., Kim, C.-G., Janiak, A. (eds.) ACIIDS 2011, Part II. LNCS (LNAI), vol. 6592, pp. 181–192. Springer, Heidelberg (2011)
20. Mitchell, T.: Machine Learning. McGraw Hill, Singapore (1997)
21. Myaeng, S.H., Korfhage, R.R.: Integration of User Profiles: Models and Experiments in Information Retrieval. Information Processing & Management 26, 719–738 (1990)
22. Nguyen, N.T.: Advanced Information and Knowledge Processing. Springer, London (2008)
23. Nemati, H.R., Steiger, D.M., Iyer, M.S., Herschel, R.T.: Knowledge warehouse: an architectural integration of knowledge management, decision support, artificial intelligence and data warehousing. Decision Support Systems 33, 143–161 (2002)
24. Riaño, D., Moreno, A., Isern, D., Bocio, J., Sánchez, D., Jiménez, L.: Knowledge Exploitation from the Web. In: Karagiannis, D., Reimer, U. (eds.) PAKM 2004. LNCS (LNAI), vol. 3336, pp. 175–185. Springer, Heidelberg (2004)
25. Rocchio, J.J.: Relevance Feedback in Information Retrieval. In: Salton, G. (ed.) The SMART Retrieval System: Experiments in Automatic Document Processing, pp. 313–323. Prentice-Hall, Englewood Cliffs (1971)
26. Suzuki, Y., Hatano, K., Yoshikawa, M., Uemura, S., Kawagoe, K.: A Relevant Score Normalization Method Using Shannon's Information Measure. In: Fox, E.A., Neuhold, E.J., Premsmit, P., Wuwongse, V. (eds.) ICADL 2005. LNCS, vol. 3815, pp. 311–316. Springer, Heidelberg (2005)
27. WordNet, A lexical database for English, http://wordnet.princeton.edu/
28. Yearwood, J., Stranieri, A.: The integration of retrieval, reasoning and drafting for refugee law: a third generation legal knowledge based system. In: ICAIL 1999 Proceedings of the 7th International Conference on Artificial Intelligence and Law (1999)
29. Zhang, D., Lee, W.S.: Web Taxonomy Integration using Support Vector Machines. In: WWW 2004, New York, USA, May 17-22 (2004)

Modeling Agents and Agent Systems

Theodor Lettmann[1], Michael Baumann[2], Markus Eberling[1],
and Thomas Kemmerich[2]

[1] Department of Computer Science
University of Paderborn
33095 Paderborn, Germany
[2] International Graduate School of Dynamic Intelligent Systems
University of Paderborn
33095 Paderborn, Germany
{lettmann,michael.baumann,markus.eberling,kemmerich}@upb.de

Abstract. In present agent definitions, we often find different names
and definitions for similar concepts. Many works on multiagent systems use abstract and informal descriptions to introduce the topic. Even
books on multiagent systems often lack a formal definition or use a self-
contained formalism. Our goal is to present a universal and formal description for agent systems that can be used as a core model with other
existing models as special cases. This core model allows clear specification of agent systems and their properties. Design decisions are made
explicitly and, by that, become a mean of comparison for different approaches. The proposed definitions for single- and multiagent systems
address all basic properties while leaving space for extensions and can
thus be used to talk about concepts using a homogeneous notation. The
comparisons of our definition to existing models show that the most-cited
descriptions can be expressed with our formalism which shows that there
is a basic consensus on fundamental properties of agent systems.

1 Introduction

In the multiagent systems community, we can find several agent and agent system
definitions, e.g. in [7,9,15,18,19,21]. Also in more general texts, like encyclopedias
many similar yet different definitions can be found [5,20]. The following informal
definition, presented in [19], is exemplary for many definitions found in literature:

> "Agents" are autonomous, computational entities that can be viewed
> as perceiving their environment through sensors and acting upon their
> environment through effectors. [...]

The core that defines an agent consists of the agent's *autonomy*, its *perception*,
and its *action* abilities. Although most of the well-known agent definitions (e.g.
[7,15,21]) agree in this informal core of an agent, they lack a precise and formal

N.T. Nguyen (Ed.): Transactions on CCI V, LNCS 6910, pp. 157–181, 2011.

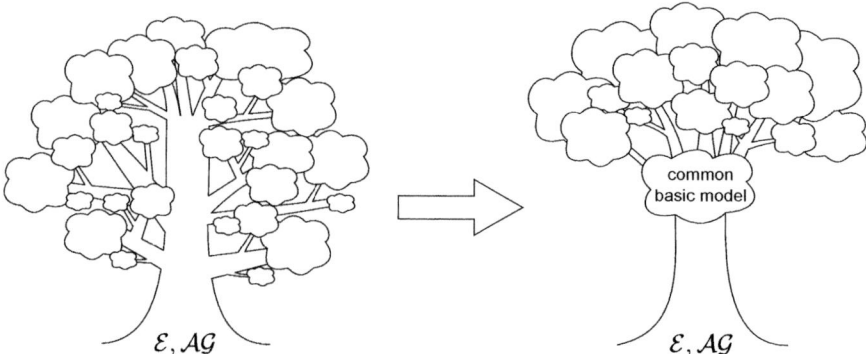

Fig. 1. Metaphorical view on the current state of the art concerning agent and agent system definitions and the intended aim of this work to provide a formal common model

notation which clearly states the understanding of an agent or agent system.[1] Therefore, this work tries to provide such formal and precise definitions which contain the formal core of agents and agent systems, as it can informally be found in the existing models used in the community.

Our basic opinion about the current situation in the community is visualized as a tree metaphor in Fig. 1. Besides an environment $\mathcal{E}$ and an agent set $\mathcal{AG}$, current models have only little in common on the first sight. This is illustrated on the left side. Beginning with these sparse similarities most models are somehow related and try to model the same issues using different notations or intentions. This leads to confusion when talking to other community members even if they work on similar problems. We intend to identify commonalities among existing models in order to establish a new basic model which could be specialized to most existing models. With the help of a formal model the designer is able to clearly specify the system and its properties. This may support the embedding of a considered system into a broader context. We also consider the abstractions to be part of the modeling step and talk about specific levels of abstraction in the design process of an agent system.

In the past, there have been several attempts to reach the same goal. However and to the best of our knowledge, none of the proposed models succeeded in providing a completely formalized definition or they often resulted in non-universal definitions. In particular, there are books on multiagent systems (MAS) that do not provide a (formal) definition at all. For example the great book *Multiagent Systems: Algorithmic, Game-Theoretic, and Logical Foundations* [16] states in the introduction:

---

[1] Note that this work should not be considered as an offense to previous works, as these works constitute very important basics in this area. The goal of the article at hand is not to degrade the undebatable important influence of these works, but to condense them to a more universal basic understanding of agents and agent systems, and at the same time to provide a general formal notation.

Somewhat strangely for a book that purports to be rigorous, we will not give a precise definition of a multiagent system. The reason is that many competing, mutually inconsistent answers have been offered in the past. Indeed, even the seemingly simpler question — What is a (single) agent? — has resisted a definitive answer. For our purposes, the following loose definition will suffice: Multiagent systems are those systems that include multiple autonomous entities with either diverging information or diverging interests, or both.

We state that the mentioned inconsistency comes from two different points. On the one hand many definitions found in literature are very abstract and informal and are written from different points of view. They often lack formal models for agents and agent systems. On the other hand, although core ideas are comparable, notation and terminology often differ a lot. The quote above also helps to clarify that it is very difficult to *define* what an agent or an (multi-)agent system is because, from a systems theory point of view, it is already unclear what a *system* itself is. Hence, the MAS community faces the same problems about formal definitions like the system theory community.

Florea [8] also tries to identify commonly accepted properties of an agent. She gives an overview on the main characteristics and classifies agents into different types. Florea states that an intelligent agent can be either reactive or cognitive and that intelligent agents are a subset of computational agents. All in all, [8] does not provide a formal definition of an agent. It is left to the reader to define its own notion of agents.

The focus of this work is on *intelligent* agents that are able to learn. Therefore, we will consider learning in our model and discuss our understanding of a learning agent. Methodologies known from *open* multiagent systems, where agents may enter or leave the system, are not considered in this work. Intentionally, other additional aspects like locomotion or sensor-fusion are not considered in the work at hand.

This article continues as follows: Section 2 gives a brief systems theory point of view on agent systems and reflects known models from literature. In Sec. 3 we will provide our definitions of an environment, an agent, and a single- and a multiagent system. In this section, we will also provide a detailed description of how learning is incorporate in our agent definition. Comparisons of the proposed model to well-known models from literature will be given in Sec. 4. There, we will discuss how far we reached our aim to provide a precise and formal framework for multiagent systems. Section 5 will discuss some properties of our model focusing on the aspect of decentralization, which we consider to be essential in a multiagent system. Finally, we will conclude the article in Sec. 6 and present an outlook on future work.

2   Formal Concepts in the Literature

The landscape of agent system research is too manifold to give a complete listing of concepts and approaches. So, we will try to examine the most commonly cited definitions in the literature. Instead of drawing the line of historical evolution of agent and multiagent systems, we will use a systems theory point of view. In defining agent systems we face a similar problem as in defining systems in general. Following the discussion in Cellier's book [4] a necessary and sufficient criterion of some entity being a system is to distinguish it as a system. In analogy, an agent system is a system in which some autonomous entities can be distinguished. So, the system consists of an environment *and* agents within it. On the system level, agent systems are a paradigm, a conceptual view onto systems.

Adopting Cellier's view, a system is an entity that can be controlled and observed and, therefore, it is a source of data gained by experiments. The designer of an agent system has to devise control processes for the agents that incorporate the essence of these data and his knowledge about the system, i.e. the control processes are based on models of the system. According to Zeigler [22], modeling is the process of organizing knowledge about a given system. Following Newell's foundation of cognitive science in [13] the knowledge level is a high-level abstraction and specialization of the states and the laws of behavior for a system. According to *physical symbol hypothesis* [14] and *problem space hypothesis* [12], the design process of control processes for agents that should act intelligent can be based on a symbolic representation of a problem space view onto the system. That is why introductions to agent systems start with an abstraction of an environment which is a state transition system. Essentially, the design process of agent systems starts with a model of the system, esp. of the environment. On the level of the environment model we can also try to characterize an agent system.

Following the tradition of SOAR (State, Operator, And Result) as a symbolic cognitive architecture, Russell and Norvig [15] give a PEAS (Performance, Environment, Actuators, Sensors) description of agent systems and characterizations of environments, which reflects an observer's view onto the system. It should be noted, that for incorporated agents their position, pose, and other observable properties are part of the state of the environment. The *mental* state of agents is not observable. Agents can get knowledge from other agents by communication or by observing their behavior, but not by "reading their minds". Properties like observability are defined according to the designer's knowledge about sensors and environment. Consequently, Wooldridge [21] defines so-called runs, i.e. sequences of states of the environment and actions of the agent, that characterize the behavior of agents, that specify a notion of memorization of the past and that are basis to a definition of equivalence for agents.

On top of the environment's model an agent model is defined that deals with the *mental* processes internally in an agent. More detailed concepts are used to describe the mental state of agents. But in any case, we find built-in knowledge provided by the designer. The knowledge can be highly specialized, complete, but inflexible as for table-driven agents, it can allow the addition of goals or maximization of utility in order to have pro-activity, or learning mechanisms can be integrated for adaptivity. Looking at the control process within the "mind" of agents, we may use approaches from all fields of artificial intelligence in order to achieve intelligent behavior of agents. Therefore, definitions of an agent system usually deal with an interface of these control processes and not with the implementation itself. For implementing the mental processes within an agent, many approaches can be found in literature. They range from well-known BDI-based architectures to layered architectures in many variations and combinations for single-agent and multiagent systems.

In the context of reinforcement learning (see e.g. [17]), the systems and models are not clearly distinguished. Idealized systems are considered that exhibit the Markov property, i.e. successor states and rewards depend only on current states and actions. Thus, Markov Decision Processes deal with systems modeled by state transition systems featuring the Markov property and the agent is able to observe enough of these states to utilize this property. In this scenario, not only the state transitions of the environment often are probabilistic, the agent's policy for choosing the next action has to implement a balance between exploration and exploitation and, therefore, usually is probabilistic, too. The reinforcement learning process is described from an observer's point of view. In contrast, the implementation of such processes is integrated into the agent, the agent itself decides to "change its mind".

3   Universal Formal Model

Most models in literature state that an agent is an autonomous software entity that is situated in some environment. But what does "environment" mean? And how can we formally define an agent and an agent system? In this section we want to propose our understanding of these terms and our formal definitions as a precise framework to model an agent and agent systems.

3.1   General Approach

In designing an agent system we are facing some general issues that should be clarified before formalizing such systems. As noted in the previous section, an agent system is not easy to define on the (physical) system level. According to the physical symbol hypothesis we start describing the intelligent behavior of agent with a model of the environment that is a state transition system. We call this level the *system model level*.

The observable features of the agent (e.g. pose, position) are part of the state of the environment. An agent is not only incorporated in some environment, it is part of it. In Fig. 2, we changed Russell's and Norvig's graphical representation of agents to emphasize this view.

The design process for agents starts on a system model level. A formal description of the behavior of an agent system is always based on some system model. PEAS descriptions and agent runs characterize agents from an observer's point of view on a system model level. For physical environments, it is impossible to give such a characterization on the system level. The more exact a formalization reflects the functionalities of a system, the harder it is to deal with these formalizations. (What are the actions necessary for taking and throwing a dice?)

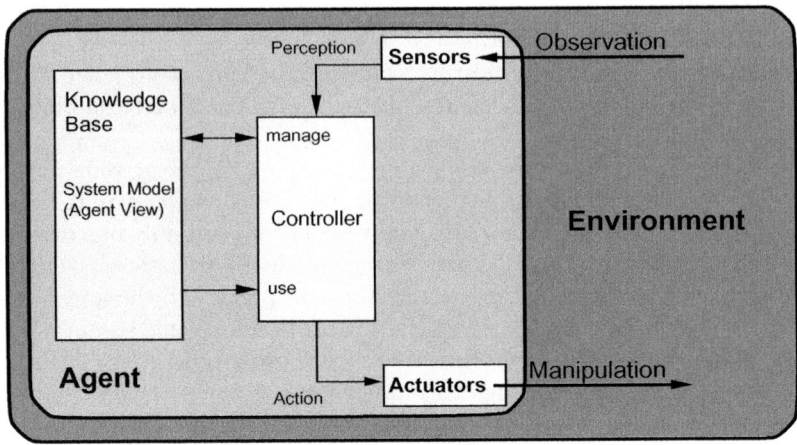

Fig. 2. Classical view of agent systems

Nevertheless, the resulting description always is a model of the real system. Even in toy problems (agents playing a game) or for software agents we start on a system model level.

Usually, designers define a system model only implicitly and in combination with the design of the agents. In using a state transition system as a system model, actions of an agent no longer initiate processes that change the environment, actions are reduced to their results, they change the state of the environment instantaneously. (Only the outcome of throwing the dice is of interest.) On the system model level, interaction of an agent with the environment can be defined by perceptions (parts of states of the environment) given by sensors and commands controlling actuators. Even though we use a state transition system as a model of the environment, this does not mean that we define this system explicitly. In general, we do not need to enumerate states or to give rules of state transitions. The system model level only serves as a conceptual view onto the agent system, that allows us to design the agent itself, i.e. a control process that is based on an internal model of the system enriched by perceptions and that is issuing actions. With this system model level and with an internal model of the agent we are dealing in the formal definition of an agent system. Figure 3 visualizes the three involved levels.

The system level in Fig. 3 shows an observer's view onto the system consisting of agent and environment. We are aware of the sensors and actuators that build the interface between mental processes within the agent and the system. On the system model level we deal with abstract perceptions and actions and no longer with realistic observations and manipulations. The mental processes of the agent take place on the agent model level. The agent interprets perceptions and chooses actions with respect to its mental state, which is (at least partly) explicitly represented as knowledge.

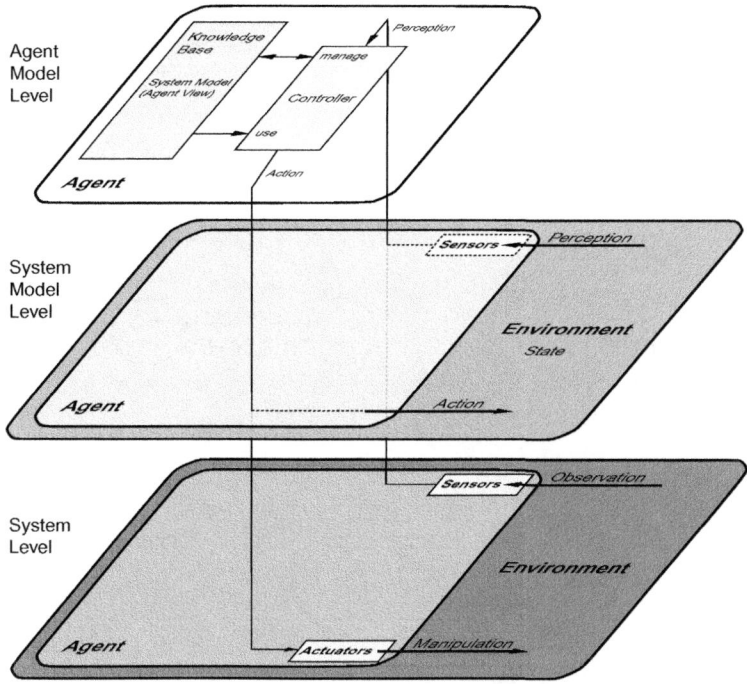

Fig. 3. Designer's view of agent systems

In Fig. 4, we provide a simple example to clarify the aforementioned general approach[2]. On the system level of this example, i.e. in the real world, a simple robot should control the temperature in a room to be between $21°C$ and $23°C$. The robot can sense the temperature in the room and is able to perform two actions: turn on or turn off a radiator. As it is common sense, we assume for our environment that the temperature increases if the radiator is turned on and that the temperature falls if the radiator is turned off. However, there might also be situations in which the temperature decreases although the radiator is turned on (e.g. if windows are opened in cold winter days). Clearly, the temperature can also increase although the radiator is off (e.g. during hours of sunshine). The actual temperature hence is influenced by the state of the radiator as well as by other processes/events in the environment.

The second layer of Fig. 4 shows one possible state transition system model of the aforementioned problem. In this example, we decide to completely neglect the functionalities of heat absorption and heat loss within the system. Transitions are labeled with heat and cool down abstracting the environment's processes/events and with the switch on and switch off actions of the robot. Perceptions are provided as values from $\mathbb{R}$ that represent the observed temperature.

---

[2] By intention, the figure is kept as simple as possible as it is intended only to visualize those elements that are of key interest for the following explanations.

Knowledge Base
System Model (Agent View)
Designer A: temperatures modeled as intervals

Knowledge Base
System Model (Agent View)
Designer B: temperatures modeled as integers

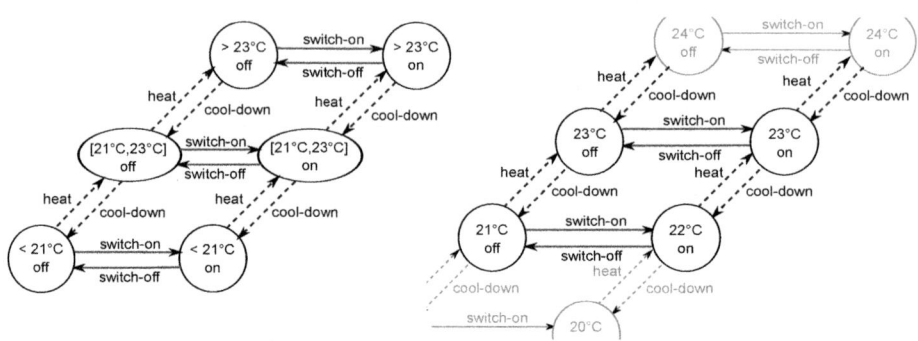

Agent Model Level

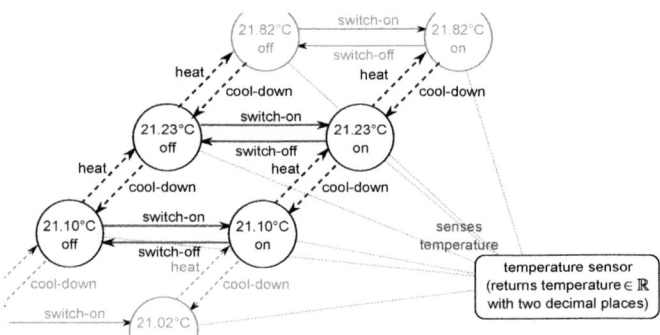

System Model Level

System Level

— agent action   ---- environment event   ◯ environment state

Fig. 4. Example of the mentioned levels and possible differences on the Agent Model Level

The system states are abstractions of the environment based on temperature values from $\mathbb{R}$ (two decimal places) and the state of the radiator (on/off). Note that the designer does not need to specify the state transition system explicitly. Indeed, it is the conceptual decision of using a state transition system with a certain temperature precision that matters at this point. Accordingly, the system model level given in the figure should be considered as an attempt to visualize this concept, only.

Finally, the third level specifies the agent's model of the world, i.e. a system model from an agent's point of view. Here, the conceptual system model level provides us with a formal perception (temperature value from $\mathbb{R}$). Then, the designer has to map a perception to an agent internal representation of temperature according to the agent's internal system model states. Note that the latter model has to be defined formally based on the concept provided at the lower system model level. As Fig. 4 indicates, concrete agents (of different designers) may have different interpretations of the system model level concerning e.g. perception handling, state structures, or state sets.

When looking at virtual systems on the other hand, we see that agents and environment by their very nature are already constructed at a certain level of abstraction. A formal definition of the system level might be available to the designer. Thus, the system model level also can be — but not necessarily has to be — fully specified and might even be equivalent with the system level.

3.2   Dynamic Environment

Before we start to define agent systems, we want to point out the strong connection between agents and environments. Both are tightly coupled entities, where one can not be defined without defining the other. Ferber [7] terms this relation for situated agents "the agent/environment duality".

Accordingly, our formal definitions for dynamic environments (Def. 1) and for agents (Def. 2) contain links between each other that will be highlighted at the respective text passages. For clarity, note that throughout this work, we use $\mathcal{A}$ to denote a single agent out of the set of agents $\mathcal{AG}$. We use $\mathcal{A}$ as index to indicate that the respective element is part of agent $\mathcal{A}$'s definition. Please also note that $\Pi(X)$ denotes the set of probability distributions over a variable X.

Next, we give a formal and precise definition of our understanding of a dynamic environment. Based on the view introduced above, we decided to explicitly model agents in an environment by considering the influence of their actions, only. Definition 1 summarizes our dynamic environment definition and the remainder of this section discusses it.

Definition 1 (Dynamic Environment). *An environment $\mathcal{E}$ is described as a tuple $\mathcal{E} = (\mathrm{S}, s_0, \mathrm{A}, \mathrm{E}, \tau)$ where*

- *$\mathrm{S} = \{s_0, s_1, \dots\}$ is a countable set of environment states with an initial state s_0.*
- *$\mathrm{A} = \underset{\mathcal{A} \in \mathcal{AG}}{\bigtimes} \mathrm{A}_{\mathcal{A}}$ denotes all joint actions (of agents) that can be performed in the environment. Here, for each agent $\mathcal{A}$ from the set of agents $\mathcal{AG}$ situated*

in this environment, $A_{\mathcal{A}}$ is a countable set of actions which contains at least an element no-action that should be used whenever the agent does not perform any action.
- E is a countable set of events that may occur in the environment. The set contains at least an element no-event, that is used whenever no event happens.
- $\tau : S \times A \times E \rightarrow \Pi(S)$ is a probabilistic state transition function, which defines the probability that the successive state will be $s' \in S$, if the current state is $s \in S$ and a joint action $\mathbf{a} \in A$ and an event $e \in E$ take place. For brevity, we write $\tau(s' \mid s, \mathbf{a}, e)$ to denote such a particular probability.

Note that we do not explicitly introduce sets of environment objects other than agents, since all (observable) information of these objects are considered to be incorporated into the set of environment states S. Figure 5 visualizes a single-agent system. Here, the wooden box is an example for an object that is modeled within the environment state set.

The environment $\mathcal{E}$ starts in an initial state $s_0 \in S$, where S is a countable set, either finite or infinite. In a particular system, depending on the designer's decision, this set can of course be finite. Although conceptually S could also be an uncountable set (e.g. containing parts represented by values in $\mathbb{R}$), we will deal with countable subsets only, when simulating such systems on a computer. The same argumentation holds for all countable sets in the remaining definitions.

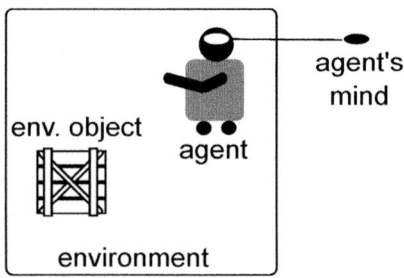

Fig. 5. Point of view: environment, objects, agent, and mental state ("mind")

The discrete states of the environment are influenced by (environment) events as well as by joint actions of the agents. This influence is reflected in the probabilistic state transition function τ, which defines the reaction of the environment to actions and events. Actions are performed simultaneously by all agents and thus establish a joint action $\mathbf{a} \in A$. To simplify the definition of the state transition function τ, our model requires the no-operation action no-action$_{\mathcal{A}}$ for each agent, as this allows joint actions that may contain "idle" agents. Given the current state $s \in S$, the joint action $\mathbf{a} \in A$ and the event $e \in E$, the function τ returns the probability that the resulting state will be state $s' \in S$. Due to the probabilistic nature of the state transition function it is easy to model dynamic environments that do not behave deterministic in the same situation but respond with different answers for the same inputs. Essentially, we defined our environment to exhibit the Markov property as it is a natural assumption. However, using a meta-model approach for the environment allows us to encode finite state-action sequences as states in the meta-model.

To clarify the role of the state transition function τ, reconsider the system model level of the temperature example from Sec. 3.1. For instance, for state $\langle 21.10, \text{off} \rangle$, action switch-on and event heat, the probability to transition to state $\langle 21.23, \text{on} \rangle$ might be $\tau(\langle 21.23, \text{on} \rangle | \langle 21.10, \text{off} \rangle, \text{switch-on}, \text{heat}) = 0.95$. However, with a smaller probability the system may transition to another state, e.g. to $\langle 21.82, \text{on} \rangle$ if the heater's influence to the temperature differs from the expectations underlying the state transition model.

Note that the state transition function τ is not responsible for the actual selection of a successive state, but only returns a probability $\tau(\text{s}' \mid \text{s}, \mathbf{a}, e)$ for each possible successive state $\text{s}' \in \text{S}$. A state selection mechanism (like e.g. the Roulette wheel selection [1]) based on these probabilities is explicitly not modeled as we consider it as a process at system level.

As we have now defined the environment we will next define a single intelligent agent.

3.3   Intelligent Agent

In the previous section, we defined our notion of an environment using the term "agent". However, we did not yet provide a precise formal agent definition. This will be done in the remainder of this section. As we mentioned earlier in this work, we intend to model an intelligent agent that is able to learn. Hence, the question arises what an *intelligent* agent is. Gottfredson [10] defines intelligence as follows:

> A very general mental capability that, among other things, involves the ability to reason, plan, solve problems, think abstractly, comprehend complex ideas, learn quickly and learn from experience. It is not merely book learning, a narrow academic skill, or test-taking smarts. Rather, it reflects a broader and deeper capability for comprehending our surroundings – "catching on," "making sense" of things, or "figuring out" what to do.

The Encyclopædia Britannica [6] states:

> In education, the ability to learn or understand or to deal with new or challenging situations. In psychology, the term may more specifically denote the ability to apply knowledge to manipulate one's environment or to think abstractly as measured by objective criteria.

As a conclusion of definitions from the literature we want an *intelligent* agent to be able to use knowledge to reason about the next action, to be able to deal with unknown situations and to adapt its behavior.

Next, we define an agent in Def. 2. As mentioned earlier in this work, agents and environments are tightly coupled entities in any situated agent system. Therefore, any agent according to the proposed agent definition is formally linked to its environment by the state set S of that environment. The vision function v_A of an agent $\mathcal{A}$ reflects the transition or border between what constitutes an agent and an environment in our model. Note also, that all agents constructed according to Def. 2 are element of the agent set $\mathcal{AG}$, which is used to define the environment in Def. 1.

Definition 2 (Agent). $\mathcal{AG}$ *is the set of all agents. An agent* $\mathcal{A} \in \mathcal{AG}$ *is defined as a tuple* $\mathcal{A} = (S, S_A, \mathcal{I}_A, \mathcal{M}_A, A_A, v_A, \mathrm{adapt}_A)$ *where*

1. S *is a countable set of states of an environment.*
2. S_A *is a countable set of internal representations of the environment states.*
3. $\mathcal{I}_A$ *is a countable set of* $\mathcal{A}$*'s internal states.*
4. $\mathcal{M}_A$ *is a countable set of* $\mathcal{A}$*'s mental states.*
5. A_A *is a countable set of* $\mathcal{A}$*'s possible actions containing at least one special action* no-action$_A$.
6. $v_A : S \rightarrow \Pi(S_A)$ *is a probabilistic vision function that maps the current state of the environment to a probability distribution over all possible internal representations of the environment states.*
7. $\mathrm{adapt}_A : \mathcal{M}_A \rightarrow \mathcal{M}_A$ *is an adaptation mechanism that translates the current mental state into another mental state.*

A single mental state $\mathrm{m}_A \in \mathcal{M}_A$ *is defined as a tuple* $\mathrm{m}_A = (\mathrm{i}_A, \rho_A, \pi_A, o_A, \tau_A)$ *where*

8. $\mathrm{i}_A \in \mathcal{I}_A$ *is the current internal state of agent* $\mathcal{A}$.
9. $\rho_A : S_A \times \mathcal{I}_A \rightarrow \mathcal{I}_A$ *is a cognition function that calculates the successive internal state of the agent based on the internal representation of the environment state and the current internal state.*
10. $\pi_A : \mathcal{I}_A \rightarrow \Pi(A_A)$ *is the probabilistic policy function of the agent. It defines the probability of executing action* $\mathrm{a} \in A_A$, *if the agent is in the internal state* $\mathrm{i} \in \mathcal{I}_A$.
11. o_A *is an action selector mechanism which selects an action of the agent based on the probability distribution over the possible actions.*
12. $\tau_A : \mathcal{I}_A \times A_A \rightarrow \mathcal{I}_A$ *is a state transition function. It defines the successive internal state* $\mathrm{i}' \in \mathcal{I}_A$, *if the agent performs action* $\mathrm{a} \in A_A$ *in the internal state* $\mathrm{i} \in \mathcal{I}_A$.

Like in known models from literature, we reflect that the agent is situated in some environment. As the agent is not able to sense the whole environment state through its sensors, the vision function v_A translates the real external environment state to a probability distribution over all internal representations of the environment state $\Pi(S_A)$ (cf. Def. 2(6)). This probability distribution should be used to reflect sensor noise, only. In particular, it should not be used to model random precepts. Both, the set of environment states and the set of internal representations are part of the agent (cf. Def. 2(1) and Def. 2(2)).

We decided to distinguish between the pure internal state of the agent $\mathcal{I}_A$ and its mental states $\mathcal{M}_A$, as the mental states are more than just the internal states. The mental state of an agent is everything that is important for a specific state and a specific instance of the agent cycle. The mental state therefore contains all relevant information of the agent, i.e. the internal state, the sensed environment state, the policy function, the state transition function, and the cognition function. Figure 5 visualizes our understanding of the relations between an agent that is situated in an environment and its mental state. In particular, the agent's sensors and actors are considered to be part of the environment. The agent's mental state, i.e. its "mind", is not considered to belong to the environment since the mind is what makes the agent autonomous. It issues directives to its actuators and receives data from its sensors. However, the mind neither has influence on the success of actions nor on how noisy data inputs are. Accordingly, actuators and sensors are not completely controllable by the agent and thus are considered to be part of the (uncontrollable) environment. Clearly, one can argue on this boundary definition but it seems to be useful in this work.

The special role of the agent's mental state is reflected in the second part of the agent definition 2(8) – (11). The mental state consists of the current internal state of the agent and the "mind" of the agent, that is described in detail, now. There, we have the cognition function which calculates the next internal state i_A based on the current internal state i_A^{old} and the internal representation of the observed environment state s_A (cf. Def. 2(9)). Based on the resulting internal state i_A, the policy function π_A gives a probability distribution over the possible agent actions A_A (cf. Def. 2(10)). The set of possible actions should at least contain a special operation no-action$_A$, which allows the agent to perform no action. The action selector mechanism o_A then selects which action a_A^{next} is executed by the agent (cf. Def. 2(11)). This decision is based on the probability distribution π_A over all possible actions. For instance, this can be realized using a probability-proportional mechanism like the Roulette wheel selection [1], or any other mechanism like simply selecting the action with the highest probability. Formally, this process of determining the resulting action a_A^{next} is given by

$$a_A^{next} = o_A(\pi_A(\rho_A(s_A, i_A^{old}))). \tag{1}$$

The next part of the mental state is the internal state transition function τ_A which calculates the next internal state i_A^{next} based on the current internal state i_A and the selected action a_A^{next} (cf. Def. 2(12)). According to the previous explanations, this can formally be stated as

$$i_A^{next} = \tau_A(i_A, a_A^{next}). \tag{2}$$

To further clarify this agent cycle, Fig. 6 visualizes the whole process.

The learning process is then the adaptation of the whole mental state. This is captured by the function adapt$_A$ which translates a given mental state into another one. The learning step can basically be performed at any time, especially it may happen during execution of any given method within the agent. The mental state can be changed between the perception-reasoning process or even

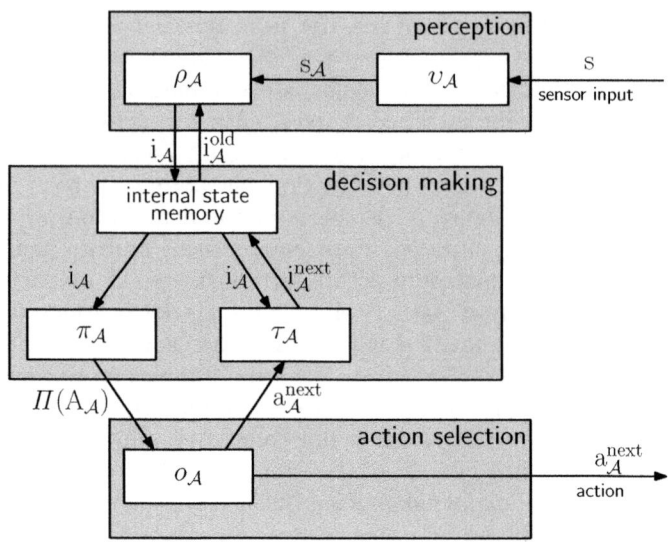

Fig. 6. The agent cycle with our agent's definition

within a process. We assume that the learning method to be used is coded in the internal states of the agents and that the adaptation function just employs this knowledge about how the agent should learn. In particular, it follows that the adaptation function itself can also be changed by a learning step. Since mental states are based on countable sets, this means that we are dealing with uncountable sets of e.g. possible adaptation functions. At this point, we do not want to limit a learning step in order to circumvent this problem. Instead, we assume (in accordance with machine learning) that complete hypothesis spaces are searched incompletely by using a preference bias. Our view on the learning mechanism is illustrated in Fig. 7. It shows which elements of Fig. 6 are influence by the $\mathsf{adapt}_{\mathcal{A}}$ function (dashed lines).

Additionally, we do not integrate an explicit performance measure as it is used in other definitions of agent systems (e.g. [15]). There is no necessity in our formal definition since we are not formalizing some concrete system. If one needs such signals from the environment (e.g. rewards), it is left to the designer to integrate this measure. We will deal with the "missing" performance measurement in our discussion section in more detail.

3.4   Multiagent Systems - Model

Up to now we have presented our understanding of an environment and a single agent. In this section we want to define a single-agent and a multiagent system. As stated in the previous section, the system consists of a single or more agent(s) and an environment. Both are part of the system. Especially, the physical representation of an agent is part of the environment as it is shown in Fig. 5. The definition of the agent only captures the mind of the agent and how a mental

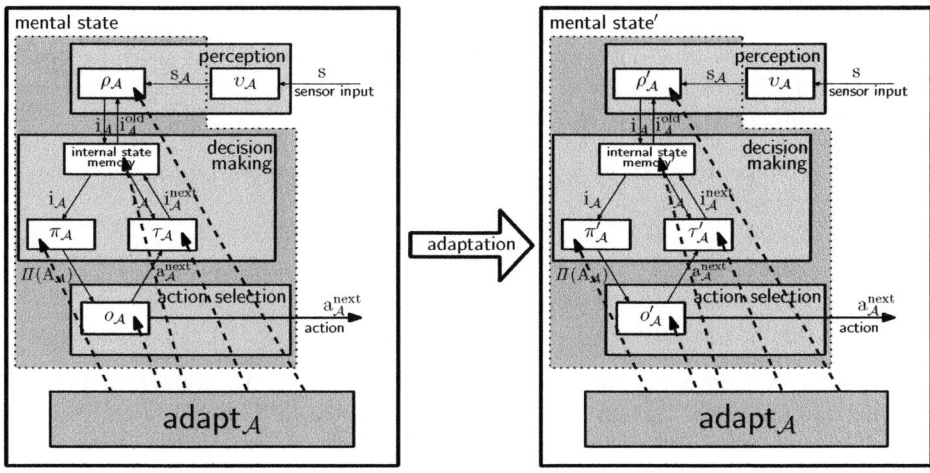

Fig. 7. The agent adapts its mental state to another mental state. The influence of $\text{adapt}_{\mathcal{A}}$ is indicated by dashed arrows.

state may look like. Therefore, the two definitions are straightforward. For simplicity we assume that agents and environment correspond to each other with respect to environment states and agent actions.

Definition 3 (Single-Agent System (SAS)). *A single-agent system (SAS) consists of exactly one agent $\mathcal{A}$ that is situated in an environment $\mathcal{E}$. Therefore, a SAS is a tuple* $\text{SAS} = (\mathcal{E}, \mathcal{A})$.

Definition 4 (Multiagent System (MAS)). *A multiagent system (MAS) consists of a set of agents $\mathcal{AG}$ that are situated in an environment $\mathcal{E}$. Thus, a MAS is a tuple* $\text{MAS} = (\mathcal{E}, \mathcal{AG})$.

A key property of a MAS is its decentrality. In particular, there should not be a central instance neither in the form of a super-agent nor any other form of external central instance. If a single-agent system is considered, it also might be the case that, on system level, we do have additional other agents. But, as those agents are not under consideration from the agent's point of view, we might decide to model these situations with a single-agent system. With a SAS we are able to concentrate on a specific agent. In a SAS no interaction, in particular neither collective nor competitive behavior, is modeled. The key issue when using a MAS instead of a SAS is the modeling of the other agents as autonomous entities. Designing the mental processes of these agents simultaneously admits controlled interaction between agents. Coordination, cooperation and communication then are additional issues that have to be considered. We do not formalize these aspects, as from our point of view they are part of the knowledge of the agents encoded in the mental states. For example a specific communication protocol is not modeled as a part of such a system as it is considered to be part of the agent's knowledge.

3.5   Exemplary Specification of a Heater-Agent

We will now show how our approach can be used to model the heater example presented in Fig. 4. It is given as a single-agent system SAS $= (\mathcal{E}, \mathcal{A})$, having the environment $\mathcal{E} = (\mathrm{S}, s_0, \mathrm{A}, \mathrm{E}, \tau)$ with:

- S $= \{\langle \text{temperature}, \text{status} \rangle \mid \text{temperature} \in \mathbb{R} \wedge \text{temperature has accuracy of}$ $10^{-2} \wedge \text{status} \in \{\text{on}, \text{off}\}\}$
- $s_0 = \langle 20.00, \text{off} \rangle \in \mathrm{S}$
- A $= \{(\text{switch-on}), (\text{switch-off}), (\text{no-action})\}$
- E $= \{\text{heat}, \text{cool-down}, \text{no-event}\}$
- state transition function $\tau : \mathrm{S} \times \mathrm{A} \times \mathrm{E} \to \Pi(\mathrm{S})$

For brevity we omit the formal specification of the state transition function τ. Assume that τ is specified such that the probability distribution over the environment states reflects the expected behavior as shown in Fig. 4 with high probability. However, with low probability other transitions may occur. The agent $\mathcal{A} = (\mathrm{S}, \mathrm{S}_\mathcal{A}, \mathcal{I}_\mathcal{A}, \mathcal{M}_\mathcal{A}, \mathrm{A}_\mathcal{A}, \upsilon_\mathcal{A}, \text{adapt}_\mathcal{A})$ is formally specified by:

- S $= \{\langle \text{temperature}, \text{status} \rangle \mid \text{temperature} \in \mathbb{R} \wedge \text{temperature has accuracy of}$ $10^{-2} \wedge \text{status} \in \{\text{on}, \text{off}\}\}$
- $\mathrm{S}_\mathcal{A} = \{\langle \text{temperature}_\mathcal{A}, \text{status} \rangle \mid \text{temperature}_\mathcal{A} \in \mathbb{Z} \wedge \text{status} \in \{\text{on}, \text{off}\}\}$
- $\mathcal{I}_\mathcal{A} = \{\text{too-cold}, \text{expecting-cooling}, \text{fine}, \text{expecting-heating}, \text{too-hot}\}$
- a mental state $\mathrm{m}_\mathcal{A} = (\mathrm{i}_\mathcal{A}, \rho_\mathcal{A}, \pi_\mathcal{A}, o_\mathcal{A}, \tau_\mathcal{A}) \in \mathcal{M}_\mathcal{A}$ with
  - $\mathrm{i}_\mathcal{A} \in \mathcal{I}_\mathcal{A}$
  - cognition function $\rho_\mathcal{A} : \mathrm{S}_\mathcal{A} \times \mathcal{I}_\mathcal{A} \to \mathcal{I}_\mathcal{A}$
  - policy function $\pi_\mathcal{A} : \mathcal{I}_\mathcal{A} \to \Pi(\mathrm{A}_\mathcal{A})$
  - action selection mechanism $o_\mathcal{A}$ is Roulette wheel selection
  - state transition function $\tau_\mathcal{A} : \mathcal{I}_\mathcal{A} \times \mathrm{A}_\mathcal{A} \to \mathcal{I}_\mathcal{A}$
- $\mathrm{A}_\mathcal{A} = \{\text{switch-on}, \text{switch-off}, \text{no-action}\}$
- $\upsilon_\mathcal{A} : \mathrm{S} \to \Pi(\mathrm{S}_\mathcal{A})$
- $\text{adapt}_\mathcal{A} : \mathcal{M}_\mathcal{A} \to \mathcal{M}_\mathcal{A}$ with $\text{adapt}_\mathcal{A}(\mathrm{m}_\mathcal{A}) = \mathrm{m}_\mathcal{A}$ for all $\mathrm{m}_\mathcal{A} \in \mathcal{M}_\mathcal{A}$

As before we omit formal specifications of some functions of the agent for better readability. For the cognition function $\rho_\mathcal{A}$ we assume that the agent wants to heat the room if it feels too cold and the temperature is too low and the switch of the heater is turned off. For the policy function we assume that the probability distribution over the actions reflects the intended actions of the agent with high probability, i.e. switch-off if it is too hot and the heater is on or switch-on if it is too cold and the heater is off, etc. However, with low probability an arbitrary action may be selected by the action selection function $o_\mathcal{A}$. For the state transition function it is assumed that the successive internal state of the agent corresponds with the expected behavior of the designer. For instance if the internal state is too-cold and the action switch-on is selected by the agent the next internal state should be expecting-heating. Note that the internal state is not only influenced by the state transition function but also by the perception of the agent as shown in Fig. 6. For the perception function $\upsilon_\mathcal{A}$ we assume that it receives with high probability the real temperature and the real status of the heater. With low probability the agent senses a lower or higher temperature and/or a wrong state of the heater. To ease the example, we use an agent that is not able to learn. This is reflected in the adapt$_A$ function that does not change the mental state of the agent. If the agent should learn, the adaptation function should change the functions of the mental state (cf. Fig 7).

As we can see, the agent system of the example can easily be specified with our universal formal model.

4 Comparison to Existing Models

In this section we will compare the presented model to well-known models of the literature and relate them to the example from Sec. 3.5. We will see that these models are specializations of our model.

4.1 Comparison to the Model of Russell and Norvig

In [15], Russell and Norvig give a rather informal description of agents and agent systems. Due to the lack of a formal definition, there exists no mapping of notations and we, therefore, compare corresponding concepts.

The authors describe several architectures of agents. Their basic concept consists of an agent that perceives its environments through sensors and may use its actuators to act in it. All presented agents are specializations of this concept. The components that compose the different types of agents are representable by the components *Controller* and *Knowledge Base* in our model (cf. Fig. 2). The basic concepts of both, our and Russell and Norvig's model, are very similar except the fact that in our model the agent is explicitly stated to be part of the environment and is not just acting upon it. In [15], the *agent function* models the agent's behavior and all presented architectures are specializations of this basic function. In contrast to this top-down approach, our model follows a bottom-up approach by defining all possible skills and properties and the creator of the agent system has to define these components adequately.

Russell and Norvig specify a *task environment* with the help of an PEAS (Performance, Environment, Actuators, Sensors) description. The *external environment* of Russell and Norvig is covered by our definition of an environment $\mathcal{E}$, whereas their concept of a *task environment* resembles our definition of an agent system. The sensors are modeled by the perception function υ_A whose output is adapted by the cognition function ρ_A and the actuators' behavior is modeled by the state transition function τ_A. The performance measure in [15] is a signal of an observer to rate the performance of the agents so that the agents are able to meet the designer's intention. It has nothing to do with learning where an internal performance measure is needed which may also be given by a sensor. In contrast the performance measure from the PEAS description is an external stimulus from outside the system.

4.2 Comparison to the Model of Wooldridge

In this section we want to compare the model presented by Wooldridge [21] to the model presented in this paper.

Wooldridge models the interaction between the environment and the agent as a form of a history which he calls *runs*. A run consists of a sequence of environment states e and actions α. With the help of a state transition function the current environment state e is translated into another environment state e' based on the agent's action α. This is very similar to the model presented here. The main difference is that we do not expect the set of environment states to be finite as Wooldridge does. Another difference is that we do not model the state transition function of the environment solely based on agent actions. We also want to be able to model other processes that effect the state of the environment. This is captured in the set of events that may occur in the environment. Without such possibilities it would not be able to define heating of a room that is the effect of stronger insolation through a window. In Wooldridge's model we are unable to capture such mechanisms. We also allow the agents to do nothing (i.e. to select no-action). In the model of Wooldridge this is simply not the default case to have a no-action. There, a succeeding environment state is reached only if all agents have selected an action. Another difference is that we explicitly see the set of joint actions as part of formal definition of the environment. Wooldridge implicitly does the same but this is only captured in his state transition function which reacts on the agents' joint action. Wooldridge also concentrates on the mind of the agent and, therefore, formalizes the agent as a kind of observer of the environment. The agent life-cycle of percept-reason-act is again similar to our definition even though his definition is less detailed then ours.

To sum up, the model of Wooldridge slightly differs from our model. The mapping of the notations in Tab. 1 underlines this similarity. One main difference is our use of infinite state sets. Thus, in the example from Sec. 3.5, we are allowed to model the state sets as integers. However, in Wooldridge's model an upper and lower bound for the temperature has to be provided in order to gain finite sets. But what happens if the temperature is outside the considered interval?

4.3 Comparison to Ferber's Model

In the book "Multi-Agent Systems" [7], Ferber discusses various approaches and formal models towards modeling agents and agent systems that can be found in literature. He also provides a "minimal common definition" for an agent and defines the concept of multiagent systems. His functional agent definition to a large extent is in a line with our formal model. Some of his requirements, like the ability to act, to (partially) percept the environment, or to have a (partial) representation of the environment can directly be found in our formal definition, too. Others, like communication or skills can be modeled using our formal sensors and actors. Also more abstract concepts like tendencies, objectives, or resources owned by an agent can be incorporated in our model using the mental state, its components and the agent's internal states.

Table 1. Comparison: Wooldridge's notation and the notation used in our universal model

Wooldridge	Description	Universal
E	Set of environment states	S
e	A single environment state	s
e_0	Initial environment state	s_0
Env	The environment	$\mathcal{E}$
Ac	Set of actions of a single agent	$A_{\mathcal{A}}$
α	A single agent's action	a
—	Set of joint actions of all agents	A
—	A single joint action of all agents	**a**
$\mathcal{AG}$	Set of agents	$\mathcal{AG}$
Ag	A single agent	$\mathcal{A}$
I	Set of agent's internal states	$\mathcal{I}$
Per	Set of perceptions of an agent	$S_{\mathcal{A}}$
see	Perception function of an agent	υ
$next$	Cognition function of an agent	ρ
$action$	Policy function of an agent	π

The multiagent system's concept provided by Ferber can be described by a tuple (E, O, A, R, Op) and some general rules that he calls the "laws of the universe". Here, E is an environment that contains a set of objects O. $A \subseteq O$ is a set of active entities/agents and R specifies the relations between objects. The set Op contains the actions of the agents that may operate on objects from O. When an action can be performed and how the environment reacts, is specified by the laws of the universe.

As we can see in Tab. 2, this concept is consistent with our formal model. Objects which are not agents can be incorporated in the environment state set S. We thus do not require an explicit set to model them. The same also holds for Ferber's set of relations R between objects, as it might be encoded in S, too. Communication or neighboring relations can be implemented by sensors and actors using (maybe partial) agent internal representations of the environment ($S_{\mathcal{A}}$). However, with the help of our model we are able to specify these abstract laws of the universe. This is illustrated in our example by the set of events and its consideration in the state transition function of the environment (cf. Sec. 3.5).

4.4   Comparison to the Model of Franklin and Graesser

In 1997, Franklin and Graesser [9] tried to figure out the essence of agency and what distinguishes an (autonomous) agent from a program. They survey and discuss several existing agent definitions used at that time. Although literature did not agree in all aspects of what agents are, Franklin and Graesser identified several properties that describe the essence of a general agent definition. they basically consider an autonomous agent to be a system that is part of an environment which it can sense and in which it performs actions according to its

Table 2. Mapping: Ferber's MAS model

Ferber	Description	Universal
E	Environment	$\mathcal{E}$
O	Set of objects	$\mathcal{AG}$, respectively encoded in S
A	Set of agents	$\mathcal{AG}$
R	Relations between objects	encoded in S; realized through sensor and actor definitions
Op	An assembly of operations of agents	A
laws of the universe	Specify operations and reactions of environment to operations	τ

own agenda. As this definition is too broad, the authors clarify that additional properties shall be taken into account in order to derive useful agent definitions.

Besides this agent definition, Franklin and Graesser also provide an operational definition for an agent system. Although they use a state transition system, they do not provide a completely formalized model. Nevertheless, similarities with our universal model can easily be identified as demonstrated in Tab. 3. As in our model, Franklin and Graesser's agent system definition also formally distinguishes between (agent) actions and events/dynamics that change the environment. Other requirements presented in [9], like sensors that may change their sensing quality over time, can also easily be reflected in our model. Therefore, the environment state has to contain some timing information, since this enables our perception function v to model the desired, time-dependent behavior. Also, Franklin and Graesser's action selection mechanism can be realized in our model. In detail, their mechanism selects an action based on sensor inputs and drives. The resulting action then will influence the environment's dynamics and thus the state of the environment. Obviously, this mechanism depends on sensed states, drives and thus on the mental state of the agent. Hence, we can refer to the corresponding parts in our definition, which include those shown in the agent cycle in Fig. 6, as well as the state transformer function τ of our environment.

In addition to these similarities, it is also worth to mention that our formal model is more flexible than the one of Franklin and Graesser. For instance, our model can be used to formalize uncertainty as many of its functions are defined over probability distributions. In the example presented in Sec. 3.5 this is reflected in the perception function and the environment state transition function.

4.5   Comparison to Markov Based Models

Markov-based models are ubiquitous in reinforcement learning in agent systems [3,17]. In their well known book on reinforcement learning, Sutton and Barto [17] consider an *agent* to be the entity that learns and makes decisions. The *environment* on the other hand is what the agent interacts with, i.e. everything outside the agent. In general, Sutton and Barto provide the rule that "anything

Table 3. Mapping: Franklin and Graesser

F&G	Description	Universal
E	Environment	$\mathcal{E}$
T	State transition function	τ
X	Environment states	S
$E(0)$	Initial environment state	s_0
A/A_j	A single agent ...	$\mathcal{A}$
A/A_j	... and at the same time the actions of a single agent	$A_{\mathcal{A}}$
P	Function that describes changes in the environment that can not be attributed to agents	E
$S(A,t)$	Sensor of agent A at time t	v

that cannot be changed arbitrarily by the agent is considered to be outside of it and thus [is] part of its environment" [17]. They also state that the border between an agent and its environment usually differs from the border between a real robot and its environment. That is, the agent's actors and sensors should be considered as parts of the environment instead of belonging to the agent. Note that this point of view matches our opinion as discussed in detail in Sec. 3.3.

In the reinforcement learning problem, agent and environment interact at discrete time steps t by invoking actions $a_t \in A(s_t)$, receiving a reward $r_t \in \mathbb{R}$ and changing the environment state $s_t \in S$. Possible actions may vary in different environment states. The goal of an agent is to learn an optimal policy π^* that maximizes the total reward over a given horizon. A policy $\pi : S \times A \to [0,1]$ returns the probability of executing action $a \in A(s)$ in state state $s \in S$. An environment has to be Markovian, i.e. the transition probability of entering state $s_{t+1} \in S$ after executing action $a_t \in A(s_t)$ in state $s_t \in S$ does not depend on the (action) history of how state s_t was reached but only on the last state and action. The reinforcement learning problem for the single agent case is investigated in the formal context of Markov Decision Processes (MDP) [3]. A Markov Decision Process can be described by a tuple $\langle S, A, T, R \rangle$, where S is a set of environment states, A a set of actions, T a state transition function and R a reward function [11]. Reinforcement learning in multiagent systems is investigated in the context of Markov games [18], also known as stochastic games, and further extensions of the MDP, such as the *Decentralized Partial Observable Markov Decision Processes* (Dec-POMDP) [2]. The latter extends the MDP by considering a set of agents, their joint actions, their joint observations, and an observation function.

General elements of our environment $\mathcal{E} = (S, s_0, A, E, \tau)$ according to Definition 1 have corresponding elements in Markov based models, except for the set of events E. Agents in Markov based models are basically reduced to actions and observations. The drive to behave such that a reward in reinforcement learning is maximized, is not formally modeled into the agents. In our model, however, learning can be realized using the adapt$_{\mathcal{A}}$ mechanism. Actions and observations/sensors can also be found in our model. What mainly distinguishes our agents from Markov based agents is the fact that our model provides the explicit opportunity to model the environment as well as a (differing) agent internal environment model. Markov based models in contrast do not clearly separate between the agent model and the environment model.

Further issues when comparing the models include the following:

1. Both models work with probability distributions over states and observations.
2. Markov based models make use of an explicit reward function. Our model, in contrast, does not provide an explicit reward function, however, it could easily be realized as part of the environment state.
3. The state transition function τ of our environment does not only depend on the joint actions of agents (respectively the action of an agent in a single-agent system) but also on events, i.e. processes, that may happen in the environment (cf. example in Sec. 3.5). Although the influence of such events might also be modeled through the probability distribution in Markov based models, the explicit usage of events allows a finer granulated modeling.
4. Partial observations realized in (Dec-)POMDPs find their counterpart in the perception function $v_{\mathcal{A}}$, the cognition function $\rho_{\mathcal{A}}$, in the internal representation of the environment state and in the agent internal state.

5   Discussion

In this section we want to discuss the proposed model. As stated in the last section, our model is basically in line with the known models from literature. We also have presented that those models are specializations of our proposed model. But what has not been considered in our model and what should be considered when modeling and building an agent system? These questions are treated in this section.

In contrast to some models known from literature, our approach does not explicitly contain a performance measure. The reasons for this are the following. As the formal model is not meant to model some concrete multiagent system one has to add a performance measure if a concrete system is considered. In literature (e.g. [15]) one finds basically two different kinds of performance measures. The first is some external signal for the agent given by some observer entity that rates the behavior of the agent in its environment. This can be incorporated into our model as an additional sensor input. The other kind of performance measures is an internal one. The agent rates its actions' outcome *itself* to perform some learning task. This can be incorporated into the mental state of the agent where the learning takes place. We decided not to model these performance measures as there is no universal schema for it. The performance may be measured over preferable states or over an entire run of the agent. Since performance measures are specific for each agent system, we thus decided to omit it in the proposed universal model.

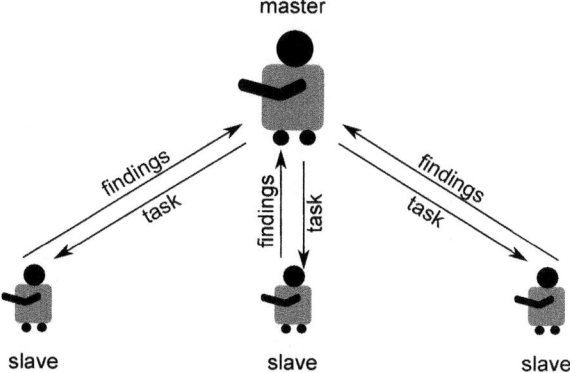

Fig. 8. Master with slave agents that submit their findings to the master agent and receive commands from it

As stated in Sec. 3 all sets that are used in the definitions can be infinite. Another worth mentioning aspect is that we want to highlight the concept of decentralism in agent systems. Therefore, it should be impossible to have a so-called *master agent* that may control all the other slave agents which then are reduced to some kind of external sensors/actors for that master. Such a master agent as illustrated in Fig. 8 would be some kind of single point of failure in an application. Besides this, if there should be a master agent then the question arises if the concept of *multi*agent systems is appropriate for such an application or if it would be better to use a *single*-agent system instead. An advantage of having countably infinite sets is the pure application of the concept. If we would limit the sets to finite ones we would also limit the possibilities of modeling real world problems. Let us again consider the temperature agent from previous sections. If the temperature is measured in integer values, it is easy to see that this is by nature a countably infinite set. If we limit the range of temperatures to a specific finite interval we would have to think about minimum and maximum values.

Our model does not contain any information about communication between agents and what has to be considered if the agents communicate with each other. In our view the communication channel is just another sensor input source, and therefore, is part of the perception function. The knowledge about the rules of communication, i.e. the communication protocol, are also part of the agents knowledge and are coded in the mental states.

Note that the mental state of an agent might be transmittable. In this case, creating a master agent is very simple, since it is possible that an agent communicates its mental state to another agent. Therefore, we should discuss the properties of a communication channel: it should be limited. Possible realizations may include a limited maximum message size that can be transmitted in one step or the storage capacities of a single agent should be bounded such that not all mental states can be stored. We want to emphasize this issue as otherwise the system would collapse to a single-agent system with a master agent.

Another aspect on the mental state deals with homogeneous agent systems, i.e. agent systems in which all agents are equal. Equality of agents means that all functions, the sensors and actuators are similar. It follows that it is no longer required to transmit the entire mental state to let one agent reason about the reasoning of all other agents. Accordingly, it is very easy to create a master agent in such systems, as a master/leader agent would only need to get all internal states of all other agents and their current internal representation of the environment.

If learning is considered in a multiagent system one can argue that no homogeneous system can exist. This is due to the fact that the learning manipulates the policy of an agent. Therefore, every agent has its own policy function after a sufficient number of iterations. In our view the learning changes the policy function itself and, therefore, formally the policy function is replaced. This is also reflected by the formal definition as no time-index is used and there is no parameter that is manipulated through the learning process.

6 Conclusion

This article proposed a basic formal model for agents and agent systems. Our main focus was on intelligent agents that are able to learn and thus are able to adapt to changes in the environment. The formal specification of an agent's mental state is an essential part of our definition. As presented in the comparison in Sec. 4 the most cited models from literature fit into our model and indeed are expressible with our definitions. We figured out the similarities and differences and can conclude that most inconsistencies are based on varying points of view. With our contribution we have a universal platform which favors discussions on specific models and leaves space for extensions.

Nevertheless, additional work should be done until the proposed model is sufficiently large to cover all facets of agent systems. Up to now neither cooperation nor coordination mechanisms are modeled in our definitions although both are very important to be considered in some applications of agent systems. For the time being, these concepts are implicitly modeled in the knowledge base and the internal state but in future work we will try to formally define cooperation and coordination and to integrate both into the formal model.

References

1. Baker, J.E.: Reducing bias and inefficiency in the selection algorithm. In: Grefenstette, J.J. (ed.) Proceedings of the Second International Conference on Genetic Algorithms and their Application, ICGA 1987, pp. 14–21. Lawrence Erlbaum Associates, Mahwah (1987)
2. Bernstein, D.S., Amato, C., Hansen, E.A., Zilberstein, S.: Policy iteration for decentralized control of markov decision processes. Journal of Artificial Intelligence Research (JAIR) 34, 89–132 (2009)
3. Buşoniu, L., Babuška, R., De Schutter, B.: A comprehensive survey of multiagent reinforcement learning. IEEE Transactions on Systems, Man, and Cybernetics, Part C: Applications and Reviews 38(2), 156–172 (2008)

4. Cellier, F.E.: Continuous System Modeling. Springer, Heidelberg (1991)
5. Encyclopædia Britannica: Agent. Website (2010),
   http://www.britannica.com/EBchecked/topic/705121/agent (visited on April 11, 2011)
6. Encyclopædia Britannica: Intelligence. Website (2010),
   http://www.britannica.com/EBchecked/topic/289766/human-intelligence (visited on April 11, 2011)
7. Ferber, J.: Multi-Agent Systems: An Introduction to Distributed Artificial Intelligence. Addison-Wesley, Longman (1999)
8. Florea, A.M.: Introduction to multi-agent systems. In: International Summer School on Multi-Agent Systems, Bucharest (1998)
9. Franklin, S., Graesser, A.C.: Is it an agent, or just a program?: A taxonomy for autonomous agents. In: Jennings, N.R., Wooldridge, M.J., Müller, J.P. (eds.) ECAI-WS 1996 and ATAL 1996. LNCS, vol. 1193, pp. 21–35. Springer, Heidelberg (1997)
10. Gottfredson, L.S.: Foreword to "intelligence and social policy". Intelligence 24(1), 1–12 (1997)
11. Kaelbling, L.P., Littman, M.L., Cassandra, A.R.: Planning and acting in partially observable stochastic domains. Artificial Intelligence 101(1-2), 99–134 (1998)
12. Newell, A.: Reasoning, problem solving, and decision processes: The problem space as a fundamental category. In: Nickerson, R. (ed.) Attention and Performance VII, pp. 693–718. Erlbaum, Mahwah (1980)
13. Newell, A.: Unified Theories of Cognition. Harvard University Press, Harvard (1990)
14. Newell, A., Simon, H.A.: Computer science as empirical inquiry: Symbols and search. Commun. ACM 19, 113–126 (1976)
15. Russell, S.J., Norvig, P.: Artificial Intelligence: A Modern Approach, 3rd edn. Prentice Hall, Englewood Cliffs (2010)
16. Shoham, Y., Leyton-Brown, K.: Multiagent Systems: Algorithmic, Game-Theoretic, and Logical Foundations. Cambridge University Press, Cambridge (2009)
17. Sutton, R.S., Barto, A.G.: Reinforcement Learning: An Introduction. MIT Press, Cambridge (1998)
18. Vlassis, N.: A Concise Introduction to Multiagent Systems and Distributed Artificial Intelligence. Morgan and Claypool Publishers (2007)
19. Weiss, G. (ed.): Multiagent Systems: A Modern Approach to Distributed Artificial Intelligence. MIT Press, Cambridge (1999)
20. Wikipedia: Multi-agent system – wikipedia, the free encyclopedia. Website (2010), http://en.wikipedia.org/w/index.php?title=Multi-agent_system&oldid=420648559 (visited on April 11, 2011)
21. Wooldridge, M.: An Introduction to MultiAgent Systems, 2nd edn. Wiley, Chichester (2009)
22. Zeigler, B.P.: Multifacetted Modelling and Discrete Event Simulation. Academic Press Professional, Inc., London (1984)

Online News Event Extraction
for Global Crisis Surveillance

Jakub Piskorski[1], Hristo Tanev[2], Martin Atkinson[2],
Eric van der Goot[2], and Vanni Zavarella[2]

[1] Polish Academy of Sciences, ul. J.K. Ordona 21, 01-237 Warszawa, Poland
Jakub.Piskorski@ipipan.waw.pl
[2] Joint Research of the European Commission, 21027 Ispra (VA), Italy
{Hristo.Tanev,Vanni.Zavarella}@ext.jrc.ec.europa.eu,
{Martin.Atkinson,Erik.VanderGoot}@jrc.ec.europa.eu

Abstract. This article presents a real-time and multilingual news event
extraction system developed at the Joint Research Centre of the European Commission. It is capable of accurately and efficiently extracting
violent and natural disaster events from online news. In particular, a
linguistically relatively lightweight approach is deployed, in which clustered news are heavily exploited at all stages of processing. Furthermore,
the technique applied for event extraction assumes the inverted-pyramid
style of writing news articles, i.e., the most important parts of the story
are placed in the beginning and the least important facts are left toward the end. The article focuses on the system's architecture, real-time
news clustering, geo-locating and geocoding clusters, event extraction
grammar development, adapting the system to the processing of new
languages, cluster-level information fusion, visual event tracking, event
extraction accuracy evaluation, and detecting event reporting boundaries
in news article streams. This article is an extended version of [20].

Keywords: event extraction, global crisis monitoring, shallow text processing, information aggregation.

1 Introduction

A massive amount of information is now stored and exchanged via the World
Wide Web, mostly in the form of free text. Therefore, natural language processing technologies which can map free text into structured data formats are
becoming paramount. In particular, the proliferation of electronic news media
has led to an emergence of publicly accessible news aggregation systems (e.g.,
Google News, Yahoo! News, SiloBreaker, NewsTin and *DayLife*) on the web for
facilitating navigation through news broadcast daily worldwide. Such news aggregation systems group topically related articles into clusters and classify them
according to various predefined criteria. Although such systems provide a more
structured view of what is happening in the world, the amount of data requiring
processing by a human remains enormous. Recently, several endeavours towards

N.T. Nguyen (Ed.): Transactions on CCI V, LNCS 6910, pp. 182–212, 2011.
© Springer-Verlag Berlin Heidelberg 2011

developing real-time news event extraction systems have been attempted, to detect key information about events from various electronic news media and summarize this information in the form of database-like structures. In this way, such systems have been successful in providing even more compact event descriptions that combine information from different sources.

This article gives an overview of the multilingual event-extraction system developed at the Joint Research Centre of the European Commission for extracting violent and natural disaster event information from on-line news articles collected through the Internet with the Europe Media Monitor (EMM) [6,5], a web based news aggregation system, which regularly checks for updates of news articles across multiple sites in different languages. Gathering information about crisis-related events over time is an important task for better understanding conflicts and for developing global monitoring systems for automatic detection of precursors for threats in the fields of conflict and health. In particular, web news reflect trends and behaviours, which constitute a powerful data source for future event prediction. The increase in security concerns since 9/11 especially those related to terrorism have significantly boosted research on developing systems for automated event extraction from news.

Formally, the task of event extraction is to automatically identify events in free text and to derive detailed information about them, ideally identifying *Who did what to whom, when, with what methods (instruments), where and why.* Information about an event is usually represented in a so called *template* which can be seen as a attribute-value matrix. An example illustrating an event template is presented in Figure 1. Automatically extracting events is a higher-level information extraction (IE) task [3] which is not trivial due to the complexity of natural language and due to the fact that, in news, a full event description is usually scattered over several sentences and articles. In particular, event extraction relies on identifying named entities and relations between them. The research on automatic event extraction was pushed forward by the DARPA-initiated Message Understanding Conferences[1] and by the ACE (Automatic Content Extraction)[2] programme. Although, a considerable amount of work on automatic extraction of events has been reported, it still appears to be a lesser studied area in comparison to the somewhat easier tasks of named-entity and relation extraction. Precision/recall figures oscillating around 60% are considered to be a good result. Three comprehensive examples of the current functionality and capabilities of event extraction technology dealing with identification of disease outbreaks and conflict incidents are given in [12], [34] and [16]. The most recent trends and developments in this area are reported in [4]. The work most similar to ours on deploying information extraction technology for merging news events from multiple news sources covering different time periods have been reported in [17] and [31].

---

[1] MUC - http://www.itl.nist.gov/iaui/894.02/related/projects/muc
[2] ACE - http://projects.ldc.upenn.edu/ace

TYPE:	killing
METHOD:	shooting
ACTOR:	Americans
VICTIM:	Five Iraqis
LOCATION:	Bagdad
TIME:	12.10.2003

Fig. 1. An example of an event template derived from the sentence *Five Iraqis were shot by Americans in Bagdad on the 12th of October 2003*

Due to our requirement that the event extraction system must be multilingual and easily extensible to new domains, a linguistically relatively lightweight approach has been chosen. In particular, we take advantage of clustered news data at several stages of the event extraction process and we assume that news articles are written in the inverted-pyramid style, i.e., the most important parts of the story are placed in the beginning of the article and the least important facts are left toward the end. As a consequence of this, only a tiny fraction of each news article is analyzed. Further, a cascade of finite-state extraction grammars is deployed in order to identify event-related information. These patterns are semi-automatically acquired in a bootstrapping manner, again via utilization of clustered news data. Exploiting clustered news intuitively guarantees better precision. Since information about events is scattered over different articles single pieces of information are validated and aggregated at cluster-level. One of the main prerequisites for the ability to digest massive amounts of data in real time is efficient processing. Therefore, an in-house extraction pattern-matching engine has been developed in order to find a good trade-off between terse linguistic descriptions and efficient processing. The system has been fully operational since 2007 and supports event extraction for several languages. The results are viewed in real time via a publicly accessible web page or via *Google Earth* application. An empirical evaluation revealed acceptable accuracy and a strong application potential. Although our domain centers around security-related events, the techniques deployed in our system can be applied to other domains, e.g., tracking business-related events for risk assessment.

The rest of this article is organized as follows. First, in section 2 the architecture of our live event extraction processing chain is described. Next, section 3 gives an overview of real-time news clustering. The process of geo-locating clusters is sketched in section 4. Subsequently, section 5 describes the structure of event extraction grammars, their creation, and multilingual aspects. Further, section 6 elaborates on information fusion. Event visualization and accessing fully-fledged event descriptions generated by the system is presented in section 7. Evaluation figures are given in section 8. Section 9 presents the results of some experiments on detecting news event reporting boundaries in a stream of news articles. Finally, we end with a summary and future work directions in section 10.

2   Event Extraction Process

This section briefly describes the real-time event extraction processing chain, which is depicted in Figure 2. First, before the proper event extraction process can proceed, news articles are gathered by dedicated software for electronic media monitoring, namely the Europe Media Monitor EMM system [6] that receives 100000 news articles from 2500 news sources in 42 languages each day. Secondly, all articles are classified according to around 700 categories and then scanned in order to identify known entities (e.g., geographical references, names of known people and organizations, etc.). This information is then created as meta data for each article. Next, the articles are grouped into news clusters according to content similarity. Subsequently, each cluster is geo-located. Further, clusters describing security-related events are selected via the application of key-word based heuristics.

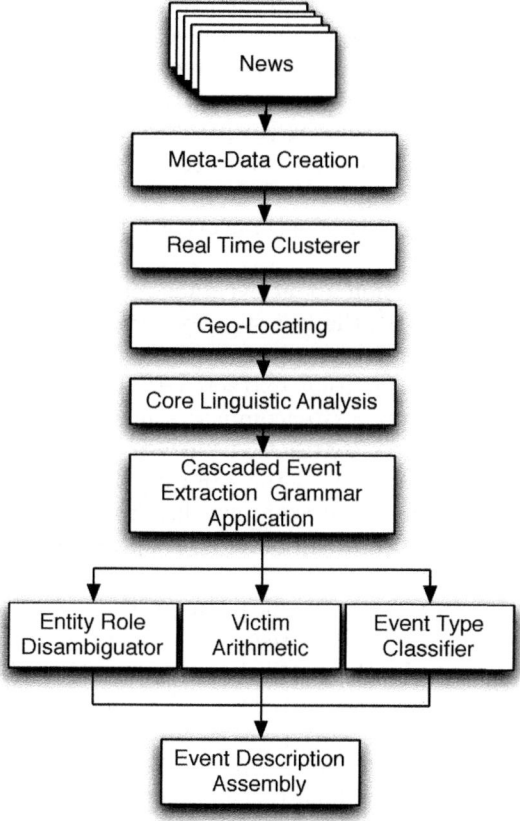

Fig. 2. Real-time event extraction processing chain

Next, each of these clusters is processed by NEXUS (News cluster Event eXtraction Using language Structures), the core event extraction engine. For each cluster it tries to detect and extract only the main event by analyzing all articles in the cluster. For each detected violent and natural disaster event NEXUS produces a frame, whose main slots are: date and location, number of killed and injured, kidnapped people, actors, and type of event. In an initial step, each article in the cluster is linguistically preprocessed in order to produce a more abstract representation of its text. This encompasses the following steps: fine-grained tokenization, sentence splitting, domain-specific dictionary look-up (e.g., recognizing numbers, quantifiers, person titles), matching of key terms indicating unnamed person groups (e.g. *civilians*, *policemen*, *Shiite*), and morphological analysis. The aforementioned tasks are accomplished by CORLEONE (Core Linguistic Entity Online Extraction), our in-house core linguistic engine [19].

Once the linguistic preprocessing is complete, a cascade of extraction grammars is applied on each article within a cluster. The patterns for the extraction grammars are created through a blend of machine learning and knowledge-based techniques. Contrary to other approaches, the learning phase is done by exploiting clustered news, which intuitively guarantees better precision of the learned patterns. The extraction patterns are matched against the first sentence and the title of each article from the cluster. By processing only the top sentence and the title, the system is more likely to capture facts about the most important event in the cluster. Figure 3 gives an example of titles and corresponding first sentences from articles reporting on a same event related to a killing of 44 people at a wedding in Turkey.

Finally, since the information about events is scattered over different articles (see the example in Figure 3), the last step consists of cross-article cluster-level information fusion, in order to produce fully-fledged event descriptions, i.e., we aggregate and validate information extracted locally from each single article in the same cluster. This process encompasses mainly three tasks, entity role disambiguation (as a result of extraction pattern application the same entity might be assigned different roles), victim counting and event type classification.

The core event-extraction process is synchronized with the real-time news article clustering system in EMM in order to keep up-to-date with most recent events.

However, in some domains, e.g., illegal migration, clustering proved to be ineffective since event reporting data seems to be more sparse, frequently coming from local news sources only, thus unlikely to form clusters. In such cases, event extraction is performed on single articles, and a larger portion of each article is analysed in order not to lose any piece of possibly relevant information [22]. Nevertheless, in this article, we focus on the description of the cluster-centric approach to event extraction, which turned out to perform good in the domain of natural disasters, violent events and other crisis-related events.

A more thorough description of the real-time news clustering, geo-locating clusters, event extraction grammars, information fusion, event reporting boundary

44 shot dead during Turkey ceremony
Eight gunmen suspected of fatally shooting 44 people at an engagement ceremony in south-east Turkey have been arrested ...
44 killed in attack in Turkey (AP)
AP - Turkish security forces on Tuesday detained eight gunmen suspected of fatally shooting 44 people, many of whom were praying, at an engagement ceremony in the rural southeast of the country ...
Turkey - Forty-four people killed at wedding party in Kurdish region
Forty-four people, including 22 women and children, were killed in an attack on a wedding party late on Monday in Turkey's Kurdish region ...
Gunmen kill at least 44 at Turkish wedding party
Masked gunmen armed with assault rifles and grenades attacked a wedding party in mainly Kurdish southeast Turkey, killing at least 44 people, authorities said ...
Masked gunmen kill 45 people at engagement party
ANKARA, Turkey – Masked assailants with grenades and automatic weapons attacked an engagement ceremony in southeast Turkey on Monday, killing 45 people ...

Fig. 3. Titles and corresponding first sentences from articles (in the same cluster) reporting on a same event related to a killing of 44 people at a wedding in Turkey

detection, issues concerning multilinguality and accessing the results produced by the live event extraction engine follows in the subsequent sections.

3   Clustering of News Articles

The real time news clustering system performs periodical hierarchical clustering on a set of news articles harvested in a 4-hour time window. A cache is maintained for twice that period in case the number of articles drops below a certain minimum, in which case the system attempts to process at least that set minimum. This process is performed every 10 minutes.

Initially each news article is considered as a cluster. The clustering process is agglomerative and uses average group linkage to determine the distances between the clusters. For calculating these distances a simple cosine measure is used. The clustering process continues until the maximum cosine distance falls below a certain set threshold (a function of the size of the term-set which can be taken as a proxy for the vector density, given a maximum word count per article).

The article feature vectors are simple word count vectors. The words used for the construction of the word-document space are selected based on various criteria depending on the amount of information available in the time window under consideration. No lemmatizing is performed and a simple bag-of-words approach is used instead.

The system maintains a constantly updated frequency table for all words found in all articles processed for a particular language over time. The system employs a technique similar to an infinite input response filter to calculate and maintain these frequencies, which can shift over time. After a fixed run-length the number of samples used to calculate the average is set. This prevents loss of accuracy, numeric overflow and gives a more realistic temporal view of the word frequencies. Additionally, a full information entropy calculation is performed over the article set in the time window every clustering run [27].

The selection criteria for the words to be used for the construction of the word-document space are as follows:

- only use words of more than 2 characters (most words of 2 or less characters do not carry any significant meaning),
- reject words that are in the 100 most frequently used words in the language (empirically this contains most of the non-significant words greater than 2 characters e.g. *the, and, for, that, said,* etc.),
- reject words that have an information entropy higher than a certain language-dependent threshold (typically 0.75) in the document set under consideration (functionally almost the same as the top 100 words removal, but now for the document set at hand removes words like days of the week, etc.),
- consider only the first 200 words (length normalisation) of each news article (most news-relevant information will be present in the first 200 words),
- only select words that appear at least twice in at least 2 documents, unless this results in a number of unique words less than a certain threshold (typically 1000) in which case only use words that appear at least once in at least 2 documents.

A cluster is only valid if it contains articles from at least 2 different sources and these articles are not duplicates.

After the clustering procedure the new clusters are compared with those calculated at $t - \Delta_t$. If there is any overlap between clusters, the articles appearing in cluster at $t - \Delta_t$ which do not appear in the current cluster, are linked to the current cluster. There are 2 possible reasons for the missing articles: either the articles have simply dropped out of the time window, or the cluster has broken up due to the changes in word-document space. This merging process can lead to internal duplication of articles, i.e. the articles are linked back into the original cluster, but also exist in a newly formed cluster. In order to avoid this duplication, the current cluster set is scanned for internal overlap and any overlapping clusters are merged.

In this way news stories consisting of large numbers of articles, far exceeding the number present in any time-window, can be tracked incrementally over time, as long as there is some reporting in the time-window.

The graph in Figure 4 shows the evolution of a cluster over time as a story. On the bottom axis is time, both left and right axis show the number of articles. The left axis shows the cumulative and 4hour sum count, while the right axis shows the instantaneous (10 minute) count. Similarly, the area in the chart shows the cumulate count of articles in the cluster and the line in the chart shows the story evolution (number of articles present in a 4 hour window) and the bars show the instant (10 minute) entry of new articles into the cluster. Red dots on the line indicate potential breaking news moments.

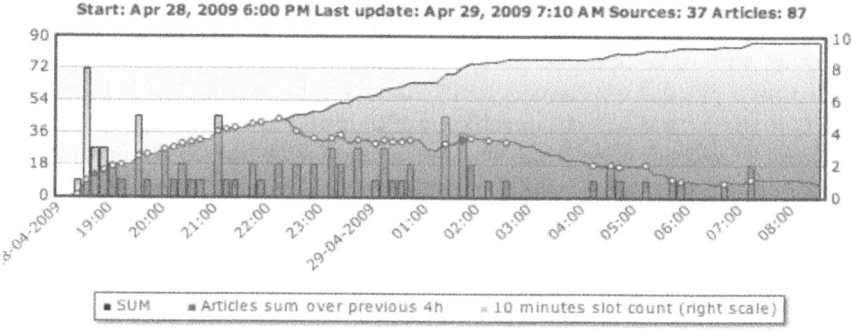

Story Edition - Specter joining Dems; shifts Senate

Start: Apr 28, 2009 6:00 PM Last update: Apr 29, 2009 7:10 AM Sources: 37 Articles: 87

Fig. 4. Evolution of a cluster over time

4   Geo-locating

Homographs pose a well-known problem in the process of geo-tagging news articles [24]. In particular, words referring to place names may:

(a) occur as person names, e.g., *Conrad Hilton* are the names of towns in the USA, New Zealand and Canada,
(b) occur as common words, e.g., *And* is a village in Iran,
(c) have variants, e.g., well known cities have language variants, e.g., *Seul* meaning alone/only in French is also the Capital of South Korea in Portuguese and Italian,
(d) refer to different locations, e.g., there are 33 places named *Clinton*.

Additional complications are caused by language inflection and capital cities referring to the reporting location.

Our latest approach is to conduct homograph disambiguation at two distinct levels, firstly at the level of individual article and secondly, when the articles have been clustered. The article geo-tagging algorithm occurs as follows: First, the problem in (a) is solved by removing previously recognized person and organization names from the toponym candidate list. Next, a multi-lingual gazetteer of place, province, region and country names (circa 600000 entries) is used to geo-match a list of candidate locations in the news articles.

In order to disambiguate homographs that are common words and place names (see (b) and (d)), the traditional approach is to use language dependent stop word lists. We use a different approach based on two characteristics maintained in our gazetteer. The first characteristic classifies locations based on their perceived size, such that capital cities and major cities have a higher class than small villages. The second characteristic maintains the hierarchical relation of place in its administrative located hierarchy (i.e., town, in province, in region, in country). The disambiguation algorithm lets high class locations pass through as well as locations that have a containment relation with other candidate locations (e.g., *Paris, Texas, USA*). To resolve (c) we remove any geo-tags that are incompatible with the language[3] of the article.

In order to handle name inflection, names are maintained with their variants encoded as a regular expression. Only matches, for which the language of the name and the article are compatible, are maintained in the candidate location list. Next, a Newswire location filtering is applied, where the word position of the candidate location is used to promote locations occurring after an initial location since the Newswire location generally appears earlier in the article.

We are currently experimenting with adding further filtering mechanisms coming from the semantics of the locative prepositional phrases, in which toponyms are usually nested. This seems particularly needed in domains, such as border security, that involve motion events (e.g. a person entity moving from place A and heading to place B possibly passing through place C), with typically multiple place name mentions, most of which are not the actual location of the event. In most of these contexts, a simple semantic analysis is sufficient to discard toponyms that are fulfilling irrelevant semantic roles (like the ORIGIN of the person involved in an illegal border crossing event), so as to largely reduce the complexity of the whole geo-location task.

At the level of the cluster all named entities and geo-tags in the articles of the cluster are gathered together. This is necessary to remove named entities that have not been matched in articles (a common reporting trait is to mention only well known names, e.g., *Clinton, Hilary Rodham Clinton, Hilary Rodham* and *Hilary Clinton*). Next, we gather the highest score for each place by maximum value (we don't sum same place values since often news wires are repeated many times and this would affect the real location that is cited in the article). Next, we cap the scores, here we look for tags that are either countries or regions and check whether any of the places cited are physically inside. When this is the case we increase the place score, i.e., some articles of the same cluster will talk more generally of an event in China while others will be more specific and will describe a location like Sechuan Province. Finally, the highest scoring place tag is chosen as the geo-location of the cluster.

Compared to the previous version of the geo-location algorithm [29] we have carried out a more thorough evaluation for English, French and Italian. The data set used were the daily clusters over three selected days. The results are presented in Table 1.

---

[3] The language of the article is primarily determined by a source related language attribute but if necessary corrected by an automatic language detector which forms part of the system.

Table 1. Precision and Recall of the Geo-Location algorithm

Lang	Cluster Size	Correct Tags	Missed Tags	False Pos.	Precision	Recall
EN	294	270	17	7	97%	94%
FR	77	76	1	4	95%	98%
IT	83	74	9	1	99%	89%

A particular system of Geo Code Identifiers (GID's) has been employed in this system. The objective of encoding the GID's is to allow fast evaluation of part of the disambiguation algorithm notably with respect to the containment functions that can be computationally intensive to evaluate using classical topographic algorithms. Here, we capitalize on the fact that our gazetteer is predefined so we use off-line processing to determine such topographic containment relations between elements in the gazetteer and higher administrative levels.

Therefore, the basic objective of encoding of the GID's is to be able to quickly determine whether two places are in the same provincial, regional and national administrative areas without having to do costly topographic calculations, index look ups or string comparisons. To fulfill this situation the GID is represented as a long integer which encodes each individual place name's administrative characteristics. In particular, country ID, regional ID, provincial ID and place name ID are represented with 10, 6, 8 and 30 bits respectively.

We start by defining GID's for our administrative area dataset, GAUL (Global Administrative Unit Layers) from the Food and Agriculture Organization of the United Nations. To encode the GAUL data set we start with all the country polygons that we assign a GID as an integer value in ascending order. For each country we then assign a sequential GID for each region inside the country again following our system outline above, then we repeat this operation for each province in each of the regions.

We then take our home grown multilingual gazetteer of place names, which has grown from a number of open source information repositories like Wikipedia and Geonames. For each location in the place name gazetteer we look for the provincial polygon that contains the place name coordinates. The GID of the provincial polygon will, by our encoding scheme, already contain the regional and national GID's. Hence we just assign a sequential number to the place name corresponding to its assignment (sequence) in the provincial polygon. Determining whether two GID's refer to places in a same country or administrative region boils down to simple bit operations.

5   Cascaded Extraction Grammars

In order to detect event information from news articles we deploy a cascade of finite-state extraction grammars. Following this approach was mainly motivated by the fact that:

- finite-state grammars can be efficiently processed, and
- using cascades of smaller grammars facilitates the maintenance of underlying linguistic resources and extending the system to new domains.

This section first introduces our in-house IE-oriented pattern matching engine. Subsequently, the structure of the current event extraction grammar for English is presented. Finally, the automatic extraction pattern acquisition and issues concerning adapting event extraction process to new languages are briefly addressed.

5.1   Pattern Matching Engine

In order to guarantee that massive amounts of textual data can be digested in real time, we have developed ExPRESS (Extraction Pattern Engine and Specification Suite), a highly efficient extraction pattern engine [18], which is capable of matching thousands of patterns against MB-sized texts within seconds. The specification language for creating extraction patterns in ExPRESS is a blend of two previously introduced IE-oriented grammar formalisms, namely JAPE (Java Annotation Pattern Engine) used in the widely-known GATE platform [9] and XTDL, a significantly more declarative and linguistically elegant formalism used in a lesser known SPRoUT platform [10].

An ExPRESS grammar consists of pattern-action rules. The left-hand side (LHS) of a rule (the recognition part) is a regular expression over flat feature structures (FFS), i.e., non-recursive typed feature structures (TFS) without structure sharing, where features are string-valued and unlike in XTDL types are not ordered in a hierarchy. The right-hand side (RHS) of a rule (action part) constitutes a list of FFS, which will be returned in case LHS pattern is matched.

On the LHS of a rule variables can be tailored to the string-valued attributes in order to facilitate information transport into the RHS, etc. Further, like in XTDL, functional operators (FO) are allowed on the RHSs for forming slot values and for establishing contact with the 'outer world'. The predefined set of FOs can be extended through implementing an appropriate programming interface. FOs can also be deployed as boolean-valued predicates. The two aforementioned features make ExPRESS more amenable than JAPE since writing 'native code' on the RHS of rules (common practice in JAPE) has been eliminated. Finally, we adapted JAPE's feature of associating patterns with multiple actions, i.e., producing multiple annotations (possibly nested) for a given text fragment. It is important to note that grammars can be cascaded. The following pattern for matching events, where one person is killed by another, illustrates the syntax.

```
killing-event :>
 ((person & [FULL-NAME: #name1]):killed
   key-phrase & [METHOD: #method, FORM: "passive"]
   (person & [FULL-NAME: #name2]):killer):event
 ->
 killed: victim & [NAME: #name1],
```

```
killer: actor & [NAME: #name2],
event: violence & [TYPE: "killing",
                   METHOD: #method,
                   ACTOR: #name2,
                   VICTIM: #name1,
                   ACTOR_IN_EVENTS: numEvents(#name2)]
```

The pattern matches a sequence consisting of: a structure of type person representing a person or group of persons who is (are) the victim, followed by a phrase (a structure of type key-phrase) in passive form, which triggers a *killing event*, and another structure of type person representing the actor. The symbol & links a name of the FFS's type with a list of constraints (in form of attribute-value pairs) which have to be fulfilled. The variables #name1 and #name2 establish bindings to the names of both humans involved in the event. Analogously, the variable #method establishes binding to the method of killing delivered by the key-phrase structure. Further, there are three labels on the LHS (killed, killer, and event) which specify the start/end position of the annotation actions specified on the RHS. The first two actions (triggered by the labels killed and killer) on the RHS produce FFS of type victim and actor resp., where the value of the NAME slot is created via accessing the variables #name1 and #name2. Finally, the third action produces an FFS of type violence. The value of the ACTOR_IN_EVENTS attribute is computed via a call to a FO numEvents() which contacts external knowledge base to retrieve the number of events the current actor was involved in the past.

We have carried out some experiments to compare the run-time behavior of EXPRESS with XTDL. In order to do this we have used the event extraction grammar presented in Section 5.2. It was converted in almost one-to-one manner into a XTDL grammar.[4] In an experiment, the grammars were applied to a 167 MB excerpt of the news on terrorism, consisting of 122 files on a PC Pentium 4 machine with 2,79 GHz. The average run-time for processing a single document (average size of 1,37 MB) for EXPRESS and XTDL interpreter was 5.57 sec. and 58.30 sec. respectively, i.e, EXPRESS was circa 10 times faster. It is important to note that the average number of matches per document amounted to ca. 60 000 and that time given above included deployment of core linguistic processing components by both engines.[5] The time consumed by pattern matcher of EXPRESS and XTDL disregarding the time needed to deploy core linguistic processing components amounted to 50.34 sec. and 2.56 sec. respectively.

A comprehensive overview of the techniques for compiling and processing grammars and the entire ExPRESS engine as well as more detailed description

---

[4] It turned to be a relatively simple task since the core linguistic components provided with EXPRESS have nearly identical functionality and I/O specification as those used in SPROUT. However, some rules had to be expressed as two rules in XTDL since XTDL rules do not allow for specifying more than one output structure directly.

[5] Both engines used the same type of components, namely tokenizers, gazetteers and morphological analysis component.

of the run-time performance comparison of ExPRESS, XTDL and JAPE is given in [18].

5.2   Event Extraction Grammars

There are two different approaches to building event extraction grammars:

- the complexity of the language is represented at the level of lexical descriptions, where each word in the lexicon is provided with a rich set of semantic and syntactic features [2,23],
- the complexity of the language is represented through different, mostly linear, patterns in the grammar, which rely on superficial or less sophisticated linguistic features [32].

Providing rich lexical descriptions like verb sub-categorization frames in [2] or ontologies in [23] requires a linguistic expertize, on the other hand, more shallow lexical descriptions will result in more patterns to encode the necessary linguistic knowledge. However, superficial patterns are closer to the text data. We believe that their creation is more intuitive and easier for non-experts than building ontologies or sub-categorization frames. Writing such patterns is easier for languages like English, where the word ordering obeys strict rules and the morphological variations are not an important issue. Therefore, we followed this approach when creating our English event extraction grammar.

This grammar in its current version consists of two subgrammars. The first-level subgrammar contains patterns for recognition of proper names, e.g., person names (*Osama bin Laden*), and small-scale structures, e.g., unnamed person groups (*at least five civilians*), named person groups (*More than thousands of Iraqis*), etc. As an example consider the following rule for detecting mentions of person groups.

```
person-group :> ((gazetteer & [GTYPE: "numeral",
                               SURFACE: #quant,
                               AMOUNT: #num])
               (gazetteer & [GTYPE: "person-modifier"])?
               (gazetteer & [GTYPE: "person-group-proper-noun",
                             SURFACE: #name1])
               (gazetteer & [GTYPE: "person-group-proper-noun",
                             SURFACE: #name2])):name
  -> name: person-group & [QUANTIFIER: #quant,
                           AMOUNT: #num,
                           TYPE: "UNNAMED",
                           NAME: #name,
                           RULE: "person-group"],
            & #name = Concatenate(#name1,#name2).
```

This rule matches noun phrases (NP), which refer to people by mentioning their nationalities, religion or political group to which they belong, e.g. *three young*

Chinese, one Iraqi Muslim, three young Maoists. The words and phrases which fall in the category `person-group-proper-noun`, `numeral` and `person-modifier` (e.g. *young*) are listed in a domain-specific lexicon (gazetteer) together with a number of other semantic classes relevant for the domain. In this way the grammar rules are being kept less language dependent, i.e., rules can be applied to languages other than English, provided that language-specific dictionaries back up the grammar. As it will be shown in Section 5.4, semantic categories can be populated semi-automatically using machine learning techniques.

Through abstracting from surface forms in the rules themselves the size of the grammars can be kept relatively low and any modifications boils down to extending the lexica, which makes the development for non-experts straightforward. Further, the first-level grammar does not rely on morphological information and uses circa 40 fine-grained token types (e.g., `word-with-hyphen`, `opening-bracket`, `word-with-apostrophe`, `all-capital-letters`), which are to a large extent language independent. Consequently, the majority of the first-level grammar rules for English can be used for processing texts in other languages. For instance, the following rule for recognition of person names (a title followed by a first name and a capitalized word) is applicable to many languages.

```
person :> ((gazetteer & [GTYPE: "title",
                         SURFACE: #title)
           (gazetteer & [GTYPE: "firstName",
                         SURFACE: #fname])
           (token &     [TYPE: "alphaFirstCapitalized",
                         SURFACE: #surname])):name
  -> name: person & [NAME: #name],
                  & #name = Concatenate(#title,#fname,#surname).
```

Clearly, some of the rules might not be applicable for some languages due to the differences in syntactic structure, but they are intuitively easily modifiable.

The second-level subgrammar consists of patterns for extracting partial information on events: actors, victims, type of event, etc. Since the event extraction system is intended to process news articles which refer to security and crisis events, the second-level grammar models only domain-specific language constructions. Moreover, the event extraction system processes news clusters which contain articles about the same topic from many sources, which refer to the same event description with different linguistic expressions. This redundancy mitigates the effect of phenomena like anaphora, ellipsis and complex syntactic constructions. As mentioned earlier, the system is processing only the first sentence and the title of each article, where the main facts are summarized in a straightforward manner, usually without using coreference, sub-ordinated sentences and structurally complex phrases. Therefore, the second-level grammar models solely simple syntactic constructions via utilization of 1/2-slot extraction patterns like the ones given below. The role assignments are given in brackets.

```
[1] PERSON-GROUP <DEAD> "were killed"
[2] {PERSON | PERSON-GROUP} <DEAD> "may have perished"
```

```
[3] PERSON-GROUP <DEAD> "dead"
[4] "police nabbed" PERSON <ARRESTED>
[5] PERSON-GROUP <DISPLACED> "fled their homes"
[6] PERSON <DEAD> "was shot dead by" PERSON <PERPETRATOR>
```

These patterns are similar in spirit to the ones used in AutoSlog [26]. They are acquired semi-automatically (see 5.3). The fact that in English the word ordering is more strict and the morphology is simpler than in other languages contributes also to the coverage and accuracy of the patterns, which encode non-sophisticated event-description phrases.

To sum up, event extraction system discards the text, which goes beyond the first sentence for the following reasons:

– handling more complex language phenomena is hard and might require knowledge-intensive processing,
– the most crucial information we seek for is included in the title or first sentence,
– if some crucial information has not been captured from one article in the cluster, we might extract it from other article in the same cluster.

In order to keep the grammar concise and as much as possible language independent, we represent in the grammar all surface-level linear patterns via pattern types, which indicate the position of the pattern with respect to the slot to be filled (left or right). To be more precise, all patterns are stored in a domain-specific lexicon (applied prior to grammar application), where surface patterns are associated with their type, the event-specific semantic role assigned to the entity which fills the slot (e.g., WOUNDED, KIDNAPPED, DISPLACED, etc.) and the number of the phrase which may fill the slot (singular, plural, or both). For instance, the surface pattern "shot to death" for recognizing dead victims as a result of shooting, is encoded as follows.

```
shot to death [TYPE: right-context-sg-and-pl,
               SURFACE: "shot to death",
               SLOTTYPE: DEAD]
```

The value of the TYPE attribute indicates that the pattern is on the right-hand-side of its slot (right-context), which can be filled by a phrase which refers to one or many people (sg-and-pl). The event-specific semantic role, assigned to each NP filling the slot is DEAD. Via such an encoding of event-triggering linear patterns, the extraction patterns [1] and [3] from the list given above are merged into one (in a simplified form):

```
dead-person :> person-group
              gazetteer & [TYPE: right-context-sg-and-pl
                           SLOT: dead]
    -> ...
```

Interestingly, we have found circa 3000 event-triggering domain-specific surface patterns for English. Clearly, the strict word ordering and relatively simple morphology allowed for easy generation of pattern variants.

5.3 Pattern Acquisition

For creating second-level grammar patterns described in previous section a weakly supervised machine learning (ML) algorithm has been deployed. It is similar in spirit to the bootstrapping algorithms described in [15,33]. In particular, the pattern acquisition process involves multiple consecutive iterations of ML followed by manual validation. Learning patterns for each event-specific semantic role requires a separate cycle of learning iterations. The method uses clusters of news articles produced by EMM. Each cluster includes articles from different sources about the same news story. Therefore, we assume that each entity appears in the same semantic role in the context of one cluster ('one sense per discourse' [11]). The core steps of the pattern acquisition algorithm are as follows:

1. Annotate a small corpus with event-specific information,
2. Learn automatically single-slot extraction patterns from annotated corpus,
3. Manually validate/modify these patterns,
4. If the size of the pattern set exceeds certain threshold, then terminate,
5. Match the patterns against the full corpus or part of it,
6. Assign semantic roles to entities which fill the slots,
7. Annotate automatically all the occurrences of these entities in all articles in the same cluster with the corresponding role this entity has been assigned in the previous step and goto 2.

An automatic procedure for syntactic expansion complements the learning, i.e., based on a manually provided list of words which have identical (or nearly identical) syntactic model of use (e.g. *killed, assassinated, murdered*, etc.) new patterns are generated from the old ones by substituting for each other the words in the list. Subsequently, some of the automatically acquired single-slot patterns were used to manually create 2-slot patterns like X shot Y. The pattern acquisition process is described thoroughly in [28].

5.4 Semi-supervised Learning of Semantic Categories

The other main step towards language and domain customization of the lexical resources deployed by extraction grammar is the population of the domain-specific semantic classes referenced by grammar rules. The task is also partially automated through application of machine learning techniques.

A semi-supervised system, *Ontopopulis*, is deployed which takes as input a small set of sample phrases belonging to a target semantic class (seed terms) and a unannotated corpus of news article, and then further populates the semantic class with new instances (terms) [30].

The learning process consists of two steps: a 'Feature extraction and weighting' stage, where context features for a category C are selected among the uni-grams and bi-grams co-occurring with any of the seed terms of C, and then weighted and ordered based on a Pointwise Mutual Information measure; a 'Term selection and scoring' stage exploiting a term feature vector representation, based on co-occurrence between candidate terms and features. The whole learning process is semi-supervised, as a minimal human intervention is required in the form of manual selection of context feature output between the two stages.

An evaluation of the learning accuracy performance was carried out for Spanish and Portuguese language on a number of semantic categories, such as Person, Weapon, Crime, Infrastructure,etc. As an example, for the classes Person and Weapon in Spanish, term precision scored 71% and 14%, respectively, while precision on the 20 top ranked terms raised to 95% and 60%, with seed set size of 56 and 22 and generative factors of 7.2 and 5.6, respectively. This shows that, while absolute accuracy is highly dependent on the target category, the tool is generally able to properly rank the learned terms based on their semantics.

5.5   Multilinguality

The English event extraction grammar described in the previous section relies mainly on a multilingual named-entity recognition grammar, language-specific dictionary of NE-relevant trigger words, and a language-specific dictionary of surface-level event extraction patterns. In this way adapting the current event extraction grammar to new languages does not require much linguistic expertise.

We have extended the system to the processing of Italian, Spanish, Portuguese, French, Russian and recently Arabic through providing the aforementioned language-specific resources. Although the system's precision was as high as expected, an empirical coverage analysis for Italian showed that there are some drawbacks when surface-level patterns are applied. This is mainly due to the free-word order and relative morphological richness of Romance languages. Further, Italian appears to be more verbose with the respect to expressing information about events, i.e., it is structurally more complex. For instance, Italian verb phrases describing events show some additional structural complexity at the linear level due to the encoding of some essential information on the event, like the 'means' or 'instruments' of a killing act, in prepositional phrases, as opposed to English which typically uses lexical content of the main verb itself to convey such information. This is shown in the following sample excerpts from Italian and English articles from cross-lingual clusters about the same event returned by EMM news aggregation system.

excite-news Monday, May 19, 2008 10:43:00 AM CEST (ANSA) - MANILA, 19 MAG - Un uomo **ha crivellato a colpi di mitra** *alcune case di Calamba, una citta' vicino Manila, uccidendo otto persone....*

cnn Monday, May 19, 2008 5:58:00 AM CEST A man **strafed** *several houses during a shooting spree early Monday in a town south of Manila, killing eight people and wounding six others...*

Consequently, we designed a slightly more linguistically sophisticated rules for Italian, Spanish and Portuguese, which cover a rich variety of morphological and syntactic constructions. This yielded better overall extraction accuracy. Some evaluation figures are given in Section 8, whereas the details of the process of adapting the system to the processing of Italian are presented in [35]. While we applied the same linguistic approach for Spanish and Portuguese, in [30] we performed a preliminary evaluation on a minimal, machine learning-oriented customization to these two languages, consisting of only a slight modification of the Italian person entity recognition grammar, together with the application of the linear pattern and semantic category learning methods introduced above. Although not impressive in absolute terms, the performance figures in both languages show a significant improvement with respect to the corresponding baseline systems, proving the effectiveness of the customization methods in addressing the multilinguality challenge.

Although we are currently developing linguistic resources for tackling the event extraction task for Arabic (EMM has some 86 different news sources in this language) and apply similar techniques as for English, our initial approach was slightly different. First, statistical machine translation systems were used for translating the articles in the Arabic clusters into English. Next, these translations were passed into the English event extraction system. In particular, we integrated two Arabic-to-English translation systems into the live processing chain, namely *Google Translate*[6] and *LanguageWeaver*[7]. We plan to compare the results of this approach with a first release of a full-fledged event extraction system for Arabic.

6 Information Fusion

Once the event extraction grammars has been applied locally at document level the single pieces of information are merged into fully-fledged event descriptions. In particular, three tasks are performed at this level: (a) semantic role disambiguation, (b) victim counting, and (c) event type classification. They are described briefly.

Semantic Role Disambiguation: If one and the same entity has two roles assigned in the same cluster, a preference is given to the role assigned by the most reliable group of patterns. The double-slot patterns are considered the most reliable. Regarding the one-slot constructions, patterns for detection of *killed, wounded,* and *kidnapped* are considered as more reliable than the ones for extraction of the *actor (perpetrator)* slot (the latter one being more generic). The pattern reliability ranking is based on empirical observations.

Victim Counting: Another ambiguity arises from the contradictory information which news sources give about the number of victims (e.g., killed) An ad-hoc algorithm for computing the most probable estimation for these numbers is applied. It finds the largest group of numbers which are close to each other and

---

[6] http://translate.google.com/translate_t?hl=en

[7] http://www.languageweaver.com

subsequently finds the number closest to their average. All articles, which report on number of victims which significantly differs from the estimated cluster-level victim number are discarded. In order to perform victim arithmetics at the document level a small taxonomy of person classes [29] is used. The article-level victim counting algorithm consists of the following steps:

1. Extract from a news article a set of NPs $E = \{E_1, E_2, \ldots, E_n\}$, which refer to individuals or groups with definite number of people and which have certain semantic role.
2. Map each E_i to a concept from the taxonomy using a list of keyword-taxonomy mappings (we denote it as $conc(E_i)$). As an example consider the text *One journalist was beaten to death and two soldiers died in the clashes in which four civilians lost their lives in total.* Three NPs referring to killed people would be extracted: *one journalist, two soldiers* and *four civilians*, and mapped to the taxonomy categories `journalist`, `serviceman`, `civilian`.
3. Delete each E_i from E, if there exist $E_j \in E$ such that $conc(E_i)$ is-a $conc(E_j)$, i.e., $conc(E_i)$ is a direct or indirect successor of $conc(E_j)$ in the taxonomy. In this manner only the most generic NPs are left in E. In our example we may identify one such relation, namely, *journalist is a civilian*, therefore we delete the NP *one journalist* from E.
4. Sum up the numbers reported from the NPs in E. In our example we have to sum up the numbers from the phrases *four civilians* and *two soldiers* (four and two).

Event Type Classification: Whenever possible, we assign a class label to the detected violent event or disaster. Some of the most used event classes are *Terrorist Attack, Bombing, Shooting, Air Attack, Man-Made Disaster, Floods,* etc. The event type classification algorithm uses a blend of keyword matching, taxonomy of event types and domain specific rules.

First, all potential event types are assigned ranks based on the matching of type-specific keywords in the articles in a given cluster (a rank for a given type is set to zero if no keyword related to this type was matched in the articles in the given cluster). Next, a non-zero valued rank of a more specific event type is boosted in case the rank of the type which subsumes it is non zero. The logic behind this step is that when some event takes place, it can be referred to at different levels of abstraction and the most specific reference should be preferred, since it is the most informative. Finally, the type with the highest rank is selected, unless some domain-specific event type classification rule (they have higher precedence) can be applied. As an example, consider the following domain specific rule: if the event description includes named entities, which are assigned the semantic role *Kidnapped*, as well as entities which are assigned the semantic role *Released*, then the type of the event is *Hostage Release*, rather than *Kidnapping*. Such rules were introduced based on empirical observations.

It is important to note that the information fusion algorithm has some limitations since it considers only one main event per news cluster, ignoring events of lower importance or incidents subsumed by the main event.

We recently replaced the simple keyword matching mechanism initially deployed with a more expressive regular expression pattern matching engine, powered with boolean operators. Experiments on French and Italian language indicate a significant comparative advantage of boolean combinations of patterns over simple keywords in terms of accuracy.

7   Live Event Tracking

Multilingual crisis-related event tracking poses a number of practical issues, mainly related to the correct geo-spatial visualization of the event together with it's principal characteristics. Another concern is to minimize constraints on end users to rely on expensive and proprietary desktop applications. We fulfill these issues by publishing the event data using current Internet standard formats, namely, KML and GeoRSS. In particular, the results of the event extraction are accessible in two ways:

- via *Google Earth* application which is passed event descriptions in KML format[8],
- via a publicly accessible web client[9] that exploits the *Google Maps* technologies and connects to our KML server

The event description interface provides elements in two languages. The title, description and the precise location of the event is presented in the native language of the event, i.e., the language of the cluster being processed. In the English language we provide the event consequences and the relative geographical path to the place. The diagram in Figure 5 shows the Google Earth user interface for French, Arabic and Italian respectively.

To provide immediate clues on the cause and effect of the event we use three visual indicators: the icon image of the event type that is geo-located on the map; the size of the icon depends on the size of the cluster; and the magnitude of the consequence of the event is indicated by a colored circle around the event. A key to the symbols used in our system is given in Figure 6.

The image in Figure 7 shows the Google Maps representation of the results of the event extraction system (in Russian). The balloon shows a heat wave event that occurred in Moscow on 28 April 2009.

8   Event Extraction Evaluation

An evaluation of the event extraction performance has been carried out on 368 English-language news clusters based on news articles downloaded on 24 January 2008. 29 violent events are described in these clusters and 27 out them were

---

[8] For English: start Google Earth application with KML:
  `http://press.jrc.it/geo?type=event&format=kml&language=en`. For other languages change the value of the language attribute accordingly.

[9] `http://press.jrc.it/geo?type=event&format=html&language=en`

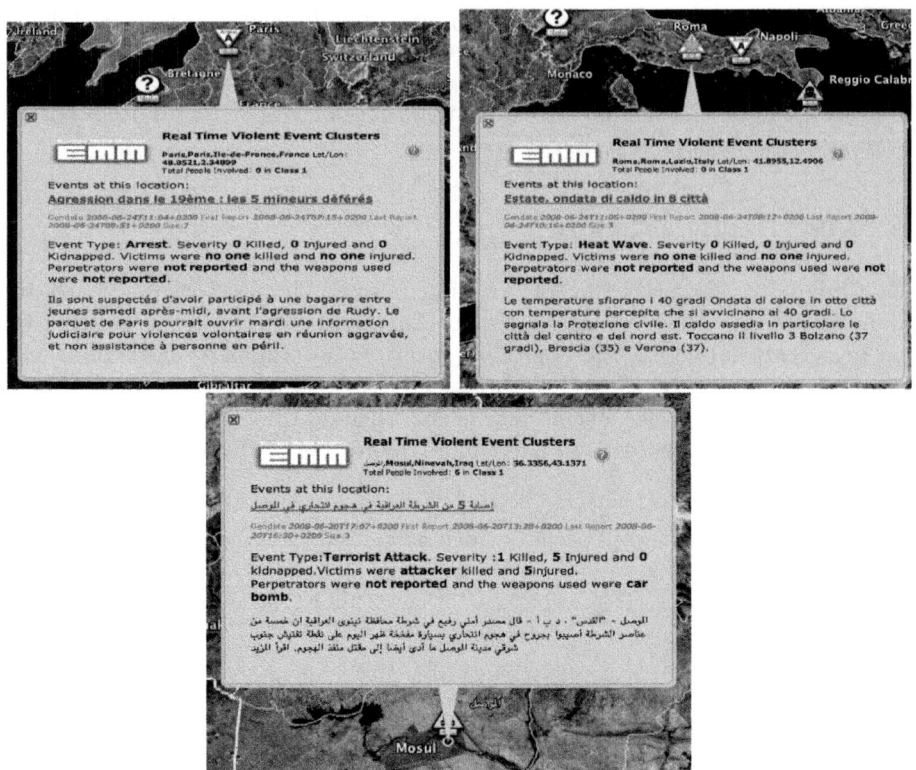

Fig. 5. Event visualization in Google Earth: Diagram showing events detected in French, Arabic and Italian. Note that the event meta data is expressed in English whilst the original, title and description are maintained.

detected by our system (**93% coverage**). In some cases several clusters referred to the same event. We consider that an event is detected by the system, if at least one cluster referring to it was captured.

Our system detected 55 news clusters which refer to 37 violent and non-violent events. 27 out of these 37 detected events are violent events (**73% precision**). In the context of crisis monitoring, discovery of disasters causing victims may also be considered relevant. Our system detected 3 man made disasters; if we consider them relevant together with the violent events, then the precision of the event extraction becomes **81%**. With respect to victim counting, for the number of dead and injured an accuracy of 80% and 93% could be achieved respectively. The event type detection performs significantly worse, i.e., only in 57% of the cases the correct event type could be assigned.

One of the most frequent errors in event classification was in case of clusters referring to terrorist bombing, which were not classified as *Terrorist Attack*, but simply as a *Bombing*. Another problem is that classification based on simple keyword matching sometimes gives wrong results, e.g., an airplane crash was

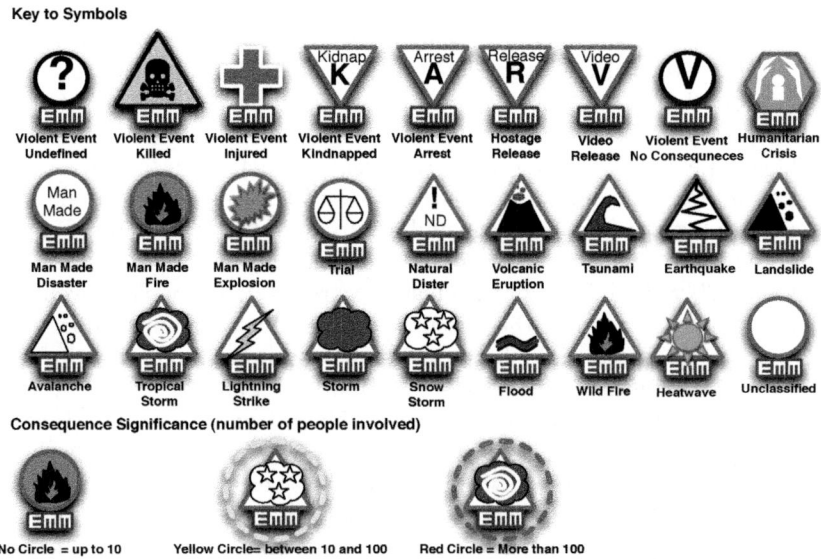

Fig. 6. Key to event type icons and magnitude indicators

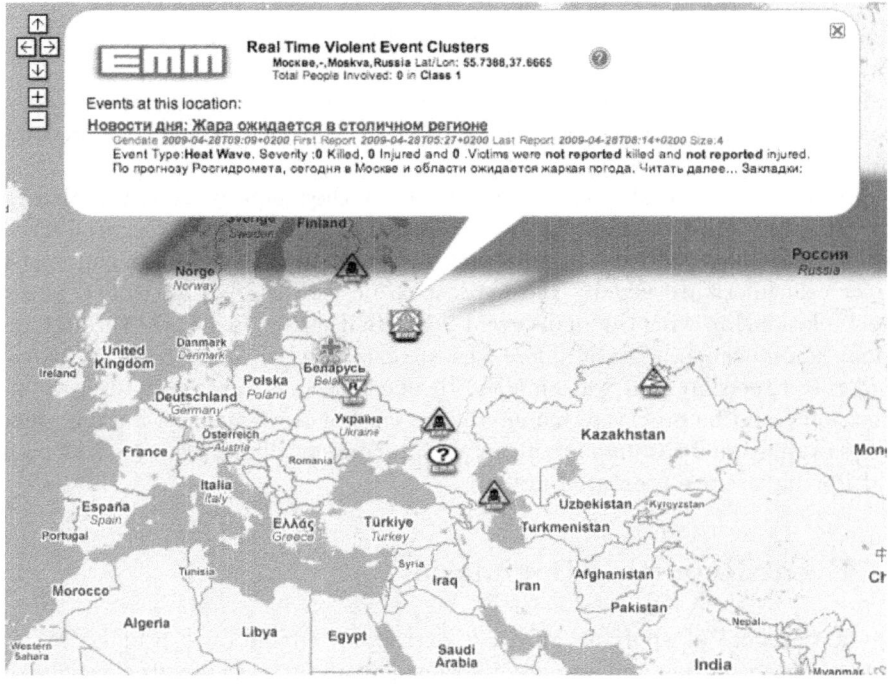

Fig. 7. Event visualization in Google Maps: The balloon shows a heat wave event that occurred in Moscow on 28 April 2009

classified as *Air Attack*, since a military plane was involved. Further, there are situations, in which two different incidents are reported as a part of one event. For example, a terrorist attack might include bombing and shooting. In such cases only one label is assigned to the whole event, although two labels would be more appropriate.

We have repeated the evaluation of the event extraction on several days, which yielded on an average similar accuracy figures to the ones reported above.

In order to evaluate the coverage and accuracy of the Italian event extraction system, we tested it on 213 clusters of news articles gathered during 4 consecutive days in July, 2008. Only part of the clusters were related to violent event stories. On this corpus, we ran both the baseline version of the system, namely the one based on linear patterns, and a hybrid version containing the more abstract rules (see Section 5.5) together with a subset of highly irregular linear patterns, which were not converted into more abstract rules. The rationale for this is that we deploy abstract rules in order to deal with productive, structurally complex language constructions, while backing off to surface level patterns to cover more idiomatic constructions. Table 2 shows a comparative evaluation of the two Italian event extraction systems. In particular, we measured precision, recall and F-measure for each role. For the sake of clarity, we define formally these measures. For a given slot type (role) T, let s_T be the number of slot values (answers) returned by the system, and let sc_T denote the number of correct answers (correct slot values) extracted by the system for the role T. Next, let all_T be the number of slot values annotated by a human expert as a value (answer) for the role T in the whole test corpus (ground truth). Then, the *recall, precision* for role T are defined as: $recall_T = |sc_T|/|all_T|$ and $precision_T = |sc_T|/|s_T|$. *F-measure* is defined as the mean of precision and recall, i.e. $F_T = (2 \cdot precision_T \cdot recall_T)/(precision_T + recall_T)$. The results of the evaluation are given in Table 2.

A clear gain in recall could be observed. A thorough analysis revealed that it was mainly due to deploying morphological abstraction and the productivity achieved through more abstract patterns. In particular, one case was interesting. *Actor* role fillers are usually the hardest to be extracted from Italian text, as their relationship with the main event verb is either to be derived through deep semantic or even pragmatic inferences, or extracted through complex two-slot patterns. Precision gain was smaller. In one particular case a deterioration in precision could be observed, namely in the case of *Arrested* role. Further details of the evaluation for Italian are given in [35]. Some evaluation figures for Spanish and Portuguese are presented in [30]

9   Event Reporting Boundaries

The major goal of applying an event extraction engine on top of EMM news clusters is to gather and update information about crisis-related events over time. Therefore, for each news story the events extracted by NEXUS at different time points are stored in a database. One of the major problems in this context is to detect duplicate events or to put it in other words, to detect new events in

Table 2. Comparison of the extraction accuracy for Italian for different roles with the baseline grammar (BL) and linguistically rich grammar (LR). P, R and F_1 stand for precision, recall and F-measure.

	Dead		*Injured*		*Actor*		*Arrested*	
	BL	LR	BL	LR	BL	LR	BL	LR
P	0.82	**0.91**	0.66	**0.77**	0	**0.66**	**0.83**	0.70
R	0.48	**0.84**	0.15	**0.53**	0	**0.25**	0.55	**0.66**
F_1	0.60	**0.87**	0.24	**0.62**	0	**0.36**	0.66	**0.67**

a news story. We consider a news story to be a sequence of news article clusters, where each such cluster contains news articles on a given topic gathered within a certain time window as the story evolves (see Section 3). Each such cluster is also associated with an event description generated by NEXUS for this particular cluster.

9.1   New Event Detection Techniques

We have explored several techniques for detecting new events in a given news story. First, we experimented with a relatively simple method, which computes the similarity between a currently extracted event and a previously extracted one (in a previous iteration) using an event similarity metric based on the content similarity of the corresponding slot values in the events being compared. In case the similarity is below a certain threshold the two events are considered to be distinct. Subsequently, this method was extended by introducing additional constraints on the confidence with which the current and past events were extracted by NEXUS. Confidence is simply measured in terms of supporting documents, i.e. documents for which NEXUS could return an event description compared with the total number of articles in the cluster. Further fine-tuning consisted of introducing some global constraints, e.g. the similarity between the current event and the average event similarity within a whole story has to be lower than a certain pre-defined threshold, otherwise the current event is considered to be a new event. We refer to the techniques described in this paragraph as OVERLAP.

Next, we investigated whether utilization of a curvature-based approach for topical segmentation of a stream of texts can improve the performance of new event detection. The basic idea behind such approaches to topic development analysis [7,13,1,25] is to compute for a given sequence of text entries $t_1, t_2, \ldots, t_k$ a sequence $s_{1,2}, s_{2,3}, \ldots, s_{k-1,k}$, where $s_{i-1,i}$ is the similarity between t_{i-1} and t_i. The latter sequence is called *similarity curve* and reflects how rapidly the content of the text stream changes between consecutive entries. In order to identify topically coherent segments one can use local minima of the similarity curve as indicators of segment boundaries, i.e. topic shift occurs at local minima. In the context of the new event detection task, our idea is to compute such a similarity curve for a given news story, and to use it for validating the decisions on tagging events as new, etc. In particular, for a given news story we compute the similarity curve for the text sequence $t_1, t_2, \ldots, t_k$, where t_i consists of the titles and first sentences of the new articles in the story cluster at time i, i.e. articles, which appeared for the first time at iteration i.[10] Subsequently, events extracted by NEXUS are tagged as new only if certain patterns in the similarity curve (indicating a topic change) can be observed (e.g., local minima). Although the briefly sketched idea of classical curvature-based algorithms for topic development analysis is effective, we have not used it for two reasons:

- it performs best in the case of text streams with 'clear' changes of topics, which is not necessarily the case in the context of news stories oscillating around one or two major topics, and
- it captures solely the pairwise relationship between two adjacent entries in the text stream, whereas capturing the global relations between entries in the text stream would provide more useful and fine-grained information in topic development.[11]

Therefore, we applied a different algorithm for computing the similarity curve, namely the recently introduced CUTS algorithm presented in [25], which captures global relations between text entries in the input stream of texts. The sequence of text entries is mapped to a curve, which reflects the topic development patterns in terms of dissimilarity between neighbouring text entries. Unlike other curvature-based topical text segmentation algorithms, which utilize solely information of pairwise (dis)similarity between adjacent entries in the input sequence, CUTS algorithm exploits broader context, i.e. 'content' dissimilarities for all pairs of entries in the input. To be more precise, the initial sequence of text entries is mapped to a 1-dimensional space so that distances between points best match the dissimilarities between the corresponding entries. The aforementioned mapping is computed through the application of a multidimensional scaling (MDS) technique [8] applied on the dissimilarity matrix for the input sequence. Next, the time dimension is added, i.e. each point in time – index of the entry in the input sequence (x-axis) is mapped to the corresponding MDS-computed value in the 1 dimensional space (y-axis). The resulting curve is called CUTS curve. A 'stable' topic in CUTS curve corresponds to an almost horizontal segment (*dominated segment*). A smooth transition from one topic to another is reflected in the CUTS curve as a sloping curve (*drifting segment*), where the gradient angle measures how fast one topic fades out and new topic fades in. Finally, interruptions, i.e. sudden and temporary introduction of a new and significantly different topic, correspond to segments with a saw tooth shape. Interruptions may either occur within dominated or drifting segments. Figure 8 illustrates a drifting segment and a dominated segment with an interruption in CUTS curves computed for some of the news stories computed by EMM.

---

[10] In case of iterations in which there are no new articles, we consider for the computation of t_i the documents which were most recently added to the story cluster.

[11] Different news media might report on the same event at different times and even the same media might re-report on the same event from time to time.

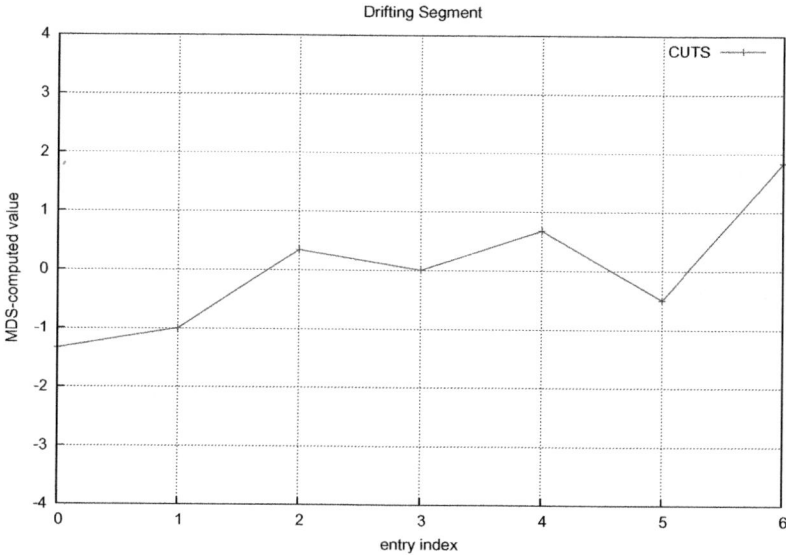

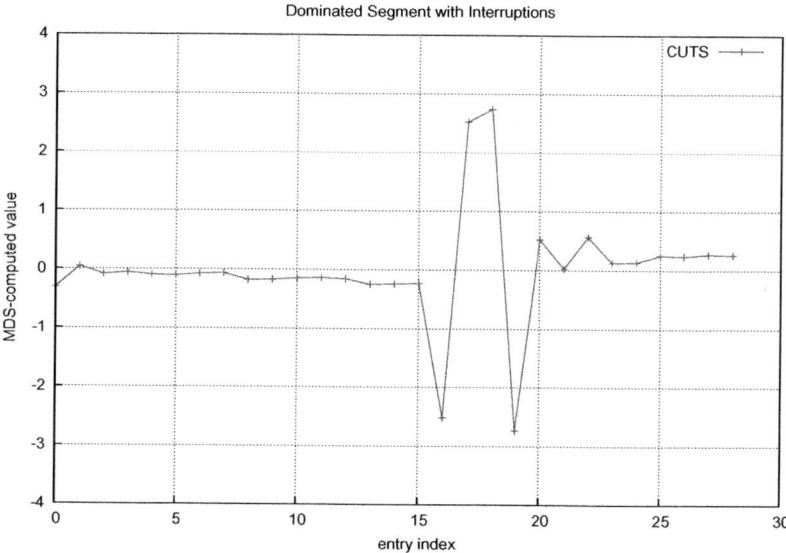

Fig. 8. An example of a drifting segment (top) and a dominated segment with an interruption (bottom) The interruption in the interval (15, 20) refers most likely to a new event or possibly to some noise in the news story cluster in this interval.

The main idea behind the CUTS-based algorithm for new event detection is that predominantly interrupted or drifting segments in the CUTS curve occur directly prior to the new event. In other words, the number of articles on a new topic or aspect of the main event of the story has reached a critical mass. Since many news stories are not stable in the initial iterations, the exact conditions (for the CUTS curve), which have to be fulfilled are slightly different for the beginning of the story and subsequent iterations, e.g., the threshold for the gradient angle in the drifting segment in order to classify an event as new is higher for the beginning of the story than for subsequent iterations.

Finally, we have combined the simple algorithms described at the beginning of this section (OVERLAP) with the CUTS algorithm (we denote this combination as OVERLAP+CUTS). To be more precise, the CUTS constraints are embedded in the OVERLAP algorithms as additional ones. Furthermore, in case the original constraints of OVERLAP algorithms do not hold, but 'almost' hold (values are within a certain distance to the thresholds, etc.) the CUTS constraints are checked, and if they hold the event is tagged as a new one. A more detailed description of the algorithms for detecting event reporting boundaries are given in [21].

9.2　Evaluation

We have carried out an evaluation of the different new event detection techniques described in the previous section. For this purpose, we have collected test data as follows. NEXUS was applied at 30 minute intervals on the English news clusters produced by EMM between 6 and 16 October 2008. In this time period 6664 different news stories were collected, where 1296 of them were related to violent and natural disaster events. About one third of the latter (442) were dynamic, i.e. at least two distinct event descriptions were generated for such stories. We have applied the different algorithms on a subset thereof, consisting of 125 stories (in which the event type changed) and we have evaluated their precision, recall and F-measure. Let E be the set of automatically detected new events in the test corpus described above and let E^* be the set of events annotated as new events by a human expert. We call the latter set the ground truth. The *recall* is the ratio of correctly detected new events and all events in the ground truth, i.e. $recall = |E \cap E^*|/|E^*|$. We define *precision* as the fraction of events, which were correctly tagged by the algorithm as new events, i.e. $precision = |E \cap E^*|/|E|$. *F-measure* is defined as the mean of precision and recall, i.e. $F\text{-}measure = (2 \cdot precision \cdot recall)/(precision + recall)$. Table 3 presents the top results obtained for precision, recall and F-measure separately. While integration of CUTS-based constraints into simple methods resulted in a significant improvement in precision, the simple methods score best in terms of recall and F-measure. As can be observed from the table there is much room for improvement. A more thorough discussion on this topic is given in [21].

Table 3. Top results obtained for detecting new events with different techniques. P, R and F_1 stand for precision, recall and F-measure.

method	P	R	F_1
OVERLAP	0.516	**0.769**	**0.615**
CUTS	0.4	0.385	0.392
OVERLAP+CUTS	**0.75**	0654	0.583

10 Summary

This article presented a real-time and multilingual news event extraction system developed at the Joint Research Centre of the European Commission. Currently, it is capable of efficiently processing news in English, Italian, French, Spanish, Portuguese, Russian and Arabic, which provide descriptions of the latest crisis-related events around the world with a 10-minute delay. The results of the evaluation on violent and natural disaster event extraction show satisfactory performance and strong application potential for real-time global crisis monitoring. In order to guarantee ease in maintenance and extensibility to new languages and domains a shallow text processing strategy has been chosen, which utilizes clustered data at different strata. The coverage and the level of sophistication of language resources used in the system varies from language to language. The results of the live event extraction are provided via a publicly accessible web page and can also be accessed with the *Google Earth* application. The system has been fully implemented in JAVA.

In order to improve the quality of the extracted event descriptions, several system extensions are envisaged. Firstly, we are working towards fine grained classification of natural and man made disasters. We also plan to improve the classification accuracy for violent events. Secondly, we aim at extending the system to new languages. This is feasible, since our algorithms and grammars are mostly language independent. In particular, we currently focus on adapting the system to the processing of Arabic news. Being able to extract information about same event in different languages and cross-linking them adds an additional navigation layer and an opportunity for fact validation and improving the accuracy of the system. Therefore, we plan to explore techniques for refining the results of event extraction, which are similar in spirit to those presented in [14]. Furthermore, we intend to study the usability of event descriptions collected over time for the same purpose. The experiments on detecting event reporting boundaries briefly reported in this article and in [21] show that there is a lot of space for improvement. Therefore, we will pursue this line of research. Next, a long-term goal is to automatically discover structure of events and relations between them, i.e., discovering sub-events or related events of the main one, as well as implementing techniques for event duplicate detection.

The range of events the system already detects is relatively wide, which makes the tool very attractive for application in various scenarios. Nevertheless, the system is currently being customized to new domains, in particular, to detect border-security related events (e.g., illegal border crossings and related cross-border criminal activities) [22] and outbreaks of infectious diseases in the public health domain. Although the accuracy of detecting certain types of events is quite satisfactory we can not fully eliminate human moderation in the process of gathering event information in a database. In order to facilitate this task a graphical interface has been implemented that allows users to correct, extend, merge, translate and store automatically extracted event information on events [22] in an event store – a specific knowledge repository on events. Finally, some work on improving geo-locating events through deployment of shallow linguistic analysis (along the lines sketched in section 4) is envisaged too.

Acknowledgments. The work presented in this article was supported by the Europe Media Monitoring (EMM) Project carried out by the Open Source Text Information Mining and Analysis Action in the Joint Research Centre of the European Commission. We are indebted to all our EMM colleagues without whom the presented work could not have been be possible.

References

1. Andrews, P.: Semantic topic extraction and segmentation for efficient document visualization' Master's thesis, School of Computer & Communication Sciences, Swiss Federal Institute of Technology, Lausanne (2004)
2. Aone, C., Santacruz, M.: REES: A Large-Scale Relation and Event Extraction System. In: Proceedings of ANLP 2000, 6th Applied Natural Language Processing Conference, Seattle, Washington, USA (2000)
3. Appelt, D.: Introduction to Information Extraction Technology. In: Tutorial held at IJCAI 1999, Stockholm, Sweden (1999)
4. Ashish, N., Appelt, D., Freitag, D., Zelenko, D.: Proceedings of the workshop on Event Extraction and Synthesis', held in Conjunction with the AAAI 2006 Conference, Menlo Park, California, USA (2006)
5. Atkinson, M., Van der Goot, E.: Near Real Time Information Mining in Multilingual News. In: Proceedings of the 18th World Wide Web Conference, Madrid, Spain (2009)
6. Best, C., Van der Goot, E., Blackler, K., Garcia, T., Horby, D.: Europe Media Monitor, Technical Report, EUR 22173 EN, European Commission (2005)
7. Brants, T., Chen, F., Farahat, A.: A System for New Event Detection. In: Proceedings of the 26tth Annual International ACM SIGIR Conference on Research and Development in Information Retrieval, New York, NY, USA (2003)
8. Cox, T., Cox, M.: Multidimensional Scaling. In: Monographs on Statistics and Applied Probability, 2nd edn., Chapman & Hall, London (2001)
9. Cunningham, H., Maynard, D., Tablan, V.: Jape: a Java Annotation Patterns Engine. Technical Report, CS–00–10, University of Sheffield, Department of Computer Science (2000)
10. Drożdżyński, W., Krieger, H.-U., Piskorski, J., Schäfer, U., Xu, F.: Shallow Processing with Unification and Typed Feature Structures — Foundations and Applications. Künstliche Intelligenz 1 (2004)

11. Gale, W., Church, K., Yarowsky, D.: One sense per discourse. In: HLT 1991: Proceedings of the workshop on Speech and Natural Language, Harriman, New York, USA (1992)

12. Grishman, R., Huttunen, S., Yangarber, R.: Real-time Event Extraction for Infectious Disease Outbreaks. In: Proceedings of Human Language Technology Conference 2002, San Diego, USA (2002)

13. Hearst, M.: Subtopic structuring for full-length document access. In: Postproceedings of SIGIR (1993)

14. Ji, H., Grishman, R.: Refining Event Extraction through Unsupervised Cross-document Inference. In: Proceedings of 46th Annual Meeting of the Association for Computational Linguistics: Human Language Technologies, Columbus, Ohio, USA (2008)

15. Jones, R., McCallum, A., Nigam, K., Riloff, E.: Bootstrapping for Text Learning Tasks. In: Proceedings of IJCAI 1999 Workshop on Text Mining, Stockholm, Sweden (1999)

16. King, G., Lowe, W.: An Automated Information Extraction Tool For International Conflict Data with Performance as Good as Human Coders: A Rare Events Evaluation Design. International Organization 57, 617–642 (2003)

17. Naughton, M., Kushmerick, N., Carthy, J.: Event Extraction from Heterogeneous News Sources. In: Proceedings of the AAAI 2006 Workshop on Event Extraction and Synthesis, Menlo Park, California, USA (2006)

18. Piskorski, J.: ExPRESS – Extraction Pattern Recognition Engine and Specification Suite. In: Proceedings of the International Workshop Finite-State Methods and Natural language Processing 2007 (FSMNLP 2007), Potsdam, Germany (2007)

19. Piskorski, J.: CORLEONE – Core Linguistic Entity Online Extraction, Technical Report, EN 23393, Joint Research Center of the European Commission, Ispra, Italy (2008)

20. Piskorski, J., Tanev, H., Atkinson, M., Van der Goot, E.: Cluster-Centric Approach to News Event Extraction. In: Proceedings of the International Conference on Multimedia & Network Information Systems. IOS Press, Poland (2009)

21. Piskorski, J.: Exploring Curvature-based Topic Development Analysis for Detecting Event Reporting Boundaries. In: Marciniak, M., Mykowiecka, A. (eds.) Aspects of Natural Language Processing. LNCS, vol. 5070, pp. 311–331. Springer, Heidelberg (2009)

22. Piskorski, J., Atkinson, M., Belyaeva, J., Zavarella, V., Huttunen, S., Yangarber, R.: Real-Time Text Mining in Multilingual News for the Creation of a Pre-frontier Intelligence Picture. In: Proceedings of the 16th Conference on Knowledge Discovery and Data Mining (KDD 2010). ACM SIGKDD Workshop on Intelligence and Security Informatics, Washington DC, USA (2010)

23. Popov, B., Kiryakov, A., Ognyanoff, D., Manov, D., Kirilov, A., Goranov, M.: Towards Semantic Web Information Extraction. In: Proceedings of International Semantic Web Conference, Sundial Resort, Florida, USA (2003)

24. Pouliquen, B., Kimler, M., Steinberger, R., Ignat, C., Oellinger, T., Blackler, K., Fuart, F., Zaghouani, W., Widiger, A., Forslund, A., Best, C.: Geocoding multilingual texts: Recognition, Disambiguation and Visualisation. In: Proceedings of LREC 2006, Genoa, Italy, pp. 24–26 (2006)

25. Qi, Y., Candan, K.-S.: CUTS: Curvature-based Development Pattern Analysis and Segmentation for Blogs and Other Text Streams. In: Proceedings of Hypertext 2006, Odense, Denmark (2006)

26. Riloff, E.: Automatically Constructing a Dictionary for Information Extraction Tasks. In: Proceedings of the 11th National Conference on Artificial Intelligence (AAAI 1993). MIT Press, Cambridge (1993)
27. Shannon, C.: A mathematical theory of communication. The Bell System Technical Journal 27 (1948)
28. Tanev, T., Oezden-Wennerberg, P.: Learning to Populate an Ontology of Violent Events. In: Fogelman-Soulie, F., Perrotta, D., Piskorski, J., Steinberger, R. (eds.) NATO Security through Science Series: Mining Massive Datasets for Security. IOS Press, Amsterdam (2008)
29. Tanev, H., Piskorski, J., Atkinson, M.: Real-Time News Event Extraction for Global Crisis Monitoring. In: Kapetanios, E., Sugumaran, V., Spiliopoulou, M. (eds.) NLDB 2008. LNCS, vol. 5039, pp. 207–218. Springer, Heidelberg (2008)
30. Tanev, H., Zavarella, V., Linge, J., Kabadjov, M., Piskorski, J., Atkinson, M., Steinberger, R.: Exploiting Machine Learning Techniques to Build an Event Extraction System for Portuguese and Spanish. LINGUAMÁTICA Journal 2, 55–66 (2009)
31. Wagner, E., Liu, J., Birnbaum, L., Forbus, K., Baker, J.: Using Explicit Semantic Models to Track Situations Across News Articles. In: Proceedings of the AAAI 2006 workshop on Event Extraction and Synthesis, Menlo Park, California, USA (2006)
32. Yangarber, R., Grishman, R.: Machine Learning of Extraction Patterns from Unannotated Corpora. In: Proceedings of the 14th European Conference on Artificial Intelligence: Workshop on Machine Learning for Information Extraction, Berlin, Germany (2000)
33. Yangarber, R.: Counter-Training in Discovery of Semantic Patterns. In: Proceedings of the 41st Annual Meeting of the ACL (2003)
34. Yangarber, R., Von Etter, P., Steinberger, R.: Content Collection and Analysis in the Domain of Epidemiology. In: Proceedings of DrMED 2008: International Workshop on Describing Medical Web Resources at MIE 2008: the 21st International Congress of the European Federation for Medical Informatics 2008, Goeteborg, Sweden (2008)
35. Zavarella, V., Piskorski, J., Tanev, H.: Event Extraction for Italian using a Cascade of Finite-State Grammars. In: Post-Proceedings of the 7th International Workshop on Finite-State Machines and Natural Language Processing, Ispra, Italy (2008/2009)

Author Index